COUNTERING WITH COMPASSION

Countering with Compassion provides educators with the tools needed to weave compassionate practice into their classrooms, schools, and wider communities. Bringing together diverse contributions, the book explores how the development of compassion across policy and practice offers a transformative pathway for both children and school staff.

A range of pertinent topics are covered, from developing a compassionate mind and compassion in children, to compassion fatigue for educators and compassionate leadership. Each chapter includes a range of exercises and activities, allowing the reader to reflect and to apply the content to their own life and work. The book puts theory into practice and encourages the reader to become a change maker in their school. It will be valuable reading for both primary and secondary teachers and school leaders.

Alexandra Sewell is a Health and Care Professions Council (HCPC) registered educational psychologist and senior lecturer in special educational needs, disability, and inclusion at the University of Worcester. Her research has been published in numerous international journals and explores the concepts of voice and inclusion in education.

COUNTERING WITH COMPASSION

A Guide to Compassionate Leadership In and Beyond School Communities

Edited by
Alexandra Sewell

LONDON AND NEW YORK

Designed cover image: Getty Images

First published 2026
by Routledge
4 Park Square, Milton Park, Abingdon, Oxon OX14 4RN

and by Routledge
605 Third Avenue, New York, NY 10158

Routledge is an imprint of the Taylor & Francis Group, an informa business

© 2026 selection and editorial matter, Alexandra Sewell; individual chapters, the contributors

The right of Alexandra Sewell to be identified as the author of the editorial material, and of the authors for their individual chapters, has been asserted in accordance with sections 77 and 78 of the Copyright, Designs and Patents Act 1988.

All rights reserved. No part of this book may be reprinted or reproduced or utilised in any form or by any electronic, mechanical, or other means, now known or hereafter invented, including photocopying and recording, or in any information storage or retrieval system, without permission in writing from the publishers.

For Product Safety Concerns and Information please contact our EU representative GPSR@taylorandfrancis.com. Taylor & Francis Verlag GmbH, Kaufingerstraße 24, 80331 München, Germany.

Trademark notice: Product or corporate names may be trademarks or registered trademarks, and are used only for identification and explanation without intent to infringe.

British Library Cataloguing-in-Publication Data
A catalogue record for this book is available from the British Library

ISBN: 978-1-032-73807-9 (hbk)
ISBN: 978-1-032-73804-8 (pbk)
ISBN: 978-1-003-46603-1 (ebk)

DOI: 10.4324/9781003466031

Typeset in Interstate
by Deanta Global Publishing Services, Chennai, India

To Will Sewell, thank you for all the brother-to-sister and sister-to-brother flows of compassion

CONTENTS

List of Contributors   ix

PART I
Framing and Foundations of Compassionate Leadership   1

1   Introduction: Re-encountering Compassion as Tradition, Praxis, and Resistance   3
    Alexandra Sewell, Kirsty Evans, and Kathryn Lynch

2   Enhancing Reflective Practice through Compassionate Leadership in Senior Leaders   15
    Jo Taylor

3   Building Compassionate School Cultures through Compassion-Focused Therapy and Mind Training   34
    Charlie Heriot-Maitland and Jo Taylor

PART II
Compassion as a Global, Multi-Cultural Professional Endeavour   57

4   Critical Compassion in Teacher Preparation: Pedagogical *Conocimientos* in Action   59
    Jesus Jaime-Diaz, Josie Méndez-Negrete, and Mary Carol Combs

5   Leading with Compassion or Control? Coaching Lessons from a Confucian Perspective   77
    Hongguo Wei, Shaobing Li, and Amer Mohammad

6   Compassionate Leadership through Self-Cognition: Insights from Moral Education in Kazakhstan   91
    Aigerim Mynbayeva, Anzhelika Karabutova, and Gainiya Tazhina

PART III
Contextualising Compassionate Leadership in Practice   111

7   Nurturing Compassion in the Early Years: Foundations for Professional Practice   113
    Angela Hodgkins

8 Rethinking Relational Leadership: Compassion with and beyond the Human 134
   Kay Sidebottom

9 Leading with Heart in Times of Crisis: Cultivating Teacher Resilience, Wellbeing, and Performance 148
   Richard Marcel

   Index 169

CONTRIBUTORS

Mary Carol Combs PhD is professor in the Department of Teaching, Learning, and Sociocultural Studies, University of Arizona. Her research interests include critical pedagogy, language planning and policy, immigration policy and education, sociocultural theory, sheltered content instruction and teacher preparation for refugee, immigrant, and citizen English-learning students. Her published work focuses on the intersection of these issues and school-based pedagogical practices.

Kirsty Evans AppEdChPsyD is an educational psychologist with an interest in emotionally based school avoidance, relational approaches and meaningful exploration of the views and experiences of pupils. She is also interested in organisational flourishing and uses coaching to support the wellbeing of teachers and leaders.

Charlie Heriot-Maitland CHM is a clinical psychologist, compassion focused therapy expert and director of Balanced Minds, specialist providers and trainers of compassion focused therapy.

Angela Hodgkins PhD is a senior lecturer at the University of Worcester. She completed a PhD in 2023, exploring early childhood practitioners' perceptions of empathic interactions with children and families. Her diverse career in working with children informs her research interests in empathy, compassion, and strength-based practice.

Jesus Jaime-Diaz PhD is assistant professor of Chicana/o studies & director of the Aztlan Research Center at Colorado State University Pueblo. His research has focused on *testimonio* and critical ethnographic methods for exploring how Mexican American community college students in Oregon use their lived experiences as a catalyst to "empower" them to pursue higher education. His current research utilises racialised social class as a unit for analysis in the schooling experience(s) of Mexican American students along the Borderlands of Arizona.

Anzhelika Karabutova is master of psychology and head of the Department of Educational Programs of the non-profit joint-stock company National Scientific and Practical Institute of Child Welfare. Her research is associated with spiritual and moral education, and psychological wellbeing of children.

x *Contributors*

Shaobing Li PhD (Miami University) is the founder and CEO of Speak Yourself. His research and practical interests focus on entrepreneurship, character-based leadership development, emotional intelligence, and strategic thinking and planning.

Kathryn Lynch AppEdChPsyD is an educational psychologist with an interest in learning and curriculum, belonging and pupil voice. She is interested in wellbeing and organisational psychology and in the use of video interaction guidance and coaching in educational settings.

Richard Marcel PhD holds an MS and PhD from the Indian Institute of Technology Madras (IITM), India. He serves on the faculty at Loyola Institute of Business Administration (LIBA), specialising in strategic management, organisational behaviour, and human resource management. His research focuses on leadership development, resilience, and compassionate leadership in VUCA and BANI environments, as well as the evolving role of leadership in the age of Artificial Intelligence.

Josie Méndez-Negrete PhD is professor emerita in Mexican American studies from the Department of Bicultural-Bilingual Studies (BBL), at the University of Texas at San Antonio. As the founder and publisher of Conocimientos Press, she continues to introduce award-winning books by people of colour in the United States, such as *Street of Too Many Stories*, by Denise Chávez. The latest forthcoming is *Eréndira: A Novel*, by Rosa M. Borunda.

Amer Mohammad is an MBA candidate at Robert Morris University, specialising in business analytics. With a background in business and commerce, he focuses on data-driven strategies for complex business challenges. He is passionate about leadership, innovation, startups, and sustainable business growth.

Aigerim Mynbayeva PhD is a doctor of pedagogical sciences and professor of the Department of General and Applied Psychology at the Al-Farabi Kazakh National University. They are a specialist in the field of higher education pedagogy, history of education, comparative education, digitalisation of education.

Alexandra Sewell AppEdChPsyD is a senior lecturer in special educational needs, disability and inclusion at the University of Worcester. A HCPC registered educational and child psychologist, she specialises in inclusive education and amplifying marginalised voices. Alexandra has co-authored and edited influential texts on SEND and contributes to educational psychology research.

Kay Sidebottom PhD is a lecturer in education at the University of Stirling, specialising in critical pedagogy, creative approaches to learning, and post humanist theory. Her research explores transformative education, social justice, and relational ethics, with a focus on challenging dominant narratives and fostering inclusive, imaginative educational practices.

Jo Taylor AppEdChPsyD is an educational psychologist, director of constellations psychology and a Churchill Fellow, completing research into compassion and caring behaviour.

Gainiya Tazhina PhD is director of the Scientific and Practical Centre for Inclusive Environment, Al-Farabi Al-Farabi Kazakh National University. Their research focuses on the issues of leadership, inclusion, professional development. They serve as a reviewer for international scholarly education journals. Their extensive industrial experience includes leading over 50 business training courses/workshops on leadership potential, teambuilding, etc. for international/local companies, HEIs and NGOs.

Hongguo Wei PhD (Case Western Reserve University) is an assistant professor at Robert Morris University. She is passionate about studying how to improve employee wellbeing and create a better workplace through the lens of emotions and leadership. Her research interests focus on leadership, emotions, workplace relationships, and ethical behaviour.

PART I
Framing and Foundations of Compassionate Leadership

1
Introduction
Re-encountering Compassion as Tradition, Praxis, and Resistance

Alexandra Sewell, Kirsty Evans, and Kathryn Lynch

Re-encountering Compassion

A call for change in educational leadership globally has been made; Fuller and Stevenson (2019) tell us that "In the face of powerful global pressures, it is easy to become pessimistic about the possibilities for resistance and the opportunities to create counter movements."

In considering how to introduce this book, I find myself recalling common critiques levied at counter movements, not just in Education but across socio-cultural domains. Those with power to lead discussion and make decisions, repeatedly use such critiques to dismiss attempts to widen discourse and action change. I wish to start this introduction here as a means of heading off, "at the pass", such common attempts.

The first is that any counter theorising is critiqued and dismissed as existing only in opposition to the dominant model. As such, it is not considered "real" or "valid" from an essentialist perspective. It is said to lack inherent legitimacy, belittled for not existing on its own merit. It is demeaned as being apart from the dominant perspective it is supposedly conceived of to challenge. An example of this style of critique is that which was levied at the development of the disability rights movement and related social model of disability. Both were initially disregarded as merely reactionary rather than as substantive paradigms in their own right (Oliver, 2013).

The second critique is that membership of counter movements (whether loosely affiliated groups, such as scholars with shared theoretical perspectives or formally organised entities, such as trade unions) lack a shared core aim beyond mere opposition. Consequently, such movements are judged as fragmented, with no central cohesion and unified direction in their critical perspective and efforts for change. They are portrayed as a disorganised rabble, lacking a singular authoritative leader and, therefore, coordination. This reflects the critics' inability to move beyond an ideological framework in which a single dominant truth must prevail over all others. It deliberately overlooks the post-structuralist emphasis on multiplicity of perspectives, for example, as seen in theories of multiculturalism. The political right's critique of the 2011 Global Occupy Movement as disorganised due to lack of central authority and an explicitly shared singular vision is one such example (Halvorsen, 2012).

This is a book of opposition; an attempt to counter the current global model of education with different perspectives. Inevitably, both dismissive critiques will be applied. The preemptive response to the first is that the propositioning of "compassion" and "compassionate practice" in education in this text is, indeed, made from a starting point of elucidating an alternative to the dominant neo-liberal Global Education Reform Movement (GERM – outlined below). However, it would be naïve to view this as arising solely from reactionary circumstances, thereby delegitimising it. Taken collectively, the arguments put forward in this edited text do not present compassion and its role in education as novel, recent, or even progressive. Compassion and its role in educational leadership is explored deeply, with each author situating it within a complex historical-cultural lineage.

For example, Jaime-Diaz, Méndez-Negrete, and Combs (Chapter 4) ground compassionate educational leadership in Latinx cultural values of *cariño* (affection, care and fondness), *respeto* (respect), and *confianza* (trust and confidence). Wei, Li, and Mohammad (Chapter 5) present a nuanced exploration of both compassionate and authoritarian leadership styles from a Confucian, southeast Asian cultural heritage. Chapters written from a Western perspective also understand compassion as a multi-cultural phenomenon, with an example found in Hodgkins (Chapter 7) that traces Compassionate practice in UK Early Years settings to compassion arising in early Buddhism. As such, while the book has been titled with the idea of "countering" the modern educative agenda, it is, in truth, an invitation for readers to *re-encounter* the emotive-social experience of compassion as a deeply embedded human value, ever-present across time and place.

Responding to the second critique requires asserting the manifold ways in which social reality is conceived. It demands clear axiomatic alignment. The response, therefore, is straightforward: this edited book is grounded in a foundation of multiple perspectives. Given the *a priori* nature of this rebuttal, it carries a strong degree of assertion. This assertion maintains that multiplicity in opinion and voice does not negate unity, as the work is not founded on the belief that educational theorising and movements require a central authoritative voice to be substantiated. As such, the following chapters begin and end with the recognition that the social-emotional world is complex. While a reductionist approach undoubtedly holds pragmatic value in education, compassion remains a complexly human, intra-personal experience. Thus, we arrive at what compassion is set to challenge. This is outlined across two concepts within educational literature, the Global Education Reform Movement (GERM) and Global Citizenship Education.

GERM: Global Education Reform Movement

Many educational commentators, academic or otherwise, have articulated a transformative trend in education typified by the application of neo-liberal principles to education systems. Put simply, neo-liberalism is an economic and political ideology of free markets, privatisation, competition, and reduced state intervention. In the context of education, neoliberalism has manifested through policies that promote market-driven approaches to competition, such as standardised testing and school performance leagues, school choice, and performance-based funding. This has been understood as the application of capitalist corporate management approaches and a commercialisation of education and commodification of learners. Proponents have argued that these ideological changes have resulted in positive progression, re-positioning education as a service for students and parents, with related increases in efficiency and accountability via measurable outcomes.

This world-movement of educational change has arguably been best encapsulated by Sahlberg (2012) who coined it as the Global Educational Reform Movement (GERM). GERM is a powerful "acronym as analogy" (Fuller & Stevenson, 2019). The neo-liberal reforms are likened to "an epidemic that spreads and infects education systems through a virus ... Education systems borrow policies from others and get infected ... schools get ill, teachers don't feel well, and kids learn less" (Sahlberg, 2012). Sahlberg (2012) originally outlined three symptoms of the GERM:

1 Competition: autonomy, improvement, accountability (school league tables, inspections).
2 School choice: marketisation, parents as consumers, corporate management values.
3 Standardised testing: learners as commodities, outcomes, curriculum standards.

The beginnings of GERM can be traced to the inter-world war and post-world war periods, where education emerged as an optimistic political focus of global significance (Biccum, 2024). It then took hold through legislation in the 1970s and 80s in neoliberal educational reforms initially implemented in the US, UK, and Chile (Fuller & Stevenson, 2019). The trend has expanded further in the 21st century, fueled by the development of cross-national comparisons of educational outcomes by global organisations such as the OECD and IEA (Maisuria, 2015). These supra-national accountability structures drive policy borrowing and market-driven reforms, further embedding GERM into an arguably increasingly globalised and homogenised worldwide education network of similar systems.

While Sahlberg (2012) originally described the application of neoliberalism to education in terms of its symptoms, framing features such as standardisation, competition, and accountability as manifestations of an illness, subsequent commentary has expanded on this perspective. Later analyses have further interrogated the depth of the malaise. Yoon (2024) describes the "maddening effect" created by the narrative of school choice, where the implicit promise of freedom and autonomy obscures the reality that choice has, in fact, been reduced. This "unseeing" masks the inequalities embedded in the system, as parents and educators fail to recognise that so-called choices are unevenly distributed. Yoon (2024) highlights how this unseeing particularly impacts those from poorer backgrounds, who experience significantly less choice. For example, in the Canadian system, the introduction of schools with specialisms is presented as an expansion of choice, yet these options are predominantly located in wealthier, white, middle-class areas, thus reinforcing existing inequities (Yoon, 2024).

Positioning parents as consumer-beneficiaries further blurs the line between political narratives and educational realities. Biccum (2024), drawing on economist Harold Innis's concept of "knowledge monopolies", expounds the complexities of the Global Education Reform Movement (GERM). Supranational and national governments are portrayed as dominating both media and educational literature, effectively controlling a knowledge economy. The influence of organisations such as UNESCO and the UN illustrates how "comparison and quantification are socially and politically constitutive and that the use of this modality of knowledge is a particular feature of ... power" (Biccum, 2024, p. 4). As a result, it is not in actuality parents, or even children and young people, who have meaningful influence over what education is or how it serves them. It is state powers and the supra-national organisations they collectively form. This is reflected in widespread parental concerns over excessive testing and increasingly narrow curricula. Many parents, in fact, "believe that education ought to be an experience for the development of critical free thinking and the building of faculties for relentless scepticism and unbounded curiosity about the nature of society" (Maisuria, 2015, p. 286).

> **KNOWLEDGE ECONOMIES**
>
> Harold Innis argued that the way societies communicate shapes their economies, emphasising how different media (like print or oral traditions) influence knowledge control and power structures. He introduced the idea of time-biased and space-biased media – time-biased preserving tradition and authority, and space-biased promoting expansion and control across distances. Innis believed that shifts in dominant communication media drive changes in economic structures and knowledge economies by determining who can access, store, and transmit information.

In summary, viewed through the lens of the GERM acronym-as-analogy, a homogenised global network of education systems has emerged. It claims to serve parents and learners, yet has, in practice, narrowed the purpose of education. This shift has intensified pressures on both students and teachers. The impact is multifaceted. While some argue that attainment levels have improved, such gains often reflect a culture of "teaching to the test" and a shrinking curriculum. Apparent rises in standards have, arguably, come at a significant cost: declining teacher morale linked to burnout (Farley & Chamberlain, 2021), increased student stress and reduced wellbeing (Davies, 2001), and a deepening of pre-existing societal inequalities (Biccum, 2024). It is within this challenging landscape that educational leaders must operate. Compassionate practice offers a potential reimagining of education's purpose and a renewed understanding of leadership as a relational, value-driven endeavour. One that prioritises wellbeing, equity, and the creation of inclusive learning environments over performative metrics and standardised outputs.

Global Citizenship Education

Global Citizenship Education (GCE) is one of many educational trends described as "many things to many people" (Barry, Waldron, & Bryan, 2024). However, a more centralised conceptualisation of GCE was established through the UN's Global Education First Initiative (2014-2017), which identified GCE as an educational approach with three core domains:

- **Cognitive**: Developing knowledge and understanding of global issues and the interconnectedness of local, national, and global systems.
- **Socio-emotional**: Fostering a sense of belonging to a common humanity, empathy, solidarity, and respect for diversity.

- **Behavioural**: Encouraging learners to act responsibly and to take informed, reflective action at local, national, and global levels

As such, GCE is viewed as a means of counteracting global, shared problems through citizenship education. At a surface level, GCE may be seen as counter to the neoliberal educational agenda. Yet, a deeper reading of the discourses surrounding it suggests that GCE can act as a willing bedfellow, providing a thought-experiment-style escape route for reconciling with, or even endorsing, neoliberalism in education. Pais and Costa (2020) dismiss GCE's claims to progressiveness as an "empty signifier" that sustains false hope and blocks the real antagonism needed for meaningful change. Educators want to believe in GCE "so that we can accept the unequal, increasingly competitive reality in which we all work as educators" (Pais & Costa, 2020, p. 11).

This is supported by Pashby, da Costa, Stein and Andreotti (2020), who found that most GCE typologies remain framed within a modern/colonial imaginary, which positions Western and European perspectives as both universal and inevitable. Such framing limits the potential of GCE to lead to genuine systemic shifts within education. Circular reasoning about GCE's purpose traps educators in cyclical debate, risking the reproduction of inequalities instead of challenging them (Pashby et al., 2020). Educators trained in this model may come to perceive the issues GCE claims to address in overly simplistic terms, promoting a new "civilising mission", where the slogan of "'making a difference' is empty; as the ones doing the 'saving' project their own beliefs as universals onto the world, creating a new form of power" (Andreotti, 2014, p. 22). Without critical reflection on these underlying assumptions, GCE risks reinforcing the very hegemonies it purports to dismantle.

Biccum (2024) argues that this drive towards global homogeneity in education clearly reflects the aims and mechanisms of the neoliberal agenda. As such, GCE becomes something to be viewed with suspicion, repurposed as a means of promoting the belief that education's primary function is to produce citizens for a productive workforce. Within this framing, GCE holds value for the neoliberal agenda insofar as it fosters critical thinking and analytical skills deemed necessary for a technologically advanced future labour market. However, Biccum (2024) challenges this perspective by asking, "in a world where people are becoming more interconnected … do they need to be more alike?" This provocation invites us to reconsider whether education should serve economic priorities or embrace a broader, more humanistic vision of global citizenship.

In summary, GCE offers only a superficial oppositional stance to an increasingly homogenised global educational practice. It provides a convenient shorthand for resistance, yet risks reinforcing the very status quo it claims to challenge. This creates space for leaders to project their own beliefs and biases onto the world. As such, GCE has become a tool of the neoliberal educational project, a means of teaching pupils the so-called "correct" global values and problem-solving skills deemed necessary to navigate the complex consequences of neoliberal globalisation. Compassionate leadership in education is presented as an antidote to this, as it shifts the focus from performative global citizenship towards relational, context-sensitive practice. This approach disrupts the individualistic focus of neoliberal frameworks by foregrounding human connection, relational accountability, and the potential for systemic change within everyday schools and local school networks.

Countering with Compassion

This edited volume proposes that compassionate leadership in education holds the potential to counter both the realities and evolving threats of GERM and GCE. The conceptualisation of compassion, and its recommended application, deliberately draws on a diverse range of global authors in an effort to foreground multiplicity of perspective. This approach seeks to safeguard against the homogenisation so often reproduced within global educational discourse, and to maintain a commitment to nuance, context, and difference.

Given this multi-faceted foundation, to comprehend how "compassion" and "compassionate practice" are articulated across the nine chapters there are five core conceptual axes to outline:

1 Foundational values/ethics.
2 Relational focus.
3 Mechanisms/processes.
4 Contextual sensitivity.
5 Purpose/aims.

The first conceptual axis, foundational values and ethics, primarily understands compassion as an interpersonal human act arising from an ethical orientation. This axis encompasses approaches such as spiritual and moral education (Chapter 6), Confucian *ren* (Chapter 5), posthuman affirmative ethics (Chapter 8), and professional love (Chapter 7). The second axis, relational focus, positions compassion as enacted through interactional styles and relationships with others. This includes the directional flows of compassion drawn from Compassion-Focused Therapy (Chapter 3), relational accountability through practices of trust, care, and respect (Chapter 4), and kinship with the more-than-human (Chapter 8).

The axis of mechanisms and processes frames compassion as a set of actionable practices and strategies. Here, methods such as reflection, coaching, and storytelling, among others, are explored as vehicles for enacting compassionate leadership. In contrast, contextual sensitivity offers a wider lens, situating compassion within sociohistorical and cultural dynamics. This includes engagement with sociohistorical analysis (Chapter 5), critical pedagogy (Chapter 4), and early years care (Chapter 7).

Finally, the axis of purpose and aims interrogates the rationale for adopting compassionate leadership. Across the chapters, the articulated aims are diverse, including the promotion of resilience and wellbeing (Chapter 3), collective thriving (Chapter 2), social justice (Chapter 4), and ecological attunement (Chapter 8). Together, these conceptual axes offer a multidimensional understanding of how compassion is defined, enacted, and situated within leadership practice across cultural, pedagogical, and philosophical contexts.

These diverse conceptualisations of compassion explored across the chapters thus resist any singular, fixed definition. Instead, they suggest compassion as a dynamic, relational, and situated practice, one that operates across different levels of interaction, context, and purpose. To honour this multiplicity while offering a coherent synthesis, the flows and frames model of compassionate leadership (developed as an overview to chapter content) can be used as a conceptual tool for navigating the varied perspectives. This model maps the enactment of compassion across four directional flows and four framing lenses. Together, these dimensions offer a means of understanding who or what compassion is directed towards, and how compassion is conceptualised, contextualised, and applied (see Figure 1.1).

FLOWS OF COMPASSION

Drawing on ideas from compassion-focused therapy and expanded through the contributions of the chapters in this book, the model identifies a series of directional flows through which compassion is enacted and experienced. These flows articulate *who or what compassion is directed towards*, as well as the relational pathways through which care, accountability, and ethical responsibility are expressed:

- **Self-to-self.** Compassion as internal process: self-awareness, self-compassion, emotional regulation, reflection.
- **Self-to-other.** Compassion as interpersonal action: empathy, care, trust-building, leadership behaviours directed toward others.
- **Other-to-self.** Compassion as received: being open to the care, feedback, and accountability of others, fostering reciprocal and relational leadership.
- **Leader-to-community.** Compassion as enacted responsibility toward the collective: recognising leadership as embedded within social relationships, moral obligations, and community wellbeing. This flow is particularly evident in Confucian conceptions of ren, as well as in pedagogical practices grounded in *cariño*, *respeto*, and *confianza*.
- **Community-to-leader (accountability flow).** Compassion as expressed through collective accountability: the community's role in holding leaders to shared ethical standards of care, respect, and trust. This flow highlights leadership as relationally answerable, not autonomous.
- **Generational / ancestral flow (past-to-present).** Compassion as historical and intergenerational: shaped by cultural, familial, and sociohistorical legacies. This flow recognises the transmission of both care and harm across time and calls for leadership practices attentive to history, memory, and the work of repair.
- **Beyond-the-human.** Compassion as more-than-human relationality: kinship, ecological attunement, and affirmative ethics with animals, land, environment, and material worlds.

Figure 1.1 The flows and frames model of compassionate leadership.

> **FRAMES OF APPLICATION**
>
> Intersecting with these flows are four conceptual frames that shape how compassion is understood and enacted within specific contexts:
>
> 1 **Cultural-historical frame.** Compassion as culturally and historically situated, drawing on spiritual traditions, ethical systems, and sociohistorical analysis (e.g. Confucian values, spiritual and moral education, intersectionality, postcolonial critique).
> 2 **Emotional-psychological frame.** Compassion as supported by psychological mechanisms such as self-efficacy, positive emotions, distress tolerance, and trust. Reflective practice, coaching, and therapeutic models fall within this frame.
> 3 **Structural-political frame.** Compassion as a mode of social justice and resistance, challenging performative, neoliberal, or authoritarian models of leadership and education. Here, critical pedagogy and relational accountability become mechanisms of disruption.
> 4 **Ecological/posthuman frame.** Compassion as relational entanglement beyond the human: acknowledging more-than-human kinship, environmental responsibility, and the ethics of interconnectedness.

Case Study: Compassionate Leadership in a Special School

Contributed by Dr Kirsty Evans and Dr Kathryn Lynch

   The Westminster School, located in Sandwell, is a specialist school that provides a nurturing and inclusive learning environment for pupils aged 7 to 19 with a range of special educational needs. It supports pupils to develop the knowledge and skills needed for life, through a broad and balanced curriculum. The Westminster School employs two Educational Psychologists (EPs) for a total of nine days per week of EP time. EPs specialise in understanding how people learn and develop, using psychological principles to support pupils, educators, and families in improving learning outcomes, addressing barriers to education, and fostering inclusive and supportive environments in schools.

Since 2020, The Westminster School has used EP time to support pupil, staff and organisational wellbeing and flourishing. This work is underpinned by EP principles for practice, which were developed through supervision:

- gaining voices;
- understanding interacting factors;
- drawing on positive psychology and exploring strengths;
- empowering others;
- discussing values and generating goals;
- personalisation; and
- commitment to anti-oppressive practice.

These principles provide a framework for supporting meaningful growth and development at multiple levels, ensuring that everyone is treated with care, respect, and dignity. Using these principles, we can promote a holistic, individualised, and compassionate approach to wellbeing.

In the early stages of EP work at The Westminster School, the senior leadership team and staff embraced training on relational approaches such as emotion coaching, which led to discussions about the kind of school The Westminster School wants to be for pupils and the school community.

As EPs, we supported the school to understand their values and engage in values-based practice. All staff were asked to complete the Values In Action (VIA) character strengths survey and we facilitated discussions with the whole staff team in relation to each of the 24 character strengths. We asked:

- Why is this important to you?
- Why is this important to the pupils and the school?

The strengths which were ranked most highly by staff were love, kindness, fairness, forgiveness and humour, which then became the school values and are arguably fundamental expressions of compassion and reflect the values of the wider community. The staff felt that love was reciprocal between pupils and staff and supported the self-esteem of pupils. Kindness was discussed as promoting honesty, openness and a sense of safety. Fairness was understood as being linked to meaningful opportunities and diversity. Humour was seen to be important for building positive relationships and supporting coping and management of emotions. For fairness, staff spoke about the importance of normalising and learning from mistakes.

These values and are not in line with punitive approaches to behaviour management and underpin the development of a unique school ethos and compassionate approach to promoting wellbeing, which now informs recruitment processes and everyday practice. New staff on arrival to the school receive training on the school ethos:

- Relationships and belonging are key to wellbeing and social and emotional development.
- Everyone is treated with empathy and compassion and approaches are person centred.
- The school motto is "safe, happy and learning together" – safety and happiness are the pre-requisites for effective learning.
- The school has a wellbeing policy and avoids purely behavioural approaches with pupils such as rewards, consequences and sanctions, in favour of relational approaches

To add another dimension to this case study, we interviewed the Executive Headteacher, Oliver Flowers, who talked about the importance of compassionate leadership in developing and maintaining this school ethos.

Oliver spoke about a compassionate approach being "values led" and about his investment in the development and maintenance of a compassionate school culture. He reflected that this takes a lot of time and that consistency is developed when it is effectively communicated, modelled through leadership and reflected in policy.

When we asked Oliver about the impact of compassionate leadership, he expressed: "it means everything; the end goal is promoting pupil wellbeing and supporting them to be compassionate individuals. This is done by ensuring pupils feel nurtured, loved and cared for." He referred to a significant decrease in physical interventions used with pupils since the development of such approaches and also spoke about the positive impact on staff retention.

During the interview, Oliver explicitly made links between pupil wellbeing and staff wellbeing as part of a whole school approach. Influenced by the work of Paul Gilbert on compassion, the role of the EP at The Westminster School has been to identify areas of need or suffering, seek to understand individual or group perspectives and work in collaboration with others to develop plans to promote wellbeing at an individual, group and systemic level. This has included staff wellbeing research on promoting diversity and supporting pupils and staff around female health challenges such as menstruation and menopause. At the individual level, EPs provide supervision and coaching for staff members focussed on wellbeing as it is acknowledged that wellbeing has a direct important on performance.

Informed by educational psychology, Oliver talked about interactions with staff in which he as head teacher utilises active listening skills, understanding, empathy and unconditional positive regard (which EPs had previously provided training on for the senior leadership team). He spoke about the importance of authenticity in such interactions to ensure meaningful connection. He referred to compassion as the "anchor" for effective leadership and reflected on his own journey of understanding and practising relational approaches (such as emotion coaching) an utilising empathy and compassion. He expressed that such approaches have impacted positively on his personal relationships as well as his leadership style.

Oliver also spoke about the challenges of maintaining a compassionate approach consistently at a systemic level when managing school and personal pressures. He referred to the emotional effort it takes for the senior leadership team and for the wider staff team to remain compassionate with others during times of stress or exhaustion. Relating to this, an important role for EPs over time has been listening to, empathising with and promoting the problem solving of the senior leadership team, staff, pupils and parents relating to complex, emotionally charged situations. Oliver also stressed the importance of some of the school values when dealing with such challenges; humour as a coping mechanism and forgiveness when people make mistakes.

In the interview we explored a perceived tension that could exist between high expectations and high compassion. Oliver expressed that a compassionate approach is not a "soft approach" and that expectations and standards should remain high for staff and for pupils. He asserted that a top down punitive approach is not the only way to lead and spoke about the demoralising and demotivating impact of leadership through fear and punitive approaches which can develop toxicity and stifle creativity.

Reflecting on the EP principles for practice five years on, there is evidence of these principles for practice infiltrating school practice at multiple levels. Here are examples relating to the first three original EP principles; gaining voices, understanding interacting factors, drawing on positive psychology and exploring strengths. Pupil voice, staff voice and parent voice are incorporated into the ethos and every day practice, formally through EP research and through forums such as student council, staff and parent surveys and informally through everyday interactions. A school wellbeing service and supporting triage system allows staff and parents to seek support for pupils and to understand the interacting factors contributing to the pupils' presentation. Working on What Works (Berg & Shilts, 2005) approaches have been embraced by staff and senior leaders, which celebrate pupils and staff's strengths and promote wellbeing.

One thing that we are sure about as EPs, which Oliver also expressed, is the importance of a holistic compassionate approach which extends to the whole school community. This takes time and work but is an investment in whole school wellbeing and belonging.

Summary

In summary, compassion is positioned not as a novel intervention or reactionary counterpoint to the prevailing global education agenda, but as a deeply rooted, culturally diverse, and historically enduring human value. While the current dominance of the Global Education Reform Movement (GERM) and Global Citizenship Education (GCE) may present themselves as progressive and solution-oriented, the analysis here highlights how both risk reinforcing neoliberal individualism, standardisation, and systemic inequity, even as they claim to promote empowerment and global solidarity.

Against this backdrop, the book does not simply advocate for compassion as resistance, but rather invites a *re-encounter* with compassion as tradition, praxis, and ethical commitment. The chapters within foreground compassion as complex and situated, simultaneously personal, relational, systemic, and ecological. Crucially, this volume rejects the notion that cohesion requires uniformity, asserting instead that multiplicity of voice, context, and perspective enriches rather than undermines the shared endeavour of compassionate leadership in education.

Through the development of the flows and frames model of compassionate leadership, the book offers a conceptual synthesis that honours this diversity. This model maps how compassion is enacted across multiple directional flows and across framing lenses. In doing so, the book seeks not to prescribe a singular approach, but to allow the reader to engage with a variety of compassionate practices that challenge performativity, resist homogenisation, and centre relational accountability. This re-encounter with compassion is not presented as an easy fix, nor as inherently progressive, but as a deliberate, often difficult, ethical choice.

References

Andreotti, V. de O. (2014). Soft versus critical global citizenship education. In S. McCloskey (Ed.), *Development education in policy and practice* (pp. 21-31). Palgrave Macmillan. https://doi.org/10.1057/9781137324665_2

Barry, M., Waldron, F., & Bryan, A. (2024). Understanding global citizenship education in the classroom: A case study of teaching practices. *Education, Citizenship and Social Justice*, 17461979241278644. https://doi.org/10.1177/17461979241278644

Berg, I. K., & Shilts, L. (2005). *Classroom solutions: WOWW coaching*. BFTC.

Biccum, A. R. (2024). What do you need to know to live in the world? Global educational reform and the democratisation of knowledge. *Globalisation, Societies and Education*, 1-20. https://doi.org/10.1080/14767724.2024.2312834

Davies, W. V. (2001). Standardisation and the school: Norm tolerance in the educational domain. *Linguistische Berichte*, 188, 393-414.

Farley, A. N., & Chamberlain, L. M. (2021). The teachers are not alright: A call for research and policy on teacher stress and well-being. *The New Educator*, 17(3), 305-323. https://doi.org/10.1080/1547688X.2021.1939918

Fuller, K., & Stevenson, H. (2019). Global education reform: Understanding the movement. *Educational Review*, 71(1), 1-4. https://doi.org/10.1080/00131911.2019.1532718

Halvorsen, S. (2012). Beyond the network? Occupy London and the global movement. *Social Movement Studies*, 11(3-4), 427-433. https://doi.org/10.1080/14742837.2012.708835

Maisuria, A. (2015). The neo-liberalisation policy agenda and its consequences for education in England: A focus on resistance now and possibilities for the future. *Policy Futures in Education*, 12(2), 286-296. https://doi.org/10.2304/pfie.2014.12.2.286

Oliver, M. (2013). The social model of disability: Thirty years on. *Disability & Society*, 28(7), 1024-1026. https://doi.org/10.1080/09687599.2013.818773

Pais, A., & Costa, M. (2020). An ideology critique of global citizenship education. *Critical Studies in Education*, 61(1), 1-16. https://doi.org/10.1080/17508487.2017.1318772

Pashby, K., Da Costa, M., Stein, S., & Andreotti, V. (2020). A meta-review of typologies of global citizenship education. *Comparative Education*, 56(2), 144-164. https://doi.org/10.1080/03050068.2020.1723352

Sahlberg, P. (2012). A model lesson: Finland shows us what equal opportunity looks like. *American Educator*, 36(1), 20-27, 40.

Yoon, E.-S. (2024). From GERM (Global Educational Reform Movement) to NERM (Neoliberal Educational Reform Madness). *Critical Education*, 13-28 Pages. https://doi.org/10.14288/CE.V15I2.186904

2

Enhancing Reflective Practice through Compassionate Leadership in Senior Leaders

Jo Taylor

> **CHAPTER AIMS**
>
> By the end of this chapter, readers will be able to:
>
> - Describe the origins of the compassion-focused coaching (CFC) model, including the theories it draws upon and key tools used to support reflection.
> - Explain the structure of the CFC process and discuss how it was received by senior leaders in education.
> - Apply compassion-focused activities to support your own reflective practice at work.

Introduction

What Is Reflective Practice?

I am a child and educational psychologist and work with children, families, educators, and organisations. A large part of my practice involves creating spaces for people to think about their work, so that they can be more effective and work more sustainably. Over the last five years, I have been exploring compassion-focused approaches as a complement to my work as a psychologist, including completing a Churchill Fellowship researching compassion as a facilitator for caring behaviour. This chapter will focus on one strand of my work with compassion: reflective practice.

Reflective practice is a phrase I'm hearing more and more. As a psychologist, I am very used to having reflective spaces that support me to do my work. In fact, psychology is one of the few professions in which reflective practice is a requirement (we call it supervision). Our registering body mandates reflective practice as essential for safe practice. We have a broad role, which involves difficult decisions, strategic thinking, hypothesising, and navigating human suffering. A reflective space to unpick these threads is important. When reading this list, you may have thought, "my job has quite a lot of those components too", or "I make difficult decisions and need to work strategically". I've noticed that many jobs and contexts have similarities to the way psychologists work, but rarely have built-in processes for facilitating reflection alongside the main job role. I think this is why facilitating reflective spaces has become such a significant part of my work as a psychologist: because they can be incredibly useful across a broad range of roles and sectors. This is likely why we've seen such a rise in sectors commissioning reflective spaces (e.g. life coaches, executive coaches, teaching coaches, love coaches).

In education, we have seen recent policy changes that have provided funding for the provision of reflective practice, through coaches for early career teachers, FE teachers, and governors (Department for Education, 2021). The white paper outlines the importance of supporting people to access personal development over time, and to develop skills while in post. As part of this, coaching was highlighted as a mechanism for personal development that could support outstanding teaching.

Adding to the momentum that reflective practice seems to have, I have co-developed a model of reflective practice based on compassion-focused approaches, called compassion-focused coaching (CFC; Heriot-Maitland & Taylor, 2024). Later in this chapter, we will use an example of providing CFC for senior leaders to explore how compassion can facilitate reflective practice. First, it is important to clarify the terms we will be using throughout the chapter.

Coaching, Reflective Practice, and Supervision

In this chapter, I will use the term *reflective practice* to describe the process of CFC. As a model, CFC shares similarities with both coaching and what psychologists refer to as supervision. Carroll et al. (2020) produced a table summarising the features of coaching, supervision, and mentoring, intended to support discussions around their differences when commissioning work in schools. I have adapted this below to help orient readers who are trying to position CFC within the wider landscape of professional learning and development approaches.

Compassion Focused Approaches: CFT, CMT and CFC

Compassion-focused coaching (CFC) is a compassion-focused reflective practice model, informed by compassion focused therapy (CFT). CFT was developed by Professor Paul Gilbert of the Compassionate Mind Foundation (www.compassionatemind.co.uk) as a psychotherapy model and has this has been successfully adapted as a model to improve the wellbeing of staff and organisations across a range of sectors (e.g. healthcare, social care, charity, business, and education).

I think using the term *reflective practice* will be most helpful when discussing CFC, as the terms *supervision* and *coaching* do not have single, agreed-upon definitions. There is long-standing academic debate around these definitions, and strong feelings about the boundaries of each approach (Flaherty, 2022; Passmore & Lai, 2020). On a practical level, these terms also carry certain stigma and popular associations. *Coaching* can make people think of sport, while *supervision* might lead readers to associate it with performance management and hierarchy.

Table 2.1 Coaching, mentoring and supervision as defined by Carroll et al. (2020).

Coaching	Mentoring	Supervision
• Enables the development of a specific aspect of a professional learner's practice • Coach is usually chosen by professional learner • Coach may have knowledge and expertise relevant to the goals of the professional learner • Process focusses on learner generating ways forward	• Supports professional learner through significant career transitions • Led by experienced colleagues with knowledge of the requirements of the role • Broker access to a range of increasingly self-directed learning opportunities	• Development of knowledge, competence and confidence for everyday context • Explores the relational aspects of the professional role • Helps to process the emotional impact of the professional role • Facilitates understanding • On-going throughout career

Language is important. When I work with schools to set up reflective practice groups, I often avoid the term *supervision* and describe the process as *reflective practice*, because it is a more neutral term. I have found that this helps people begin the process without making too many early judgements or experiencing undue anxiety. As we progress through the chapter, you can decide for yourself whether CFC is best described as a supervision or coaching model.

This chapter will cover:

- The development and application of compassion-focused approaches to reflective practice in education, through the lens of CFC – a compassion-focused reflective practice model.
- The experiences of senior leaders who participated in CFC groups between 2020 and 2023.
- Ideas for how CFC and compassion-focused reflective practice more broadly could be useful in your context.

What Is Compassion?

Compassion-focused coaching was designed with CFT and CMT at its core, so it uses the following two-part definition:

> The sensitivity to suffering and the commitment to relieve or prevent it.
> *(Adapted from Gilbert, 2009)*

In short, compassion-focused therapy (CFT) aims to help people regulate threat-based emotions and experiences by building internal feelings of safeness and developing compassion towards self and others (Gilbert, 2009; Gilbert & Simos, 2022). Compassionate mind training (CMT) was developed by Irons and Heriot-Maitland (2021) and involves approaches and tools that can be used outside of a therapeutic context – and have been applied to great effect across a range of settings.

Compassion-Focused Attributes and Skills

The two-part definition of compassion is particularly useful when considering reflective practice, as it links the worlds of awareness and action. We need both the sensitivity to suffering and the commitment to relieve or prevent it. This definition helps us to understand that compassion relies on two distinct groups of psychological processes (Gilbert, 2009; Gilbert et al., 2017; Irons & Beaumont, 2017). As we will see below, these attributes and skills can be cultivated through CFC.

Engagement with Distress

To help people, we need to have some understanding of their difficulties. Table 2.2 presents a set of attributes which facilitate engagement with suffering, getting close to suffering, to better understand it, and this can be complicated, not least because it can be draining and difficult. Engagement with distress can involve a range of attributes which I have presented in a table, alongside a description of why it can be helpful and an example of how CFC can develop it.

Alleviation of Distress

The second group of psychological processes focuses on building the skills and knowledge needed to respond to suffering – to try and improve things. CFT outlines six distinct areas that contribute to compassionate thought and action (Gilbert et al., 2017; Irons & Beaumont, 2017). These span a continuum of thoughts and feelings, including how we direct our attention to seek solutions, how we use imagination and memory to support ourselves and make action feel sustainable, and the types of behaviours we engage in. In Table 2.3, these attributes are presented alongside examples of how they can support compassion, and how CFC can facilitate their development.

Over the years of using CFC, I observed that sessions developed participants' compassionate attributes and skills (see "How has CFC been Received?" below). I also noted that these attributes and skills contributed to the increased effectiveness of reflective practice sessions. Over time, within CFC groups, we created a virtuous cycle: the reflective space enhanced participants' compassionate attributes and their ability to use compassionate skills, while simultaneously benefiting from these psychological processes.

Compassion-Focused Coaching Origins

In CFC sessions, we often talk about "creating the conditions" for compassionate thought and action. This same principle applies to the process of setting up CFC groups. The CFC

Enhancing Reflective Practice in Senior Leaders 19

Table 2.2 Key attributes for engaging with distress and suffering.

Attribute	Why it is helpful	How CFC can develop it
Care for wellbeing	Feeling motivated to care is the first step towards helping	Highlighting care for wellbeing in agenda items, using questions to explore care in discussion
Sensitivity	Attending to distress is fundamental to understanding it: in our selves and other people	Using all its members sensitivity, to direct attention to different aspects of difficulty.
Sympathy	Being moved by peoples' experiences contributes to our commitment to help	Noticing and communicating sympathy: to other group members and also for aspects of agenda items
Empathy	Taking multiple perspectives contributes to more helpful actions	Benefitting from the empathy of all its members, meaning that perspective taking can be shared and built upon.
Distress tolerance	Turning towards distress can be difficult in itself, so in order to be able to help, we need to build our tolerance.	Providing a facilitated space for the exploration of distress, the processing of suffering and the recovery from talking about agenda items
Non judgement	Moving away from criticism and judgement can help us to understand situations more clearly	Noticing, unpicking and negotiating judgements in sessions, to help participants choose alternative approaches in their work.

manual (Heriot-Maitland & Taylor, 2024) includes three key sections to support this process: *Preparing for CFC, Setting Up the Supervision Group,* and *Laying the Foundation for a Trusting Group.*

Initial Training in Compassion Theory

Over the last four years, we have adapted the way we help participants prepare to take part in reflective practice groups. A key part of this process is an initial training session. We have found that investing a little more time and depth into this early stage enables participants to begin getting more out of their sessions, earlier on. The training covers several elements, including the evolutionary functions of emotions, CFT as a therapeutic approach, how CFT and CMT have been used in education, some of the frameworks we use to explore emotions in sessions, and initial reflections on how to prepare for the first CFC session.

At the time of writing, compassion seems to be in the zeitgeist – frequently used in both my professional and social circles. However, to my ear, it is often used in different ways, typically as a synonym for empathy or kindness. For others, compassion may not be something they have considered at all – in relation to their work, their lives, or even more

Table 2.3 Skill training for the alleviation of distress and suffering.

Skill	Why it is helpful	How CFC can develop it
Attention	Learning to focus on what will be useful to us	Questions to explore alternative angles of agenda items and reframe situations
Imagery	Harnessing our imagination to produce compassion-related responses in our bodies	Using CMT activities as part of sessions to introduce participants to tools they can use in their work and life.
Reasoning	Developing our compassionate metacognition to engage with thoughts, people and situations more helpfully	Using questions to engage reasoning skills.
Sensory	Using different senses to create a fuller experience of positive emotions, so that we can feel more grounded.	Using CMT activities to explore positive emotions through different senses.
Behaviour	Combining wisdom, care and courage to act in a way which will prevent and reduce suffering and distress	Planning actions after discussing agenda items and reflecting on how plans went in future sessions.
Feeling	Practising emotions like kindness, warmth and contentment, so that they are easier to access	Highlighting these feelings during discussions, using visualisation to practice feelings throughout sessions.

broadly. This felt like an important piece of context, as it meant that CFC groups were likely to include senior leaders with very different understandings of what compassion means. As such, another important part of creating the conditions for useful CFC sessions was supporting participants to share, contrast, and align their perspectives on compassion and how it would be used in our work together.

Running initial training sessions is always a fascinating experience. It is an honour to introduce participants to compassion-focused theory, and the content often provokes powerful responses. Reflecting on this, three aspects of the day consistently stood out as particularly impactful for participants.

Exploring the evolved functions of emotions
Emotions can be a tricky part of life, yet many people don't spend much time thinking about them. Considering the evolved function of emotions can be fundamentally de-shaming, as it highlights how natural our feelings are – that they help us achieve

things and are not our fault. It can also offer hope, as it reminds us that we have in-built mechanisms for thinking, feeling, and acting more helpfully in daily life. With practice, we can get better at using these.

Introducing models of emotions from CFT and CMT
Having a shared vocabulary to talk about emotions in different situations can be an important step in developing a new relationship with our emotional experiences. Initial training introduced attendees to models from CFT and CMT – such as the three circles model of emotion and the multiple selves model. These were shared as practical tools to help explore people's motivations in various situations. For many participants, this was empowering, as it helped to make sense of actions and outcomes with colleagues, direct reports, children, and families.

Turning towards suffering
This can be a powerful "aha" moment for participants. As humans, we often instinctively turn away from suffering or distress in an attempt to protect ourselves. At times, we may actively escape it; other times, we might realise we have unconsciously distanced ourselves from a situation. These responses are rarely deliberate – it can simply feel as though it "just happened". In the initial training, we planted the seed that turning towards suffering can lead to better understanding, which can be the first step in reducing or preventing it.

Laying the Foundations for a Trusting Group

As part of laying the foundations for a trusting group, we dedicated time to helping participants consider what they would need in order to engage fully with CFC. It was important to recognise that individuals would bring different levels of familiarity and comfort when approaching reflective conversations, influenced by their professional, historical, and cultural backgrounds.

We also clarified what the group was – and was not. For example, it was framed as "a place to unpick tricky situations, but not therapy", and "a space for professional development, but not line management". These distinctions helped to set clear expectations and reduce uncertainty.

In the first session of CFC, participants created a *group agreement*, outlining what they expected of each other and from the group as a whole. They also developed a *contract*, which described what sessions would feel like when working well, and what the group would do if things weren't working effectively. During the initial training, we set aside time to help participants reflect on what makes for a good contract or agreement. This contributed to the smooth running of the first session and helped reduce anxiety around what to expect. Having facilitators present for these conversations was particularly valuable, as it allowed participants to ask questions and receive reassurance.

Skill Development

When people think about reflective practice, they often imagine talking through a scenario and leaving the session with a solution or next step. While supervision can look like this, it can also serve as a forum for developing broader skills.

Hewson and Carroll (2016) use a metaphor of supervision as a house, with different rooms you might inhabit depending on the process in use – for example, recharging in the lounge, reflecting in the office, or experimenting in the art studio. This metaphor resonated with CFC groups, who brought different goals and ways of working to each session. As a result, sessions were used in varied ways on different days.

Chapters 4 and 5 of the CFC manual focus on supporting participants to develop skills in reflective practice and compassion. Naturally, the specifics varied depending on each group's needs and preferences, but a few trends emerged over time. One such trend was that the first few months of a CFC group were often spent engaging in psychoeducation, developing psychological skills, and being introduced to models and techniques from compassionate mind training.

Psycho-education in CFC Sessions

People can have very different experiences of emotions, varying levels of emotional awareness, and differing needs when it comes to processing emotions. This is true not only for individuals participating in reflective spaces, but also for their colleagues, clients, and stakeholders. Early in their CFC journey, senior leaders were supported to use models from CFT and CMT to help them recognise and understand the emotions being experienced in the situations they brought to the group. This was useful on a number of levels.

One of the first models participants are introduced to is the *three circles model of emotion*, which helps individuals explore the feelings and motivations they might hold in particular situations. The model was developed as a tool for use in compassion-focused therapy (CFT) (Gilbert, 2009), and it simplifies decades of experimental research into mammalian emotional drives carried out by Jaak Panksepp (Davis & Montag, 2019). In short, it suggests that mammals share a set of common emotional systems, each with evolved functions designed to help us navigate our lives.

Another model used in CFC to support emotional exploration is *multiple selves* (Irons & Beaumont, 2017). This model helped participants begin to build relationships with their emotions. For some readers, this may sound unusual, a relationship with an emotion? But the principle is widely recognised across therapeutic disciplines such as cognitive behavioural therapy, mindfulness-based stress reduction, and narrative therapy.

It can be a helpful approach because, by creating a distinction between ourselves and our emotions, they often become less overwhelming. This makes it easier to make conscious choices about how to interpret and respond to them. Over time, most CFC participants were able to develop this skill, gaining insight into how their emotions might be trying to help in a given situation, as well as recognising the unintended consequences those emotional responses could bring. For example, the angry part of me might be trying to help right an

Enhancing Reflective Practice in Senior Leaders 23

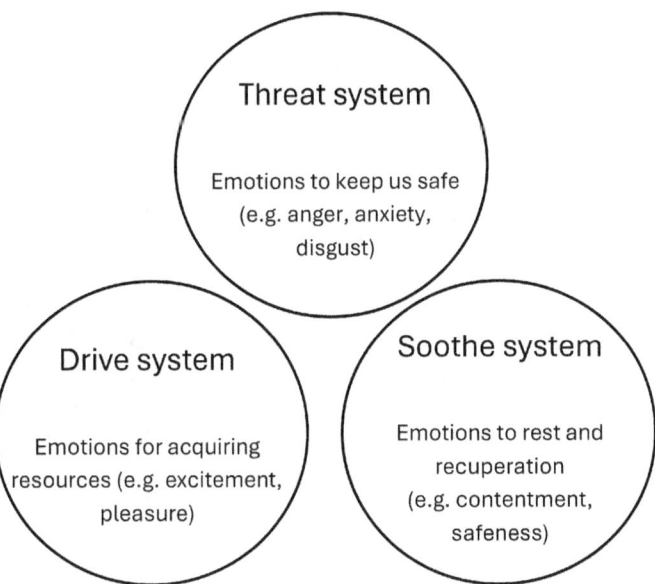

Figure 2.1 The three circles model of emotion.

injustice by pumping me up to act bravely, but my actions might be making the people I manage feel a bit disconnected from me.

> **REFLECTIVE ACTIVITY: MEET YOUR MULTIPLE SELVES**
>
> One of the things which CFC facilitators can do across sessions is help participants to get to know their different "selves". As Table 2.4 outlines, we can have different parts of ourselves which add different thoughts to situations and can want different outcomes from interactions. So, having a greater awareness of what these different parts of us are like can help us to make wiser choices in our work (and life). It can also start to open up another layer of understanding around other people's actions ("I wonder if that was their angry-self talking?", "this email looks like it might have been written by someone's anxious self" etc). The process of getting to know our multiple selves and using them to unpick situations at work can take time and careful facilitation. However, if you are curious then I've included an activity which will help provide an introduction to your angry, anxious and sad selves, so that you can get a sense of how they feature at work.

Table 2.4 The Multiple Selves in practice. Example situation: a child threw a chair in my lesson.

Angry Self	Anxious Self	Sad Self
Thinks: "They could have hurt a classmate, or me! Nobody should have to teach with this kind of behaviour, it is not fair!" Wants: Justice, change, to be heard.	Thinks: "I think my colleagues were talking about it in the staff room. They probably think I am a bad teacher." Wants: Safety, certainty.	Thinks: "I heard they had an argument with their foster carer in the morning, I know things have been difficult at home recently." Wants: Care, time alone

1. You will need a piece of A4 paper, something to draw with and perhaps something to add colour with.
2. Draw three simple outlines of a person, to represent the three multiple selves we will be introducing (angry, anxious, sad).
3. Add in some detail, so that you can tell them apart. What kinds of faces do they have? Do they have any props or items of clothing which help you know who they are? Or, that you associate with how they navigate life and work? (e.g. my angry self has bright red hair which flames when particularly incensed).
4. Is there anything else associated with them (colours, sounds, textures)?
5. Do they get involved at work? If so, write where/when each of them tends to feature most (e.g. *when the photocopier has broken and time is running out before an important meeting*, or *as I am about to run a meeting for the people I manage*, etc.).
6. Write some key words to describe what each of them wants at work.
7. Is there anything you find difficult about how they show up (associated feelings, physical responses, recovering, compensating etc)?
8. Is there anything helpful about these different selves? If so, write some words which capture how they help at work.
9. Choose one of your multiple selves (perhaps the one which shows up at work the most?) Next time you are at work, you might be able to notice when they are arriving in a situation. So, now we are going to plan a way that might be helpful to respond (e.g. thanking them for their input and saying goodbye, writing down their contribution, so you can think about it later, inviting another multiple self to contribute a different perspective, etc.).

Developing Psychological Skills in CFC Sessions

In CFC, participants develop their ability to engage in wise, strategic thought. Before this, they can often rush to offer solutions when people describe a difficulty. I see this with lots of senior leaders in education and my interpretation is that it's because people really care: care about the people in the group, care about the work, care about the cause or clients. An early transition in CFC is helping people move from a place of speed ("I need to help as quickly as possible") towards a place of wise action ("I want to understand better so that we can choose the most useful way forward").

Another key development which participants go through is improving their ability to ask useful questions. As a CFC supervisor, in early sessions, there was a focus on supporting participants to ask more, open questions. Over time, this developed into a more curious stance in sessions, with participants leaning away from offering immediate advice and moving towards unpicking situations a bit more. If we think back to our definition of compassion: the first half revolves around the awareness of suffering and distress. Where, we need to understand the difficulty so we can best help. In CFC, learning how to ask questions was a step towards being able to help reduce and prevent suffering, more effectively. This shift in questioning also provided a foundation for the layering of compassion-focused theory, where participants were able to choose questions which might be influenced by models from CFT or CMT.

For CFC participants, building a foundation which included an increased awareness of emotions, the ability to unpick the emotions in situations and the skill to ask really useful questions meant that they were able to make session time more useful, more quickly.

REFLECTIVE PROMPT: ASKING MORE, POWERFUL QUESTIONS

Questions can be a powerful tool and choosing the right tool is important. I see educators use questions as part of their pedagogy all day. However, I see questions used less in meetings with adults.

Let's do a thought experiment. Imagine something has happened at work. Something tricky, which you feel stuck with and you want some help from colleagues.

First, imagine a scenario where you describe the situation, briefly, just the headlines and then the person you are speaking to replies with some advice (e.g. "you should try ...", "something similar happened to me and I ...").

Next, lets imagine the same tricky situation but when you approach your colleague for help they ask you questions to understand the situation a bit more, before you think about next steps.

In each situation, consider, how you feel, about the situation and about the colleague? What kind of next steps do you leave with?

I am not framing either scenario as good or bad. I am highlighting the fact that they are different, and that you might arrive at different places as a result, questions are a tool, we can choose to use.

If you are interested in exploring how the use of questions can impact meetings or interactions in your context, I have included some examples of questions, which you could add to your tool box.

> **OPEN QUESTIONS TO EXPERIMENT WITH**
> - What impact is this having?
> - Who is the owner of this issue?
> - What do you need from this conversation?
> - What is the ideal outcome?
> - What do you need to make something happen?
> - Who do you need to talk to, to move forward?
> - What needs to be said, which has not been said?

Compassionate Mind Training

One of the distinctive features of CFC is that it incorporates elements of compassionate mind training (CMT), offering a dual benefit: developing participants' psychological skills while also facilitating deeper and more meaningful reflection. CMT is a rich and varied approach, introduced in the previous chapter (Irons & Heriot-Maitland, 2021; see also www.balancedminds.com). This section zooms in on specific processes and models that featured prominently in the senior leaders' CFC groups.

Practising the Giving and Receiving of Compassion

Compassion can flow in three directions: from self to other, from other to self, and from self to self (Gilbert et al., 2017). Most participants had not encountered this model before joining CFC and had not considered how compassion might flow in their lives and work.

Early sessions focused on developing awareness in this area. Initially, this occurred naturally alongside other processes, for example, supervisors highlighting moments of compassion as they arose during discussions. As participants grew more familiar with the concept, they began to intentionally direct compassion toward other group members and name when they felt they were receiving it. This practice often felt good, as well as being psychologically beneficial, and became an intentional part of group culture.

Facilitators also encouraged group members to reflect on what their *compassionate selves* might say in response to a scenario. These kinds of prompts often accessed insights that weren't immediately conscious, enriching the flow of compassion within the group. Over time, participants began to initiate this themselves, asking reflective, compassionate questions and expanding their repertoire of tools for navigating difficult situations.

Creating the Conditions for Compassionate Thought and Action

The pace and pressure of professional life, especially in leadership roles, can easily inhibit reflective, strategic thinking. For many senior leaders, this was simply "how things are". However, when we are in a state of threat or heightened arousal, cognitive processes like empathy, imagination, and metacognition are harder to access. In those states, we tend to seek fast answers and binary choices, helpful in emergencies, but limiting when the goal is compassionate leadership.

In CFC, considerable effort is invested in creating the right conditions for compassion to emerge. This often involves *slowing things down*, physically (e.g. through grounding or breathing exercises) and psychologically (e.g. using questions to explore before offering solutions).

For many participants, this slower pace felt counterintuitive, particularly in caring professions where the impulse to help quickly is strong. CMT offered a suite of tools, especially visualisation and soothing techniques, that helped facilitators guide participants into a more grounded, reflective space, where wise and compassionate responses were more likely.

The Compassionate Self

A key element of CMT is the development of the *compassionate self*, a version of oneself that embodies the core attributes of compassion: wisdom, courage, and a commitment to caring behaviour (Irons & Beaumont, 2017).

In CFC sessions, we helped participants build a working relationship with their compassionate self. This began by noticing and naming moments where these qualities emerged in discussions. As awareness grew, participants started using the concept more proactively, for instance, asking "What would my wisest self say in this situation?" or "How might I act if I were led by compassion rather than urgency?"

Over time, participants developed a rich and vivid sense of their compassionate self, sometimes supported by visualisation exercises. They reflected on posture, tone of voice, presence, and how others might respond to this version of themselves. These details made it easier to imagine their compassionate self during sessions and, increasingly, in day-to-day leadership roles.

This internal character became both a guide and a resource, someone to turn to for wise, caring, and sustainable action. (You might revisit the reflective prompts on open questions from earlier in this chapter and try asking: "What would my compassionate self say?")

How Was CFC Used?

CFC sessions were used differently by different groups. One of the strengths of the model is its flexibility, it creates space for participants to explore the challenges they are facing in their work. In the CFC manual, Chapters 6 to 9 were dedicated to four key areas of focus: self, student, colleague, and leadership/systemic (Heriot-Maitland & Taylor, 2024).

Self-Focus

Throughout this chapter, I've described several areas in which individuals developed through CFC sessions. One of the most frequent uses of CFC was to help participants cultivate greater compassion for themselves.

Table 2.5 Multiple selves can include our compassionate self. Example situation: a child threw a chair in my lesson.

Angry Self	Anxious Self	Sad Self	Compassionate Self
Thinks: "They could have hurt a classmate, or me! Nobody should have to teach with this kind of behaviour, it is not fair!" Wants: Justice, change, to be heard.	Thinks: "I think my colleagues were talking about it in the staff room. They probably think I am a bad teacher." Wants: Safety, certainty	Thinks: "I heard they had an argument with their foster carer in the morning, I know things have been difficult at home recently." Wants: Care, time alone.	Thinks: "How can I help boundaries feel like they are about safety and not about punishment?" Wants: Connection, a solution which can suit everyone, to keep all parties safe.

A key strand of CFT is *de-shaming*, helping individuals understand the evolved functions of their emotions and recognising that we navigate life with brains and bodies not optimally adapted to modern contexts. For senior leaders, who carry high levels of responsibility, this understanding can be both challenging and deeply supportive.

CFC sessions gave participants space to unpick their own experiences and responses, often using CFT and CMT models to better understand the emotional drivers within a situation. Sessions also offered an opportunity to practise activating their soothe system, and to give and receive compassion.

Student Focus

Teaching is difficult and teaching in marginalised or disadvantaged communities presents additional challenges.

Between 2020 and 2024, the majority of senior leaders who engaged in CFC worked in Alternative Provision, settings that support children who struggle to access mainstream education. These students often had complex needs and presented with heightened threat-based responses.

CFC sessions enabled leaders to explore ways to support these students, better understand the roots of conflict, and develop responses grounded in wisdom, courage, and care. As with self-focused work, CFT and CMT models were used to look beneath behaviour, exploring underlying motivations, thoughts, and unmet needs.

Colleague Focus

Working with people can be both rewarding and complex. When I first began offering reflective spaces for educators, I expected most agenda items to centre on personal emotions or challenges related to supporting children. However, I was struck, though, in hindsight, not surprised, by how many participants brought issues relating to colleagues.

In CFC sessions, participants used the space to unpick responses to interactions with others across the professional hierarchy: from senior leaders to peers and direct reports. The CFC manual includes sections on directing compassion towards colleagues, receiving support from others, and helping team members manage their own threat-based emotions.

Leadership/Systemic Focus

Another benefit of CFC is its capacity to be used flexibly across all layers of a participant's professional ecosystem. There is no single 'correct' way to use a reflective space.

In my experience, after participants had used CFC to explore personal, student-related, and relational agenda items, they often became curious about applying the approach to broader, systemic leadership challenges. (This was explored in more detail in the previous chapter, so I will keep this section brief.)

Examples of leadership-related uses of CFC include:

- Preparing for difficult conversations with direct reports.
- Reflecting on the emotional impact of school systems and processes.
- Exploring ways to use compassion-focused approaches to support the wider school community.

An exciting development was that some participants began using CFC sessions to support their own facilitation of reflective spaces for others. This ranged from structuring compassionate conversations and creating psychologically safe conditions, to formally leading reflective groups. These experiences not only developed the participants' own practice, but also brought a new dimension to CFC sessions, focused on the challenges and learning involved in holding reflective space for others.

How Has CFC Been Received?

CFC was evaluated at the end of each year, with findings summarised and analysed in detail by Heriot-Maitland and Taylor (2024).

The evaluation involved annual survey data, including both quantitative ratings and qualitative feedback. Results from the first three years indicated increases in:

- Perceived resilience.
- The ability to be compassionate towards self, students, and staff.
- The ability to de-escalate challenging behaviour.

Participants reported impact across the four areas of focus set out in the CFC manual: self, student, colleague, and leadership. One participant reflected:

> The biggest impact for me was on my own responses to challenging behaviour in school… conversations really helped me to reflect on what my emotions were in the

situation, what the child might have been communicating … Also, I have grown in confidence in terms of being able to support colleagues in those conversations, particularly in my line management role.

(Heriot-Maitland & Taylor, 2024, p. 12)

The evaluation also highlighted the acceptability of CFC being delivered by multiple supervisors, supported by initial training and the CFC manual. This provides a foundation for training more practitioners in the approach, allowing a wider range of educational settings to access CFC.

Looking ahead, Heriot-Maitland and Taylor (2024) identified opportunities for CFC to shape practice in areas such as student behaviour management, pastoral care, and safeguarding (p. 18). As described throughout this chapter, CFT and CMT are flexible frameworks that support understanding and navigating complex professional situations. It will be interesting to see how CFC continues to evolve and what further applications may emerge.

> **REFLECTION ACTIVITY: COMPASSIONATE REFLECTION**
>
> I designed this activity to support people in reflecting at the end of an academic year, although it can also be used at other points in the academic calendar. The resource was created with the intention of:

- Avoiding negativity bias.
- Reflecting in a meaningful and supportive way.
- Highlighting moments of connection and contentment within a busy life.
- Recalling times of courage and wisdom.
- Exploring the flows of compassion in your life.

These intentions draw on many of the ideas explored earlier in this chapter – such as the *three circles of emotion*, the *three flows of compassion*, and the *qualities of compassion*.

Below, I've included eight coaching-style questions to give a flavour of how compassion can be woven into reflective practice.

> **REFLECTION PROMPTS**
>
> Respond to the prompts below in whatever way feels helpful, write, draw, doodle, or mind map.

- A time when you felt connected to others at work.

This might be a memory of connection, or even a vision. It could involve collaboration, shared purpose, or honest feedback.

- *A time when you felt content at work.*

What does contentment feel like for you? A quiet hum? A soft glow? How do you know when you're feeling it?

- *A time when you did something courageous at work.*

Courage might mean stepping outside your comfort zone, choosing short-term discomfort for long-term benefit, or speaking truth to power – even saying "no" to something.

- *A time when you were wise in your work.*

Wisdom could involve strategy, long-term thinking under pressure, or moments when you felt guided – by experience, mentors, or even ancestral strength.

- *A time when you were caring in your work.*

Who benefitted from your care? How did you show it? What was the impact, and how did you notice?

- *A time when you were compassionate to someone else.*

How did you notice their distress or suffering? What did you do in response? How did they react?

- *A time when you received compassion from someone else.*

Who offered support? What did they do or say? How did you feel before, during, and after?

- *A time when you were compassionate to yourself.*

How did you notice your own need? What did you do in response? What happened as a result?

Summary

Compassion-focused approaches have been used to create a model of reflective practice known as *compassion-focused coaching* (CFC). Drawing on tools and models from compassion-focused therapy (CFT) and compassionate mind training (CMT), CFC provides a structured space to develop the attributes and skills required for compassionate thought and action.

CFC supports the development of effective questioning skills and provides psychoeducation about emotions. It also incorporates practices from CMT to help participants create the conditions for meaningful reflection. Through this process, participants are supported to cultivate the compassionate qualities of courage, wisdom, and a commitment to caring behaviour. A key feature of the model is the development of the *compassionate self*, who can be intentionally accessed to guide thought and action throughout the working day.

CFC can be used with a range of focal points – including the self, students, colleagues, and leadership or systemic issues. Evaluation data collected over four years showed that senior leaders experienced increased resilience, improved capacity to give and receive compassion, and greater confidence in de-escalating challenging behaviour.

Further Reading

Irons, C., & Beaumont, E., (2017) *The compassionate mind workbook: A step-by-step guide to developing your compassionate self*: Robinson.

For readers who are interested in knowing more about compassionate attributes and skills, they could read section 5 of Chris Irons and Claire Beaumont's *The Compassionate Mind Workbook*. Alongside each attribute and skill, they present questions and activities to help the reader to connect with and reflect on each one.

Heriot-Maitland, C., & Taylor, J. (2024). Developing a compassion focused supervision model for senior leaders in education. *OBM Integrative and Complementary Medicine*, 9(2), 033. https://doi.org/10.21926/obm.icm.2402033.

For a deeper introduction how CFC groups can be set up you could read sections 1-3 of the CFC manual. If you are interested in how CMT is introduced and the supervision processes which can be facilitated during a CFC session, you could refer to sections 4 and 5 of the CFC manual. For readers looking to know more about how CFC can be used with a self-focus, student-focus, colleague-focus or leadership/systemic-focus, they can read sections 6-9 of the manual.

References

Carroll, C., Brackenbury, G., Lee, F., Esposito, R., O'Brien, T., (2020) *Professional supervision: Guidance for SENCOs and school leaders*. UCL Centre for Inclusive Education. https://discovery.ucl.ac.uk/id/eprint/10090818/1/Carroll_SENCO%20Supervision%20Guidance%20February%202020.pdf.

Davis, K, L & Montag, C (2019) Selected principles of Pankseppian neuroscience. *Frontiers in Neuroscience*, 12.

Department for Education (2021) *Skills for jobs: Lifelong learning for opportunity and growth*. White Paper. Retrieved from https://assets.publishing.service.gov.uk/government/uploads/system/uploads/attachment_data/file/957856/Skills_for_jobs_lifelong_learning_for_opportunity_and_growth__web_version_.pdf.

Flaherty, J. (2022). *Coaching: Evoking excellence in others*. Routledge.

Gilbert, P. (2009). Introducing compassion-focused therapy. *Advances in Psychiatric Treatment*, 15(3), 199-208. Retrieved from http://apt.rcpsych.org/content/15/3/199.full.pdf

Gilbert, P., Catarino, F., Duarte, C., Matos, M., Kolts, R., Stubbs, J., Ceresatto, L., Duarte, J., Pinto-Gouveia, J., & Basran, J., (2017) The development of compassionate engagement and action scales for self and others. *Journal of Compassionate Healthcare*, 4(4). https://doi.org/10.1186/s40639-017-0033-3

Gilbert, P., & Simos, G. (2022). *Compassion focused therapy: Clinical practice and applications*: Routledge.

Heriot-Maitland, C., & Taylor, J. (2024). Developing a compassion focused supervision model for senior leaders in education. *OBM Integrative and Complementary Medicine*, 9(2), 033. https://doi.org/10.21926/obm.icm.2402033.

Hewson, D., & Carroll, M., (2016) *Reflective practice in supervision*: MoshPit Publishing.

Irons, C., & Beaumont, E., (2017) *The compassionate mind workbook: A step-by-step guide to developing your compassionate self*. Robinson.

Irons, C., & Heriot-Maitland, C. (2021). Compassionate mind training: An 8-week group for the general public. *Psychol Psychother, 94*(3), 443-463. https://doi.org/10.1111/papt.12320

Passmore, J., & Lai, Y. L. (2020). Coaching psychology: Exploring definitions and research contribution to practice. In J. Passmore & D. Tee (eds), *Coaching researched: A coaching psychology reader* (pp. 3-22). John Wiley.

3

Building Compassionate School Cultures through Compassion-Focused Therapy and Mind Training

Charlie Heriot-Maitland and Jo Taylor

> **CHAPTER AIMS**
>
> By the end of this chapter, readers will be able to:
>
> 1 Understand and apply compassion-focused theory and frameworks within your own leadership context.
> 2 Identify and critically engage with the four key pillars for building compassionate organisational cultures.
> 3 Engage with practical activities to deepen your understanding of how compassion-focused approaches can support leadership and workplace wellbeing.

Introduction

This chapter is for individuals interested in compassionate leadership and in creating compassionate cultures within organisations. It explores the underlying theory that explains why compassion matters in leadership and highlights practical ways to embed compassion into organisational life. The chapter is rich with reflective tools and structured activities designed to help leaders develop their compassionate capacities, enhance team dynamics, and shape organisational culture. It also includes case studies to illustrate real-world applications and offers further reading to deepen understanding and support continued learning.

Defining Compassion for Leadership

Compassion means different things to different people. In this chapter we will be defining compassion as:

> The sensitivity to suffering and the commitment to relieve or prevent it.
>
> *(Adapted from Gilbert, 2009)*

DOI: 10.4324/9781003466031-4

This definition builds on social and religious understandings, particularly from Buddhism, which describes compassion to navigate the suffering around us (Dalai Lama, 1995). The dual aspects of openness and commitment highlight compassion as action oriented. This is particularly relevant as leadership is where awareness and action align.

Compassion-Focused Approaches

Practitioners have developed therapeutic and personal development frameworks using theory and empirical research into compassion. In this chapter, we will be looking at organisational case studies which draw heavily on two approaches: compassion-focused therapy (CFT) and compassionate mind training (CMT).

Compassion-focused therapy was developed by Professor Paul Gilbert of the Compassionate Mind Foundation (www.compassionatemind.co.uk) as a model of psychotherapy. CFT aims to help people regulate threat-based emotions and experiences (such as anger and anxiety) by building internal feelings of safeness and developing compassion towards self and others. As such, CFT can offer a useful framework for environments that are fast-paced and high-stakes, such as education. In this chapter, we will explore the flexibility and usefulness of this framework for leaders.

In 2015, Irons and Heriot-Maitland developed an eight-week compassionate mind training (CMT) course, based on Gilbert's (2009) model of CFT (Irons & Heriot-Maitland, 2021; see also www.balancedminds.com). This course comprises eight sessions, each lasting 2.5 hours, and helps people to learn about compassion and relationships through an evolutionary understanding of "tricky brains", emotions, and motivational systems, with application across the three flows of compassion (self-to-other, other-to-self, and self-to-self) (Irons & Heriot-Maitland, 2021). Evidence for the benefits of participating in CMT groups has been demonstrated across a variety of populations, including teaching staff (Matos et al., 2022), healthcare staff (Martin, Beaumont, Norris, & Cullen, 2021), care staff in youth settings (Santos, Pinheiro, & Rijo, 2023), and the general public (Irons & Heriot-Maitland, 2021).

CMT has been shown to be a flexible tool that can be applied to groups such as families, teams, and organisations. In the section below, you will read about how CMT has been used to support staff development and wellbeing, including details about the course structure and how tools and activities can be applied in a professional leadership context. Compassion-focused approaches can also be used at a systemic level. As a starting point, we will think about our body as a system and then about how individuals interact with the systems around them at work.

The Brain-Body Link

People often consider the brain to be the controller of the body. While this is accurate in some respects, it is also somewhat simplistic. There is a bi-directional feedback loop between our brains and bodies. This dynamic relationship can both cause difficulties and create opportunities, particularly in the context of leadership and the workplace.

Before we consider how compassion-focused approaches can be applied at a systemic level, it is helpful to understand how the brain, body, and environment interact. This understanding allows us to better conceptualise how compassionate cultures can support more effective working environments. Our brains are part of our bodies and operate within a complex, multi-layered system.

For example, when we feel threatened, our logical and conscious thinking processes can be overridden, allowing us to respond more quickly. This is a process often taught in undergraduate psychology courses and was evocatively described by Daniel Goleman (1995) as an "amygdala hijack". It is also widely recognised in popular culture, where people talk about "acting without thinking" in emergency situations.

These examples are important because they challenge the idea that humans are always in conscious control. While it may feel as though we are in the pilot seat of our minds, there are times when the body or environment acts upon us, rather than the other way around.

Evolutionary Perspectives

This process makes a lot of sense from an evolutionary perspective. In a moment of life-or-death stakes, there will probably be a need to act quickly and not consider nuance. For example, if I need to escape from a lion, I probably don't need to think about how my actions might impact the trustee meeting next week (e.g. "Did I demonstrate the organisational values during my escape?" or "Do I need to reach out to the stakeholders who like cats?").

Threats have changed for most people living in modern context, but we still have the same software and hardware designed to keep us safe. One of the interesting features of our threat system is that it can activate in response to psychosocial experiences, even when there is no physical danger (e.g. remembering past situations or imagining things that might happen). The impact on us can feel the same as if there were physical danger, and it can affect how our brain functions, making it harder to use complex cognitive processes like planning, perspective-taking, and logical reasoning.

Brains are amazing: very quickly, in the moment, humans can judge the threat level of a situation and, if it is not considered life-threatening, re-engage their rational faculties, allowing for conscious thought, deeper analysis, and the use of skills like metacognition. While this switching can take time and be draining, it means that we don't have to remain stuck in a threatened state.

Using the Body to Influence Thought (and Vice Versa)

We can use our bodies to create the conditions for wiser thought and action. Just as our bodies can prepare us for a life-saving response to threat, often making it more difficult to think clearly, we can also use physical techniques to slow the body down and support more thoughtful, considered responses. For example, extended exhalations can activate the parasympathetic nervous system and slow the heartbeat, creating an internal signal of safeness and allowing us to re-engage our rational faculties.

This is possible because the feedback loop between the brain and the body is bi-directional. In other words, the brain influences the body, and the body influences the brain. For instance, recalling something frightening or frustrating can cause your body to tense up and your breathing to quicken, making it harder to think clearly. Conversely, being physically relaxed, such as when you're surrounded by supportive loved ones, can help create a sense of spaciousness in the mind, making it easier to access calm, reflective thought.

Application in High-Pressure Environments

This feedback loop can be powerful for people aiming to complete work to a high standard in fast-paced environments. When things feel stressful and busy, we still want to be able to access all our skills and perform at our best, so it is important to have strategies for creating the conditions that support wise thought and action.

At one end of the application scale, we see this feedback loop used by the military and law enforcement to navigate life-threatening situations (Röttger et al., 2021). At the other end, psychologists use similar approaches to help people increase their sense of safeness, prevent their threat systems from activating, and enhance access to skills such as logical reasoning, empathy, and imagination. We will explore this in more detail below, with a description of CMT.

Having considered the brain-body relationship, we can now explore how individuals interact with the systems around them; personal, professional, and systemic. Systems theory and workplace ecosystems have a well-developed research base. Ungar (2018) explored the barriers and facilitators that influence how people access resources within their ecosystem, showing how this can support resilience and long-term wellbeing. Doughty and Moore (2021) used an ecosystemic lens to examine how inclusive teams can be created and better understood.

Just as the brain and body engage in a top-down/bottom-up dance, so too do individuals and systems. People can be supported or limited by the systems they are embedded in, whether through HR policies, key performance indicators, or professional standards. These effects are not uniform; systems are interpreted through a person's history, social context, personality, and psychology.

For leaders, helping individuals and teams to shape their environments with this in mind can support the cultivation of a compassionate workplace culture. The case studies that follow offer examples of how systems can be analysed and iteratively developed in practice.

Potential Barriers to Creating a Compassionate Culture in Organisations

Compassion-focused approaches have been associated with an increased ability to cope with failure, reduced stress, heightened positive emotions, and even improved athletic performance (Gilbert et al., 2017; Mosewich et al., 2019). Yet, compassion is often misunderstood and can feel intimidating.

When delivering compassion-focused training to senior leaders, we sometimes encounter initial apprehension. At other times, participants express concern about how their colleagues might perceive them if they are seen as a "compassionate leader". With this in mind, and before exploring the case studies, we will address three common misconceptions about compassion.

MISCONCEPTION ONE: COMPASSION IS TOO SOFT FOR LEADERSHIP

Gilbert's research into fears of compassion found that many people associate it with weakness. This belief is often linked to the idea that success requires toughness, which can become a barrier to self-compassion (Gilbert et al., 2011, p. 248).

In our work with leaders, we regularly encounter the view that compassion is "soft" or incompatible with leadership. These assumptions often shift over the course of training. While it's important to address such concerns with sensitivity and context in mind, the core message is clear: compassion is not weakness. It involves facing difficulty, seeking understanding, and taking meaningful action. What could be stronger?

MISCONCEPTION TWO: THERE ISN'T TIME IN MY FAST-PACED WORKPLACE FOR COMPASSION

Some people believe compassion takes too much time, slows things down, and is therefore incompatible with busy work environments. I've spoken with professionals uncertain about how compassion-focused approaches could fit into their daily routines. Gilbert et al.'s (2011) research supports this, showing that a common fear of self-compassion is the belief that being kinder to oneself will lower personal standards (p. 248).

However, research suggests the opposite. Self-compassion has been linked to higher performance and sustainable working. Mosewich et al. (2019) found that greater self-compassion was associated with better goal progress, as it enabled more accurate reflection and effective coping with failure. Breines and Chen (2012) also suggest self-compassion may be more predictive than self-esteem when it comes to bouncing back after setbacks. Furthermore, compassion supports long-term high standards and can protect against burnout (Matos et al., 2022).

MISCONCEPTION THREE: HUMANS ARE NATURALLY COMPETITIVE AND OUT FOR THEMSELVES; COMPASSION IS NAIVE

I've often heard the argument, both professionally and socially, that humans are fundamentally self-interested, and that compassion is naïve. It's easy to point to examples where self-centred competitiveness is rewarded with power, money, or recognition, making the argument seem persuasive at first glance.

However, research increasingly shows that human emotional drives are more nuanced. Gilbert's (2009) *Three Circles Model of Emotion* explains that we are equipped with three core systems: the threat system (to keep us safe), the drive system (to pursue goals), and the soothing system (to rest, connect, and recover).

This model shows that just as we are wired for competition and self-preservation, we are also wired for connection, cooperation, and compassion. Anger, anxiety, ambition, contentment, and empathy are all part of our evolved psychological toolkit, each serving a function. Compassion is not an add-on; it's a natural, adaptive part of being human.

Gilbert has built on this understanding by highlighting the interplay between social and psychological processes. Social processes shape the organisation of the mind, what we attend to and how we think (Gilbert, 2021). He describes how competition-focused social processes can inhibit caring behaviours, orientate us towards controlling others, and attune the mind to potential threats. The opposite is also true: we can create social processes that promote cooperation and caring behaviour (controlling and holding vs sharing and caring).

In short, humans have the capacity for both competition and cooperation. Both are innate, evolved functions. Furthermore, broader research evidence suggests that orientating towards helping others supports happiness and health (see Crocker et al., 2017). For leaders, the key question becomes: can we harness the interaction between our evolved hardware/software and the social context to create compassionate cultures that lead to positive outcomes for teams?

Summary

Compassion prevents and reduces suffering. It is possible to create organisational cultures, systems, and processes that promote cooperation, caring behaviour, and increased wellbeing. We will explore four case studies illustrating how compassion-focused approaches have been applied across different levels of leadership and organisational practice. These case studies centre on four key pillars for creating a compassionate culture:

1. Staff wellbeing and personal practice.
2. Team meetings, policies, and procedures.
3. The physical environment.
4. Compassionate leadership training and coaching.

Reflecting on the three misconceptions discussed earlier, these case studies will demonstrate how compassion can:

- Help people better understand the difficulties their clients are experiencing, enabling more effective collaboration.

- Support those doing emotionally demanding work, so they can continue helping others more sustainably.
- Shape physical environments that encourage cooperation and connection.
- Guide teams in managing their emotions and navigating workplace challenges more effectively.
- Improve how meetings are prepared for and conducted.
- Enable more nuanced caseload management.
- Foster alternative workplace processes that feel more empowering.

My hope is that, by reading this chapter, you will see how compassion can sit at the heart of effective leadership, and leave with ideas for how you can shape the systems around you to create a more compassionate work culture.

Creating a Compassionate Culture in Organisational Projects for Vulnerable Children

This section outlines four key pillars for creating a compassionate culture within organisations. Case studies are provided to illustrate how these pillars have been applied in various settings. The examples are drawn from four large-scale organisational projects delivering services to vulnerable young people across sectors including care, housing, and education.

All four projects adopted CFT (Gilbert, 2009; Gilbert & Simos, 2022) as the overarching model and framework guiding their approach. One of the authors (CHM), a clinical psychologist and CFT expert, was involved in the design and development of these projects, as well as the staff training and consultation. As this chapter aims to provide a general, descriptive overview of the broader approach, the names and locations of the projects have been anonymised and will instead be referred to by their service area (see Table 3.1).

Staff Wellbeing and Personal Practice

A key aspect of creating a compassionate culture is helping staff to develop their own compassionate motives and competencies, both towards themselves and one another. Starting with compassion for staff is crucial, as this forms the foundation from which all practice,

Table 3.1 Four pillars of compassionate culture, and illustrative case study examples.

Pillar of compassionate culture	Case study setting
1. Staff wellbeing and personal practice	Children's Social Services Youth Support and Housing Charity
2. Team meetings, policies and procedures	Children's Social Services
3. The physical environment	Children's Secure Care Home
4. Compassionate leadership training and coaching	Children's Social Services Leadership Programme for Senior Teachers in alternative provision (AP)

interventions, and interactions with vulnerable young people are approached. It is essential to help staff feel safe and supported, giving them space to develop the capacity and confidence for wise and compassionate engagement in their work.

One way to support staff in this is by offering structured personal practice courses, which not only deepen emotional self-awareness but also develop competencies and the ability to be compassionate towards self and others. In these case studies, this personal development was operationalised through CMT (Irons & Heriot-Maitland, 2021).

The CMT course combines taught content with experiential exercises and practices (e.g. mindfulness, imagery, and compassionate mind skills development). Participants learn how to access and strengthen their "compassionate minds", using these skills to reduce self-criticism, regulate strong negative emotions (such as anger, anxiety, and shame), and develop compassion for themselves and others. Specifically, CMT participants learn:

- How our minds are naturally prone to getting caught in negative thinking-emotion "loops".
- The "three emotion systems" model, and how emotional imbalance can arise.
- What compassion is, what attributes support it, what can block it, and how to train the mind in it.
- That compassion flows in three directions: to others (compassion for others), from others (compassion from others), and to ourselves (self-compassion).
- Skills to regulate emotions by developing mindfulness and compassion.

Participants also develop practical skills in:

- Mindfulness: exploring the power of attention and awareness, and practising a variety of mindfulness exercises to build greater attentional stability.
- Breathing: learning how specific breathing rhythms can help soothe and calm both body and mind.
- Compassion: engaging in practices that develop the compassionate mind, including those involving memory, imagery, embodied action, emotion, and thought.

One of the key challenges in implementing a personal practice model within an organisation is sustaining this practice over time. It is therefore important for teams to identify and develop their own "in-house" facilitators, leaders and "compassion champions" who can support their colleagues. In organisational projects using CMT, the typical approach is to train a group of employees to become facilitators of compassion training for their peers, as illustrated in the following case studies.

Case Study: Children's Social Services

In this project, a local authority aimed to offer CMT personal practice courses to every member of its workforce. Not just those in direct client-facing roles, but also staff in business operations and administrative positions. The service initially piloted the eight-week

CMT course (Irons & Heriot-Maitland, 2021) in selected areas, including with social workers and foster carers. However, for a full organisational rollout, it was recognised that eight weeks was too time-consuming for many staff. As a result, a slightly adapted version was introduced: four weeks of personal practice (i.e. applied to self), followed by two weeks of client-focused practice (i.e. applied to work with children and families). All staff across the organisation completed the four-week personal practice course, while those in direct client-facing roles completed the full six weeks.

A team of in-house facilitators attended intensive "train-the-trainer" sessions, equipping them with both the theoretical knowledge and practical skills required to deliver the course to their colleagues. Supervision was also provided to support the new trainers as they led their first sessions.

Case Study: Youth Support and Housing Charity

In this project, a youth charity provider aimed to offer CMT personal practice courses to all staff, many of whom were residential care workers, but also including health and wellbeing practitioners, as well as management, domestic, and administrative staff. For this project, the CMT course was adapted to be delivered over two full days, with a week's gap in between to allow for personal practice.

The service also identified a small team of seven or eight in-house trainers, all of whom had the appropriate skills and interest to facilitate the personal practice courses. Unlike the approach taken in the Children's Social Services project, this initiative did not use a supervision model for new facilitators. Instead, the new trainers co-facilitated their first course alongside an experienced CMT provider and trainer, learning through live observation and feedback.

Team Meetings, Policies, and Procedures

The personal practice of CMT lays the foundation for a self-aware and self-reflective workforce. Although the courses are primarily focused on improving staff wellbeing, they can also support staff in bringing a compassionate approach to all aspects of their work, including interactions with children and families, as well as with one another. The CMT framework provides both a structure and shared language that can extend into all areas of service operations and delivery, from meetings (e.g. team meetings, supervision, reflective practice, and line management) to procedures and policy documents.

Creating the Conditions for Staff Meetings and Interactions

If a meeting takes place while staff are in "threat mode", this can significantly affect how the conversation unfolds. A threat-based mindset is more likely to lead to impulsivity, rushed decision-making, top-down imposition rather than collaborative discussion, and reinforcement of power hierarchies within the team. At higher levels of threat, meetings may descend into blaming, polarisation, splitting, or even dissociation.

A compassion-informed approach can help by fostering internal feelings of safeness and affiliation in staff, thereby creating the conditions for a more productive and meaningful conversation. This might involve starting meetings with a brief body-based or breathing exercise. In CFT terms, activating the body's soothing system to calm the threat response. In essence, this is about using the body to support and prepare the mind. Such practices help staff engage with:

- compassion towards self and others;
- mentalising;
- reflective and reflexive thinking;
- noticing and naming emotions;
- identifying patterns; and
- emotional conflict resolution.

Creating a Shared Language for Meetings, Policies, and Procedures

Another way in which CMT personal practice can shape the wider organisational culture is through the development of a shared, compassionate language. CMT provides staff with a non-judgemental framework for noticing and naming difficult emotions, situations, and conflicts. This allows teams to approach challenges mindfully and without blame.

For example, the "three circles" model (red, blue, green) can be used to help teams articulate their emotional states. They might ask, "How are our team's three circles balanced at the moment?" or "What factors are activating our team's threat system?" This language supports teams to reflect on shared struggles, have difficult conversations, and revisit them over time, e.g. "How are our three circles balanced now, three months later?"

The concept of multiple selves also offers a helpful way of acknowledging emotional complexity and supporting reflective practice. For example, team members might ask themselves, "Which parts of me were active during that difficult family conversation?" or "What's going on in my angry self?" or "If I connected with my sad self, what would it be saying or want to do?" This framework becomes particularly useful in supervision and reflective practice meetings, enabling teams to access not only emotional insight but also their collective compassionate motivation and wisdom. The "compassionate self" becomes the guiding stance from which the team can respond.

These ideas from CFT and CMT can also be applied to written materials, such as policy documents (e.g. those covering sickness, grievances, absence, performance management, and disciplinary processes). Compassionate principles can be embedded directly into the language of the policy, or offered through supplementary guidance to support managers in applying their "compassionate self" when enacting those policies.

A truly compassionate culture may even favour co-production in policy development. Consider the difference between a team being told, "These are the rules," and one being asked, "What would you like to see in the rules?", "How would you like this service to run?", or "If things were working well, what would we notice?"

Case Study: Children's Social Services

In this project, each unit of four to five social care practitioners held weekly practice meetings to discuss the progress of their caseload of children and families. During these meetings, staff were encouraged to reflect on their own emotional systems (three circles), multiple selves (e.g. angry, anxious, sad, compassionate), and any fears, blocks, or resistances to compassion, particularly in relation to the families and individuals they were supporting. The meetings were facilitated in a way that created space for mutual support and fostered a sense of belonging and connection within the team. This helped to establish a safe foundation from which staff were enabled to make wise, often difficult decisions in the best interests of children and families.

Staff were provided with a practice manual that included guidance on structuring these meetings. Prompts included:

- Where are the family at? How is the intervention going for them? What's next? What are we not hearing, and how can we access this?
- Where are we? (What emotion/system is activated for us?) How are we feeling towards the family as a whole, and towards individuals?
- In what ways are we finding compassion difficult?
- Which compassionate qualities will be important to draw upon (e.g. non-judgement, empathy, distress tolerance, monitoring our own emotional reactions/urges)?
- Checking in with our multiple selves.
- Looking out for one another and noticing examples of compassionate practice, for example, asking, "What examples of compassion have I seen from colleagues this week?"

To support training, video demonstrations of practice meetings were created. In these clips, social workers are shown checking in with their own multiple selves when reflecting on a family conflict, before connecting with the wisdom of their compassionate self.

The Physical and Social Environment

Creating a compassionate culture requires attention to the contexts in which compassion can flourish. In the social environment, this includes fostering affiliative, supportive relationships within the team, as well as a sense of belonging, connectedness, and shared purpose or direction. Having a shared language within the organisation (as described in the previous section) can support this, and a basic understanding of evolution-informed CFT psychoeducation (e.g. "tricky brains", "loops") helps foster a culture of:

- Common humanity: recognising the things we all share as humans.
- De-shaming: understanding that it's not our fault we struggle with these tricky brains of ours.

In terms of the physical environment, this involves considering the sensory impact of colours, sounds, objects, smells, and so on, acknowledging how different environments can evoke emotional responses in the body that may either inhibit or support compassion. A useful starting point is to guide staff through exercises that raise awareness of how different spaces influence them, using the three circles model (threat, drive, soothing). An example of this is described in the case study.

At the most basic level, the CFT model suggests that our threat system can block or inhibit compassion, while creating neurophysiological experiences of safeness, linked to the soothing system, can support or facilitate it. However, when considering the environment, it is important for teams to seek a helpful balance between all three emotion systems, as compassionate care often requires input from all three.

REFLECTIVE ACTIVITY: DESIGN A CHILDREN'S HOME

This exercise invited staff to reflect on how the physical environment can influence emotional experience and behaviour, both for themselves and for the young people they support. Drawing on Gilbert and Simos's (2022) three emotion systems model (threat, drive, and soothing), staff were asked to explore how different environments may activate different emotional responses.

To make this concept more accessible and engaging, the team used the metaphor of Instagram filters, each one representing one of the three systems, to design an imagined space, such as a children's home or a classroom.

Engage in the task for yourself. Design a [children's home / classroom] through each of the following three "filters":

- **Red (threat system):** What would an environment look like that activates a sense of threat or danger? Think about noise, lighting, colours, layout, and sensory input.
- **Blue (drive system):** What would an environment look like that stimulates goal-oriented behaviour, achievement, and excitement? Consider stimulation, reward systems, and visual cues.
- **Green (soothing system):** What would an environment look like that promotes calm, connection, and safety? Think about warmth, quiet, sensory comfort, and relational cues.

Below are examples of design notes taken from staff members.
   Red filter design notes:

- Big gates, high walls, locked doors.
- Plain white, stripped back rooms.
- Tight rules, no visitors.
- Bars on windows, barbed wire.

- Staff dressed in armour.
- Drill sergeant, boot camp.
- Robotic-like staff, no humour.
- No soft furnishing, no risky plants/nature.

Blue filter design notes:

- Welcoming and enthusiastic.
- Themed days.
- Reward charts, doing everything for prizes.
- Upbeat music (house), high fives on entry.
- Task focused (go, go, go).
- Certificates on walls.
- Staff of the month award.
- Florescent colours, bright.

Green filter design notes:

- Pastel colours, soft furnishings.
- Low-level, adjustable lighting.
- Calm voice tones, whale music (spa).
- Plants and outdoor area.
- Animals, pets.
- Pyjamas, onesies.
- Buddy system.
- Personalised room decoration (e.g. own photos, memories).

Compassionate Leadership Training and Coaching

The success of creating and sustaining a compassionate culture ultimately rests with compassionate leadership. Leaders set the vision and values of an organisation; they allocate time and budgets for staff training and personal development; they shape meeting structures, policies, and procedures; and they control funding for environmental features and design. Perhaps most importantly, leaders also influence the interpersonal (self-to-other) dynamics between staff, which in turn shape patterns of self-to-self relating. These relational patterns may be oriented around threat and competitive social mentalities, or around compassion and care.

Compassionate leadership training and coaching involves developing self-awareness. This includes awareness of oneself, one's brain, and one's emotional systems. To shape a compassionate culture, a leader must first be able to recognise when their own threat system is activated, and when they are leading from that place. This is not about blaming or shaming leaders. It is about understanding the nature of our tricky brains and acknowledging how these dynamics affect all of us in our roles.

Workshops typically begin with an introduction to compassionate leadership and a discussion around what staff would see or feel if they were truly experiencing it. The workshop then moves into a more experiential phase, focusing on self-awareness (e.g. recognising our own threat system), identifying leadership values and motives (e.g. pro-social, curious, supportive), and creating a visual image of what those values would look like in practice (e.g. collaboration, co-production). Leaders are supported in translating their values into motives and actions, and in developing a self-compassionate inner guide to help move towards these.

The workshop helps leaders connect with their authentic motivations for forming relationships, collaborating, and co-producing with others. Crucially, it also encourages curiosity and learning from the wisdom and diversity within their teams.

As part of the training, leaders engage in experiential exercises that guide them through a difficult leadership situation or conflict, using each of their multiple selves (e.g. angry, anxious, sad, compassionate). This helps leaders to first cultivate compassion in their internal world, before embedding it in the structures and relationships within their teams.

Following compassionate leadership training, a series of coaching sessions can support leaders in embedding the training into their everyday practice. These sessions use real-life examples of leadership challenges, conflicts, and dilemmas to help leaders practise applying their compassionate mind in context.

The coaching helps leaders to recognise when their threat system is activated in day-to-day situations and to practise activating the patterns that support their compassionate mind. Leaders are also supported in learning how to hold and tolerate the discomfort of conflict or disagreement, without rushing to find a solution or "fix". A key learning point is that compassionate leadership is often less about having immediate answers, and more about using one's authority to remain curious and collaborative in the face of complexity.

REFLECTIVE ACTIVITY

Think of a recent leadership conflict or dilemma. Take a moment to recall where you were, who was there, and what happened. If helpful, close your eyes to picture the scene.

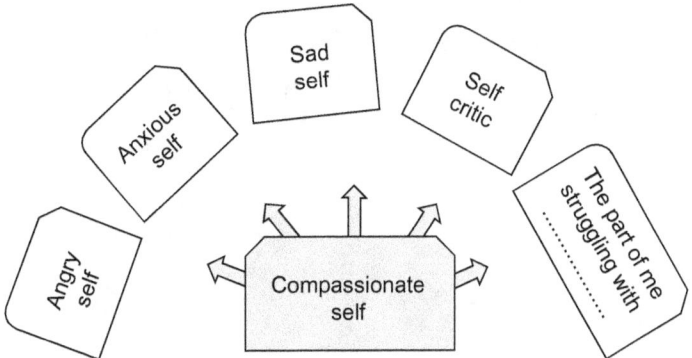

Figure 3.1 Self-supporting compassion in self-to-self relationships.

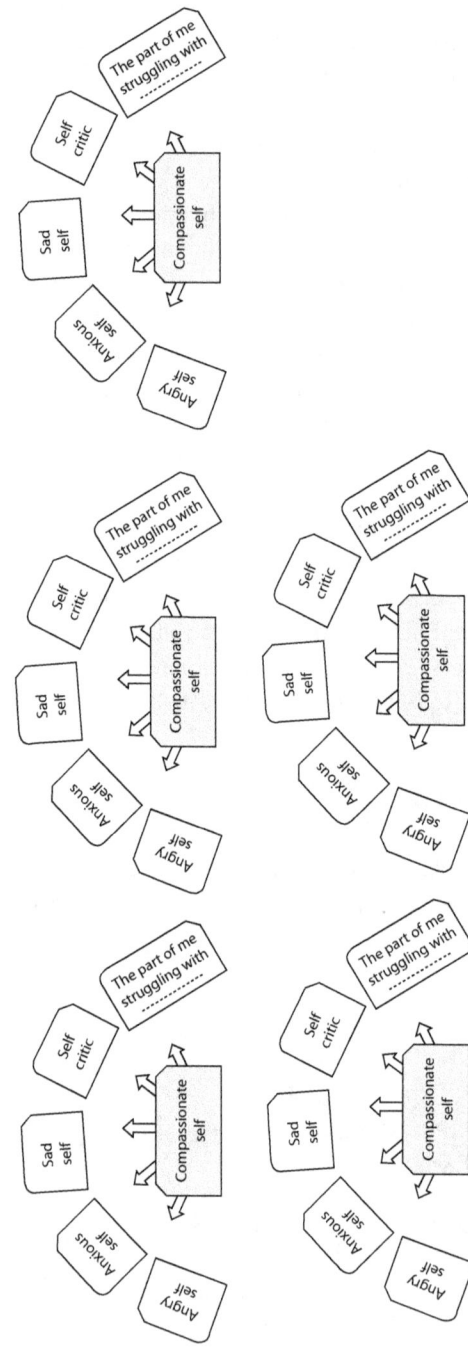

Figure 3.2 Compassionate self-experiential exercises.

Building Compassionate School Cultures   49

You'll now explore this situation through four emotional "selves": angry, anxious, sad, and finally, your compassionate self. For each self, reflect on the following:

1 Thoughts: What is this part thinking?
2 Feelings in the body: Where and how do you feel this?
3 Behaviour / urge: What does this part want to do?
4 Desired outcome: What result does this part want?

Record your reflections in the table below for each self.

Self	Thoughts	Feelings (Body)	Behaviour / Urge	Desired Outcome
Angry Self				
Anxious Self				
Sad Self				
Compassionate Self				

Transition to Compassionate Self

After reflecting on the first three selves, pause and centre yourself:

- Sit upright, feet grounded, and take a few slow breaths.
- Connect with your breath, allowing the body to settle.
- Bring to mind your compassionate self, with qualities like wisdom, strength, and caring commitment.

Now revisit the same situation. While staying grounded in your compassionate self, complete the final row in your table. Consider:

- What does your compassionate self think and feel?
- What does it want to do?
- What outcome would it seek?

This exercise supports emotional awareness and helps shift perspective in challenging leadership moments.

Case Study: Children's Social Services

In this project, all organisational leaders attended an initial workshop called "Compassion Focused Systemic Training for Leaders". Middle managers participated in a full-day workshop, which was run twice to ensure everyone could attend. Team Leaders and Practice Leaders attended a similar full-day session, tailored slightly to reflect their distinct roles and responsibilities, and also delivered twice.

These training sessions introduced CFT and systemic ideas, exploring how these models could be integrated to form a framework for leadership. The training offered tools to support self-awareness among leaders and guidance on how to embed compassion-focused principles into team meetings, organisational processes, working relationships, and one-to-one line management.

Following the training days, middle managers participated in a series of six follow-up coaching sessions titled "Reflexive Practice Sessions for Middle Managers in Social Care" (held monthly, each lasting 90 minutes). Depending on group size, sessions were designed to begin in smaller breakout groups of three to five leaders with a facilitator, lasting around an hour, before rejoining the larger group for shared reflections. This structure aimed to create a dual experience: a safe, confidential space to explore challenges in depth, while also maintaining a sense of connection and belonging to the wider leadership team.

Agenda topics for these sessions included emerging leadership issues such as staff shortages, team workload, high sickness levels, managing performance, and tensions like, "My priorities as a leader conflict with staff priorities" or "As a leader, I can't be as present as I'd like to be". There were also reflections on common fears around compassionate leadership, including concerns like "I'm not clinically trained to manage people's distress" or "If I'm seen as too compassionate, people may take advantage of me". While exploring these topics, facilitators encouraged leaders to regularly check in with their multiple selves and created space for both giving and receiving compassion among the group.

Case Study: Leadership Programme for Senior Teachers in AP

In this project, senior leaders in schools were offered a full day of training, followed by fortnightly coaching sessions in small groups (3-4 people, 90 minutes each) over a two-year period. These sessions were initially titled "Compassionate Leadership Coaching", but the name later changed to "Compassion Focused Coaching (CFC)" (Heriot-Maitland & Taylor, 2024).

During the initial months of CFC, the focus was on cultivating compassion within *self-to-self* and *self-to-student* relationships. However, towards the end of the two-year programme, the emphasis shifted more towards leadership development.

The *CFC Manual* and *Supervisor Guidance* provide support for leaders in distinguishing between *criticism* and *compassionate correction*, and between *antisocial* and *prosocial* leadership styles (Gilbert & Basran, 2019). The guidance also helps leaders to explore and develop their self-identity as Compassionate Leaders by clarifying their values and learning how to activate evolved motivational systems to act in line with those values.

The manual also includes strategies for building compassionate cultures within schools, covering areas such as meetings, interpersonal interactions, and the physical environment, in alignment with the ideas outlined in earlier sections of this chapter.

Building Compassionate School Cultures 51

Ultimately, the goal of CFC is to empower school leaders to recognise and develop their own compassionate facilitation skills, so they can take these approaches back into their schools. This includes applying compassion through line management, emotional support for staff and students, and broader wellbeing initiatives

Utilising Compassion: Activities for a Compassionate Leader

This section is intended to help bring to life some of the approaches and tools which have been mentioned above. Below you will find two activities, which can support with the cultivation of compassion in different ways:

- The Wheel of Compassion, a reflective and planning tool, aimed at exploring compassionate qualities and the direction compassion is flowing in situations.
- A practice which will help with connecting with your Compassionate Self, as a leader.

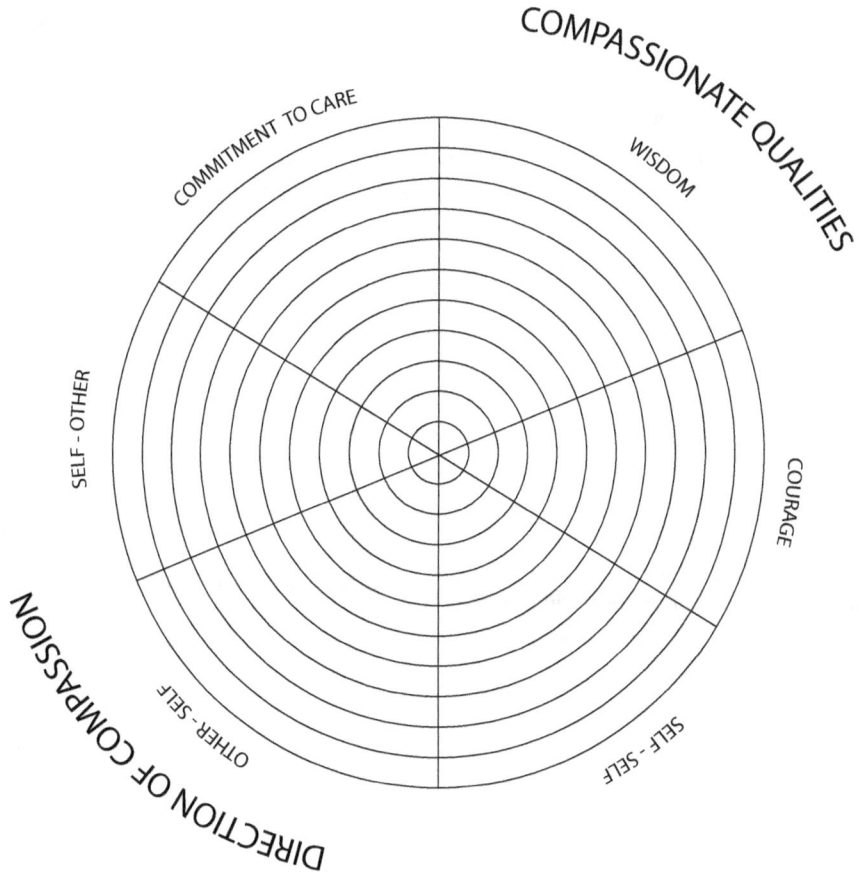

Figure 3.3 The Wheel of Compassion.

REFLECTIVE ACTIVITY: THE WHEEL OF COMPASSION

The *Wheel of Compassion* is a reflective activity I use personally, as well as in training and supervision sessions. You might recognise it as similar to the *Wheel of Life*, a coaching tool attributed to Paul Meyer, which is often used to assess areas of work and life in terms of "where they are now … and where you would like them to be". I designed the Wheel of Compassion to help you check in with:

- how much compassionate qualities have been showing up in your life and work; and
- the strength and direction of compassion flow between yourself and others.

The Wheel of Compassion supports you in centring compassion in your work, so that you can do your best, more sustainably. It draws on two frameworks to create a simple and accessible structure: *compassionate qualities* (Irons & Beaumont, 2017) and *directions of compassion* (Gilbert et al., 2017). The activity includes three steps and takes around 10 minutes to complete.

I've outlined the steps below so you can give it a try and see whether it would be useful in your leadership or workplace. This is a practical activity that can support you in building a compassionate culture in your workplace. It may also be useful for colleagues or those you lead, helping them check in with these key aspects of compassionate working.

Step 1: Compassionate Qualities

These qualities help us notice and reduce suffering and distress. Using the wheel, shade in the layers of each segment for:

- Commitment to care.
- Wisdom.
- Courage.

The more layers you shade, the more that quality has been present recently.

Example: if you remember being particularly courageous this week, you might shade in more layers in the "Courage" segment.

Step 2: Directions of Compassion Flow

Compassion can move in three directions:

- From you to others.
- From others to you.
- From you to yourself.

Using the second wheel (or adding to your drawing), shade in each segment based on how much you've experienced each direction of compassion recently.

Example: if you've received a lot of compassion from others lately, you might shade in more layers in that segment.

Step 3: What Next?

Looking at your completed wheel, choose one area you'd like to develop. This might be a compassionate quality you'd like to connect with more, or a direction of compassion flow you'd like to strengthen. Set a small intention for the coming week to support this.

Example: "I'd like to try and notice when others are being compassionate towards me," or "I'll pause and take a breath to see if something wise comes to mind."

> **REFLECTIVE ACTIVITY: CONNECTING WITH YOUR INNER COMPASSIONATE LEADER**
>
> Compassionate qualities help us to engage in compassionate thought and action (Irons & Beaumont, 2017). As part of CMT, participants can use activities to cultivate and connect with their compassionate self. Below, I've included a script which gives a flavour of how this might be incorporated into your work.

You might use this activity as a reflective or planning tool, either on your own or with your organisation. It will take at least 15 minutes and could take longer if you choose to take notes or discuss each stage. You may wish to try it alone in a quiet space the first time.

Imagine that you've woken up on a very special day. Today, you are at your most compassionate and are going to walk through your workplace as a compassionate leader.

We are going to use the power of imagery and visualisation to strengthen your connection to your inner Compassionate Leader. First, we will imagine what your day might be like as a leader expressing each of the three compassionate qualities: courage, wisdom, and a commitment to caring behaviour. You will imagine how people react to you when these qualities are dialled up to 100. Finally, you will get to experience walking through your workplace as a compassionate leader with all of these qualities turned up to the maximum.

First, let's focus on the compassionate quality of courage. Imagine it's Monday morning and someone has added a courage tonic to your cornflakes. You can feel the courage coursing through your veins as you arrive at work. At your most courageous, how are you holding your body? What is your posture like? As you greet your colleagues, what does your voice sound like? What kind of thoughts are popping into your courageous mind? What actions are you taking at work, as a leader, when you're at your most courageous? How is this courage received by the people you work with and lead? As you talk with them and move through your day, how do they respond to you?

Next, let's focus on the compassionate quality of wisdom. Imagine it's Tuesday, and someone has whispered words of wisdom into your mind overnight. You can feel this knowledge in your brain, ready to emerge and solve problems as a leader at work. At your wisest, how do you hold your body? What is your posture like? As you greet your colleagues, what does your voice sound like? What kind of thoughts are in your wise mind? What actions are you taking at work when you're at your wisest? How is this wisdom received by your colleagues? As you talk with them and move through your day, how do they respond?

Now let's focus on the compassionate quality of commitment to caring behaviour. Imagine it's Wednesday, and someone has charged your heart with a caring cable. You can feel the commitment to care pulsing in your chest, ready to be expressed at work. At your most caring, how do you hold your body? What is your posture like? As you greet your colleagues, what does your voice sound like? What thoughts enter your mind when you are at your most caring? What actions are you taking as a leader committed to caring behaviour? How is this commitment received by the people you work with? As you interact with them throughout your day, how do they respond?

Finally, imagine it's Thursday and you wake up as your inner compassionate leader. All the qualities from the week, courage, wisdom, and caring, are dialled up to 100 out of 100. You finish your breakfast and head into work, fully embodying your compassionate self. How do you hold your body? What is your posture like? As you greet your colleagues, what does your voice sound like? What thoughts arise in your mind when you are this compassionate leader? What actions are you taking? How are you received by the people around you?

Take a moment now to let your imagination settle. You might wish to jot down anything that felt interesting or important. What parts of your inner compassionate leader might you want to reconnect with or channel the next time you're at work?

Summary

Compassion is the sensitivity to suffering and the commitment to relieve or prevent it. It is not soft or fluffy. Compassion means getting up close to the difficult things in life, working to truly understand them, and taking meaningful action to improve the situation. As an approach, compassion aligns powerfully with leadership and the shaping of organisational culture.

Compassion-focused approaches have been shown to increase people's ability to cope with failure, reduce stress, enhance positive emotions, and even improve athletic performance. These benefits have been observed across a range of populations, including teaching staff, healthcare professionals, care staff in youth settings, and the general public.

For leaders interested in creating a compassionate workplace culture, there are four key pillars to focus on:

1 Staff wellbeing and personal practice.
2 Team meetings, policies, and procedures.
3 The physical environment.
4 Compassionate leadership training and coaching.

Further Reading

Heriot-Maitland, C., & Taylor, J. (2024). Developing a compassion focused supervision model for senior leaders in education. *OBM Integrative and Complementary Medicine*, 9(2), 033. https://doi.org/10.21926/obm.icm.2402033.

For an insight into how practitioners are trained to support leaders to use compassion in schools, see section 9 of the CFC Manual (Heriot-Maitland & Taylor, 2024). As described in the case study in this chapter about a leadership programme for senior teachers in AP, this manual helps leaders to explore aspects of compassionate leadership and creating compassionate organisations and systems.

Gilbert P (2021) Creating a compassionate world: Addressing the conflicts between sharing and caring versus controlling and holding evolved strategies. *Front. Psychol.*, 11. https://doi.org/10.3389/fpsyg.2020.582090

For an academic exploration of how social structures can shape our thoughts and feelings, read Gilbert (2021), which describes two opposing approaches for shaping society and offers a route towards creating a more compassionate world.

References

Breines, J., & Chen, S., (2012) Self compassion increased self-improvement motivation. *Personality and Social Psychology Bulletin*, 38(9), 1133-1143.

Crocker, J., Canevello, A., Brown, A, A. (2017) Social motivation: Costs and benefits of selfishness and otherishness. *Annual Review of Psychology*, 3(68), 299-325. https://doi.org/10.1146/annurev-psych-010416-044145

Dalai Lama (1995). *The power of compassion*. New Delhi: HarperCollins.

Doughty, S, E., & Moore, J, R,. (2021) Understanding inclusive organizations through ecological systems theory. *International Journal of Research in Business Studies and Management*, 8(1), 7-14. https://doi.org/10.22259/2394-5931.0801002

Gilbert, P. (2009). Introducing compassion-focused therapy. *Advances in Psychiatric Treatment*, 15(3), 199-208. Retrieved from http://apt.rcpsych.org/content/15/3/199.full.pdf

Gilbert P (2021) Creating a compassionate world: Addressing the conflicts between sharing and caring versus controlling and holding evolved strategies. *Front. Psychol.*, 11. https://doi.org/10.3389/fpsyg.2020.582090

Gilbert, P., & Basran, J. (2019). The evolution of prosocial and antisocial competitive behavior and the emergence of prosocial and antisocial leadership styles. *Front Psychol*, 10, 610. https://doi.org/10.3389/fpsyg.2019.00610

Gilbert, P., Catarino, F., Duarte, C., Matos, M., Kolts, R., Stubbs, J., Ceresatto, L., Duarte, J., Pinto-Gouveia, J., & Basran, J., (2017) The development of compassionate engagement and action scales for self and others. *Journal of Compasssionate Healthcare*, 4(4). https://doi.org/10.1186/s40639-017-0033-3

Gilbert, P., McEwan, K., Matos, M., & Rivis, A (2011) Fears of compassion: Development of three self-report measures. *Psychology and Psychotherapy: Theory, Research and Practice*, (84) 239-255

Gilbert, P., & Simos, G. (2022). *Compassion focused therapy: Clinical practice and applications*: Routledge.

Goleman, D. (1995). *Emotional intelligence*. Bantam Books.

Heriot-Maitland, C., & Taylor, J. (2024). Developing a compassion focused supervision model for senior leaders in education. *OBM Integrative and Complementary Medicine*, 9(2), 033. https://doi.org/10.21926/obm.icm.2402033.

Irons, C., & Beaumont, E., (2017) *The compassionate mind workbook: A step-by-step guide to developing your compassionate self*: Robinson.

Irons, C., & Heriot-Maitland, C. (2021). Compassionate mind training: An 8-week group for the general public. *Psychol Psychother*, 94(3), 443-463. https://doi.org/10.1111/papt.12320

Martin, C. J. H., Beaumont, E., Norris, G., & Cullen, G. (2021). Teaching compassionate mind training to help midwives cope with traumatic clinical incidents. *British Journal of Midwifery*, 29(1), 26-35.

Matos, M., Albuquerque, I., Galhardo, A., Cunha, M., Pedroso Lima, M., Palmeira, L. ... Gilbert, P. (2022). Nurturing compassion in schools: A randomized controlled trial of the effectiveness of a Compassionate Mind Training program for teachers. *PLoS One, 17*(3), e0263480. https://doi.org/10.1371/journal.pone.0263480

Mosewich, A. D., Sabiston, C. M., Kowalski, K. C., Gaudreau, P. (2019) Self compassion in the stress process of women athletes. *The Sport Psychologist*, 33. https://doi.org/10.1123/tsp.2017-0094

Röttger, S., Theobald, D. A., Abendroth, J. *et al.* (2021). The effectiveness of combat tactical breathing as compared with prolonged exhalation. *Appl Psychophysiol Biofeedback, 46*, 19-28 https://doi.org/10.1007/s10484-020-09485-w

Santos, L., Pinheiro, M. D. R., & Rijo, D. (2023). The effects of the compassionate mind training for caregivers on professional quality of life and mental health: Outcomes from a cluster randomized trial in residential youth care settings. *Child Youth Care Forum*, 1-21. https://doi.org/10.1007/s10566-023-09749-6

Ungar, M., (2018) Systemic resilience: principles and processes for a science of change in contexts of adversity. *Ecology and Society*, 23(4). https://doi.org/10.5751/ES-10385-230434

PART II

Compassion as a Global, Multi-Cultural Professional Endeavour

4

Critical Compassion in Teacher Preparation

Pedagogical *Conocimientos* in Action

Jesus Jaime-Diaz, Josie Méndez-Negrete, and Mary Carol Combs

> **CHAPTER AIMS**
>
> By the end of the chapter, readers will be able to:
>
> - Explore teacher-student engagements with attention to how schooling interactions may reproduce uncritical forms of consciousness.
> - Critique normative teaching practices by identifying the absence of critical pedagogy in instructional approaches.
> - Evaluate and consider alternative pedagogical frameworks, including critical compassion from an empowered and transformative perspective.

Introduction

This chapter explores the ways in which high school teachers understand their students in relation to their own racialised social class backgrounds. It problematises ethnic outsider inabilities to engage teaching philosophies and practices, which render teachers unable to create constructive dialogues with students that have been marginalised in the culture of schooling. Given classed, raced, and gendered past practices in education and their schooling trajectory, which have historically truncated their potential mobility, this study is mediated by racialised social class positions, which veil issues that intersect with structural inequalities.

At the turn of the nineteenth century, the structure of schooling in western nations focused on economic productivity. This was a direct result of the Industrial Revolution, which focused on production that mirrored factory assembly lines (Jaime-Diaz & Combs, 2025). Schools thus took on the task of socialising youth, a role previously assumed by the nuclear family (Arum et al., 2021). The structure of schooling became a fundamental tool in the reproduction of the social class structure. Immigrant labour was welcomed, however, language, culture, race, and identity were viewed as barriers to Americanisation and the acquisition of standardised English language as favourable practices of Anglo-Conformity (Combs et al., 2014; Orosco, 2016). Students who failed to meet imposed expectations of production levels were viewed as unintelligent and deficient in their preparation to ascend the ranks of factory management (Anyon, 2011; Ball, 2013; Foucault, 1977; Griffin, 2013; McLaren, 2005; Oakes, 2005). Within such dynamics of power, teachers served as both normative agents and labour brokers and purveyors of cultural norms ensuring compliance to ideological doctrines of power (Giroux, 1992; Torres, 2009).

It is not our intent to argue that schools lack the option for teacher resistance to schooling norms, as its practice is guided by traditional expectations embedded in symbolic ideology. Our aim is to advance a conversation mediated by Sociohistorical and Intersectionality theories and explore race and social class discourses in the structure of schooling when the teacher has the awareness and is conscious of their social location, and then they are unaware and negate the structural differences that reproduce inequality. Furthermore, we problematise school culture and the normalisation of social inequity within such structures, given the lack of literature about race and social class, and lack of intersectionality within education (Codiroli & Cook, 2019). We offer that education has been and continues to be a mechanism of discomfort imposed by an economy that promotes inequity as a norm, whereby the majority of poor people in rural and urban communities are Black or Latino (Anyon, 1980; Kozol, 2012).

There is an urgent task in the twenty-first century, and that is to critically and radically challenge and change the dominant foundations, and conceptions as to what gives meaning to education, which is ideologically imparted through a master narrative reinforced in contemporary times by way of neo-liberalism, whereby principles of free markets, limited governmental intervention, meritocracy, and personal responsibility (Oakes et al., 2018; Stetsenko, 2023). According to Dafermos (2023) Neo-liberalism has encroached upon spheres of education and has imposed a doctrine of competition, consumerism, and has redefined education as a commodity of marketisation. Pavlidis (2023) supports such position by asserting that through the neo-liberal mode of capitalist accumulation teachers are undergoing proletarianisation. Through such economically driven ideological views teachers are being de-professionalised and their labour power has been devalued from skilled to average. According to Ball (2013) contemporary schooling serves as an apparatus of intensification with heightened insecurity for both students and teachers through standardised, the use of test scores to evaluate teacher effectiveness, and scripted curriculum enforced by the state. Within such schooling environments a critical compassion is demanded in the pursuit of the common good, where teachers and students can both be authentic and centre themselves on the inward immediacy of living and learning together (Rabois, 2016).

To frame the schooling experience and its dynamics of power within a social structure, we begin with an overview of sociohistorical and Intersectionality theory. Then, we outline schooling in the context of race and social class background, and teaching, as these intersect in the refinement of social reproduction. We examine contemporary literature on critical pedagogy. Thereafter, we present the methodology and participants in this study, with a subsequent analysis of the themes that emerged, concluding with implications for future research. We argue that there is a continued need to scrutinise the ways in which racialised social class influences teacher-student engagement by exploring modes of inquiry concerning teacher-to-student pedagogical engagements across circumstances, framed by the following questions:

1 In what ways does social class background influence teachers' beliefs about their students?
2 In what manner do teachers' family beliefs influence their early interactions with peers?
3 By what means did teachers arrive at an understanding about the race and class difference in schooling?

Sociohistorical Theory and Intersectionality

From a sociohistorical paradigm, this chapter draws upon the theoretical contributions of critical education scholars (Anyon, 2011; Illich, 1970; McLaren, 2005; Oakes, 2005; Willis, 1977). This necessarily calls to interrogate epochs in history, as we observe, critique, and problematise the repetitive sides of the discipline. Important to critique how social stratification is reproduced and manifested through social class, race, gender, age, religion, disability, and how forms of oppression are interrelated and can be understood as intersectional (Crenshaw, 2019; Hill Collins, 2017). Sociohistorical paradigm is the dynamics of power in the schooling process that is actively influenced by ideas transmitted directly from the past: "Consciousness is reproduced not only directly through the individual's contact with work and membership in a particular class, but also through these institutions of reproduction" (Bowles et al., 2015, p. 101). These theories complement Marxist feminism, which postulate that oppression occurs within different spheres of identity in which privilege resides (Davis, 1983).

According to Belkhir (2001) it is imperative to struggle against historical social inequalities that have derived from race, class and gender. Such an imperative suggests that analyses of racism, sexism and classism must be unified within a Marxist critique of capitalism where such intersectional oppressions are drawn upon to make sense of different forms of inequality within social structures. This provides a dialogical lens for making sense of the sociohistorical centrality of the ways in which intersectional disempowerment prolongs inequality, exploitation, cultural subordination and domination. As such, we can set out to amend past errors that foresaw intersectional disempowerment as antagonistic in the class struggle.

Carpenter and Mojab (2023) advise for the articulation of intersectional forms of oppression as class struggle to explore the dialectics of reform and revolution within educational spaces, articulating them through social relations of difference. Carpenter and Mojab (2022) go on to affirm that a Marxist feminist extension delineates the concretisation of capitalism and the immense proliferation of social difference by which capitalist social relations are dependent upon.

Ethnocentrism as Social Reproduction

Teacher educators need to interrogate selective perceptions that trigger their social distance from students, particularly when traditional education requires them to impart taken for granted beliefs from their traditional socialisation which perceive difference as a threat (Carignan et al., 2005). When teachers fail to become aware of their cultural knowledge, they must recognise how ethnocentrism or "the tendency to judge other groups, societies,

Table 4.1 Sociocultural concepts shaping perceptions of difference and inclusion.

Ethnocentrism	Judging another culture exclusively from the perspective of one's own experience
Selective perception	Projected upon other groups of people what an individual expects to only see. Imposing what is good/bad, or morally correct
Social distance	Degree of intimacy a person is willing to accept with members of other groups
Institutions of social reproduction	Family origin, language, work, education, religion

Source: Healey and O' Brien (2022)

by the standards of one's own culture" (Healey & O'Brien, 2022), impedes their practice, which implicates dehumanisation and the disconnection of the body, mind, and spirit in a closed environment (Bowles & Gintis, 2011). Healey and O'Brien warn about the pitfalls of judging others through deficit perspectives (Table 4.1).

The objective of a teacher in a classroom then becomes one of monitor, in which she or he must produce learning outcomes for students, with an understanding that some will fail while others will succeed (Ball, 2013). In such mechanical learning environments, the underlying message is one closely aligned with the reproduction of labour: a reflection of an economy that is predatory in relation to the limited number of jobs to fill and embedded presumptions about whom shall occupy such spaces. Within the Western tradition, the reality for many students in schools is one where an authoritarian figure restrains their feelings and spirits' in their ability to understand the world (McLaren, 1995).

Critical Pedagogy

Contemporary structures of schooling in the United States were transformed from traditional pedagogies and influenced by philosophies of education and essentialism, to ones that argue students become prepared for basic positions in society (Anyon, 1980; Oakes et al., 2018). Such pedagogical approaches have been argued as outdated in contemporary US schooling (Bartolome, 2004). Critical pedagogues have called for changes in the preparation of educators. They argue that with fluctuations in the structure of schooling, the critical importance is the preparation of teachers, along with the scrutiny of practical skills of teachers in credential program, while teacher assumptions, values, and beliefs are examined (Bartolome, 2004; Sleeter, 2017). These traditional ideological notions are directly transmitted from the past and have been early tools of socialisation whereby teachers apprehend and relate to "difference" as products of society (Linley, 2017; Lynch, 2018).

Critical pedagogues offer that teaching is a political act and not an objective one where content is solely delivered (Freire, 2005, 2000; Graziano, 2008; Licona, 2004). For these reasons, hierarchies must be dismantled, as teachers collaborate with their students to create a community of learners built upon a mutual respect, whereby culture, language, and

Table 4.1 Methodological overview and practitioner pathways: applying a culturally grounded case study approach to educational research.

Component	Method/approach used	Purpose	Recommendations for reader use
Overall design	Qualitative case study using **ideal types** from five teacher narratives	To examine how teachers conceptualise race, class, and education	Use case studies in your setting to explore contrasting teacher worldviews on structural inequalities
Cultural approach	**Conocimiento** and **Pláticas** (Chicana feminist methods)	Build relational trust and culturally grounded dialogue; connect family/community histories to classroom experience	Adopt culturally relevant conversation methods to foster authentic reflection and relationship with participants
Research context	Working-class, majority-Mexican community high school ("Vigilancia")	Highlight context of economic marginalisation and cultural identity shaping schooling	Consider how your school/community's socio-cultural context shapes teaching identities and student experience
Participants	5 teachers (1 math, 4 English; 2 Chicanas, 2 white females, 1 white male); recruited via principal after IRB approval	To ensure participant diversity and ethical engagement	Ensure ethical research practices (informed consent) and attend to intersectionality in participant selection
Data collection	Semi-structured interviews- **Pláticas** (tape-recorded and transcribed)- Participant observation	To explore lived teaching experiences and racialised social class interactions	Use multiple data sources (interviews, conversations, observation) to deepen understanding of teaching practices
Data analysis	**Appreciative Inquiry** (feminist, strength-based)- Holistic coding- Topic coding linked to upbringing, neighbourhood, and ideology	To co-create knowledge that centres teacher experience, and trace how early life shapes views of difference	Apply strengths-based inquiry and link emerging themes to wider sociocultural histories of participants
Theoretical frame	Intersectionality + Marxist feminism	To interrogate how race, class, gender intersect in shaping teacher ideologies	Use intersectional theory to analyse how systems of oppression shape classroom dynamics and teacher-student relations

customs are valued as resources in the production of knowledge through holistic dialogue (Cresswell, 2016; Jaime-Diaz, 2019; McIntyre et al., 2001; Méndez-Negrete, 2013; Orozco & Jaime-Diaz, 2016; Orozco & Lopez, 2015; Ovando & Combs, 2018).

We further the discussion by borrowing from critical race and whiteness theories, including the *pedagogy of fear*, which Leonardo and Porter (2010) have conceptualised in classroom contexts as fear of disrupting the peacefulness of dominance. The pedagogy of fear is further enacted within what Castagno (2014) termed the *culture of nice*. Classroom environments, like the educators within them, are discursively positioned as *nice* because they work with children and youth. Nice educators invest in the creation and maintenance of *niceness* within their classrooms. Hence, discussions about controversial or uncomfortable topics in nice classrooms will take place within safe/nice spaces. Nice educators may initiate challenging dialogues, to be sure, but they also risk the immediate reaction by those whose peacefulness, organised by oppression, may be disrupted. Finally, we draw from Martin Luther King, Jr.'s call for the construction of "creative tension" as a means of confronting and overcoming prejudice and racism in higher education contexts.

We draw from Martin Luther King, Jr.'s *Letter from a Birmingham Jail* (1963), in which he expressed frustration with the city's white clergy because they criticised demonstrations against segregation, urging civil rights activists to wait for a more auspicious moment to protest.

> This "wait" has almost always meant "never". It has been a tranquilising thalidomide, relieving the emotional stress for a moment, only to give birth to an ill-formed infant of frustration. We must come to see with the distinguished jurist of yesterday that "justice too long delayed is justice denied.
>
> (King, 1963, p. 5)

King also argued that nonviolent direct action in pursuit of human equality had to generate "creative tension" within the white community because whites had consistently refused to confront racial segregation. Creative tension was constructive and necessary to help people "rise from the dark depths of prejudice and racism to the majestic heights of understanding and brotherhood" (p. 4). We draw from the work of critical race scholars Zeus Leonardo and Ronald Porter (2010) to analyse the concept of *safe spaces*:

> One of the main premises of safe-space discourse is that it provides a format for people of color and whites to come together and discuss issues of race in a matter that is not dangerous as well as inclusive. Thus, the conventional guidelines used to establish a safe space, such as being mindful of how and when one is speaking, confidentiality, challenge by choice, and speaking from experience, are used to create an environment where fundamental issues can be broached and no one will be offended.
>
> (Leonardo & Porter, 2010, p. 139)

We frame the following questions to consider throughout the chapter:

1. If civility means an atmosphere of control or politeness, how courteous or polite must we be to individuals who express racism, sexism or homophobia? Should we be "nice" to aggressive, domineering individuals?
2. Does the enforcement of "niceness" in the classroom reproduce or reinforce the dominance of some groups over others?
3. How might instructor complicity and silencing (re)produce oppressive and perilous environments in classroom settings?
4. How can instructors and students alike facilitate critical conversations in "brave spaces" that educate and transform even as they challenge and disrupt?
5. Critical race scholars often talk about what they call "white fragility." How do you understand this idea?
6. Do we have to "comfort" white students in order to support them in difficult conversations about race, class, gender and homophobia? How do we "comfort" students of colour when such conversations do not take place?

A Note on the Research Underpinning this Chapter

This chapter relies on a qualitative case study approach. The project was conducted with five high school teachers, from which two ideal types have been created. One supports the sharing of lived experiences as ways to engage race and class as systems of oppression, while the other with diverges from that point of departure, perceiving education as an Americanisation process (Creswell, 2007; Hesse-Biber & Leavy, 2011).

Table 4.2 details how the research was conducted for the reader more interested in research approaches and methods. In keeping with the goal to make theory actionable, we also recommend ways in which this can inform practice in your own setting.

Important Themes and Outcomes from the Work

In this section, we present themes that emerged from the study: (1) the obscurity of ethnocentrism, (2) critical compassion and *cariño*/affection, (3) *respeto*/respect and *confianza*/trust. We then conclude with implications for racialised social class and education research, relying on a *conocimiento* approach that has retrieved the family and community legacy of the teachers who participated in this study.

The Obscurity of Ethnocentrism

Maestra Acero (pseudonym) traced her origins to the far eastern United States. Coded as a steel personality, one related to rugged individualism, her persona and character were often difficult to engage. She claimed to not see racial difference in her everyday interactions with the local African American community. In her view, *Vigilancia* is not giving students a "real" education. She did not agree with the exaggeration of the word critical in education, and tokenised the request for her to participate in the study with her response, albeit she agreed to participate. "I'll participate in your 'little' interview." Because they were not problematic, as she "knew her job." *Maestra Acero* rejected intersectionalities under examination. In our *plática*, she said:

> Where Black people lived – we knew it was segregated. Yeah, not on purpose; it's just how it was ... People had their neighbourhoods; we had our neighbourhoods. Black people were poor, most of them were poor. I made friends, if people talked to me I would talk to them. I just wasn't Ms. Social Butterfly.

With this example, *Maestra Acero* spoke about social and racial class segregation in a notion of otherness that is normalised through early socialisation and family upbringings. However, she failed to acknowledge the ways in which her family reinforced power differences and supported the segregation of people by race.

For her, waving at Black people when she would pass by at the bottom of the hill in her neighbourhood, signified a type of friendship, framing her pedagogical approaches in the classroom, and marking the social distance she practiced with her students, particularly objectifying the ways in which she related to them. In the classroom, *Maestra Acero* displayed a tight-knit inclusiveness with a few students who looked like her, while demonstrating distance and distrust in those who were least like her. Her teaching practices emerged to show the ways in which she internalised relationship with others, illustrating the social distance of just how she projected difference in her teaching. Although she spoke with concern about treating everyone equally, the norms of social inequity were reinforced in her classroom, there was no need to make adjustment, things were as good as they were.

Through observation, *Maestra Acero* favoured those who were obedient and loyal to her. The day she was interviewed, she asked five students to re-state and affirm her beliefs and ideas (Ball, 2013). While *Maestra Acero* claimed she did not see or express difference, her narrative spoke otherwise, as she recalled her own schooling.

> You knew which kids were the favourite, they were the popular kids. We didn't really have a social economic issue in our school; we were all lower middle to middle. In my school, the poor kids were the brown kids. But I never saw them as different, that is why I would talk to them. I knew they were Black – that is obvious – we didn't have Hispanic students in our neighbourhood. We didn't have anybody else in our neighbourhood.

While she found points of connection with lighter complexioned blacks, in her teaching, *Maestra Acero* actively imparted a colour-blind approach, in her denial of failure to recognise and resisted the structural inequality embedded in racism. She reproduced the culture of home, and adhered to traditional views of schooling, stating that race and class did not warrant scrutiny. Her actions denied the perceived irrational and emotional experiences of her students through controlling measures that repressed identity. Avoidance thus becomes a tool with which controversial topics are engaged, to only disrupt a discourse of niceness within white normative teaching practices (Orozco, 2019a).

Critical Compassion and Cariño/Affection

In the art of teaching, it is vital to activate critical thinking, which calls for reliance on critical compassion in the schooling context. Thus, they must shed traditional order of operation to adopt self-reflexive ways of teaching and understanding what it means to enact a liberatory practice in teaching, and they must be mindful about their students' lived experiences. To carry out their practice, teachers must rely on their emotions as sources of connection, to engage and examine interactions with their students (Rabois, 2016). This calls for them to authentically care for their charges, by integrating a social justice framework, which values the dignity of students, by recognising their experience. It is indispensable that educators advance a critical compassionate intellectualism, which requires them to acknowledge and develop learning interactions where students are co-creators and subjects in the schooling process (Romero, Arce & Cammarota, 2009).

Toward this end, Freire (2000) posited that problem-posing education allows for students and teachers to dismantle subordination by collaborating in the educational process, with an open up dialogue that mediates the learning process between teacher/learner. When students understand the meaning of injustice through critical pedagogy, they problematise their world, departing from a heightened social consciousness. In contrast to homogenised common sense view of teaching, we present a critical examination provided by one of the few Chicana teachers in this study.

Maestra Corazón Mágico evidences and demonstrates love and value for students, and treats them with compassion and respect, allowing them to express their emotions. During lunch break, she stays in the classroom, hanging out with students, to expand their perspective about class, and often draws students from other classes. She builds on her early upbringing growing up in the barrio, as this allows her to engage the knowledge they have in common:

> As a child, I didn't have anybody there for me. So, it was hard. I found solidarity with my friends but even then struggling all through life. But I made friends. I was a social person and it wasn't the same. My mom would come home irritable, tired. So, I don't have memories of my mom asking me, "How was your day? Let's talk about school, let's do this, let's do that." My mom was exhausted, [and as a mother] I emulate my mom's behaviour.

She has a strong social life, expressing and validating a Chicana identity. However, with her own children, *Maestra Corazón Mágico* continues to reproduce her family upbringing experiences, but her reflections about motherhood provide her tools for critical compassion and empathy. Congruent with Freire and Macedo (2005), she asserts that human beings can locate themselves through their histories into the present, and, with reflection, teachers must engage the struggle for human life and freedom. As such, *Maestra Corazón Mágico* relays knowledge to her students, whereby she attentively monitors and continuously checks on her students' learning. During a class observation, in a class of about twenty-five students, she consciously used space in an effort to reach all students. Constant movement, in addition to reflecting on their common experiences as working-class people, verified the ways in which she affirmed their communal knowledge as social resources in their schooling.

Critical pedagogy stimulates thought-provoking engagement, when students understand the wrongs of the past, they create a better future. Toward that end, *Maestra Corazón Mágico* problematises the tools utilised in the social control exercised within confined spaces, in the culture of schooling (Foucault, 1977). Within structures of schooling there also must be ways to challenge feelings of confinement, which restrict self-determination. For students to understand detrimental boundaries that impede their self-empowerment, an alternative space must be created.

In observation, *Maestra Corazón Mágico* created space for disagreement among students, as she fashioned venues to challenge. At times, she did not intervene in heated arguments that mattered to students. Around issues that were critical to dismantling oppression, such as gender and immigration, she interacted and created the ambiance for students to reach collaborative resolutions. She also created space, when not in the classroom, and there were times when students showed up to create a space of unity, finding sanctuary in the creation of knowledge because it was a brave space. Within these pedagogical approaches, "difference" among students is not tolerated as deficient, inferior, or unequal. Instead, her pedagogical praxis democratises schooling space to broaden a moral vision of education (Giroux, 1992).

These two teachers problematise that in the structure of schooling, the learning environment must necessarily examine the experiences of working class/poor or underprivileged communities, and how they cope with poverty, despair, and violence. This can be facilitated through an environment of self-awareness and insight into the community of which they are part. This ensures youth do not to internalise poverty or fall into a culture of shame, as such space allows students to attribute cultural capital to their family life and educational experience (Yosso, 2005).

Respeto *and* Confianza *(Respect and Trust)*

At the forefront of a conversation, *respeto* and *confianza* mutually inform Mexican-immigrant culture (Valdés, 1996). Historically, schooling in the United States has focused on the deculturalisation and aggressive assimilation of minoritised groups who are perceived as outside the norm (Elenes, 2003; Spring, 2016). Within this ideology, failure and success in schooling are positioned as the sole responsibility of the individual. What is seldom interrogated is traditional educational philosophies that trump the education of minoritised students in regimented schooling spaces designed to limit freedom of movement (Foucault, 1977).

Maestra Corazón Mágico includes *respeto y confianza* in the curriculum, she articulated:

> Students were disrespectful, but people have different tolerances of what is respectful. Teachers perceived it as you are being disrespectful, "so, get out of my room," or you're being disrespectful, "so, go sit outside in the hall." It was traumatising,

teachers were very punitive. Everything was punitive, one female teacher who had the audacity to treat us like human beings, took us outside to say, "let's talk about it." "Okay come back inside," and that was it. The rest of them definitely had that power trip of humiliating people in front of the class.

In her own experience and in her teaching, *Maestra Corazón Mágico* spoke about the ways in which teachers disrespected students. She demonstrated the ways in which *confianza* was articulated outside of the classroom and never modelled as an alternative for students. For her, social classification replicates the other. Such dogmatic practices thus become tools of social control in colonial practices (McLaren, 1995).

Critical scholars in education studies have countered deficit stigmas and have argued that poor marginalised communities can rely on social networks to make healthy choices in the development of their communities. They argue that a shift of consciousness can take place when youth engage racism and understand privilege, power, and difference, thus not repeating cycles of harm (Méndez-Negrete, 2006; 2013). Consequently, to engage their students, teacher's constantly manifest or navigate racial/class privilege to disrupt structures of control (Orozco, 2019b).

Conclusion: Implications for Social Class and Education Research

We have argued that critical praxis and pedagogical engagements are central in teaching, about racialised social class within the structure of schooling. Through *pláticas*, semi-structured interviews, and participant observations, we have illustrated the ways in which social reproduction takes place in schooling practices, when teachers' lived experiences are not interrogated and shared, to model self-knowledge and reflexivity among students as critical thinkers. Education must provide students opportunities to understand the world in which they participate, to transform it (Méndez-Negrete, 2013).

Future teachers must recognise that social transformation will not come by changing the schools, but by cultivating an education that is politicised and simultaneously unlinked to the status quo (Méndez-Negrete & Gibson, 2014). Change will only come when society transforms the systemic apparatus of schooling into an organic social movement that shares its struggle with the working-class experience (Torres, 2009).

Critical theory offers that all human being are born with their own unique gifts. Within such heightened consciousness, a learner challenges ideology, unmasks power, overcomes alienation, and learns about liberation as facets of democracy (Brookfield, 2004). There is a danger in pedagogical practices that restrict the organic human experience to one of privilege, power, and difference. West (2003) warns, "Nihilism is...the lived experience of coping with a life of horrifying meaninglessness, hopelessness, and (most important) lovelessness. This usually results in a numbing detachment from others and a self-destructive disposition towards the world" (p. 596). This is what happens to a person when their schooling experience devalues their self-worth in a world where a person is labelled a failure (Ter Borg, 1988).

To counter nihilism demands having a deepened empathy of the world, a critical compassionate thinking is reason grounded by empathy and valuing the wellbeing of all those who inhabit the world with us (Rabois, 2016), departing from an insightful and conscious sense of self in relationship and interaction with others. Rector Aranda (2019a) advises care must be linked to cultural and political underpinnings, while offering a thread of caution for avoiding the tendency to enact shallow forms of compassion. Such approach regarding student-teacher relationships should be established within a context of care and trust (Rector Aranda, 2017), where students feel brave by their voices and experiences being incorporated into class discussions, written reflections and collaborative activities which draw upon critical pedagogy (Rector Aranda, 2019b).

Romero and Arce (2009) further the cultivation of critical compassion by creating an authentic and caring educational environment guided by appreciation and respect for the Chicana/o community, its culture, and historical struggle for educational equality. Romero (2008) additionally affirms the importance of naming oppression as part of critical compassion. Furthermore, an in-depth articulation of how oppression has manifested itself into the social reality of the student-teacher, and within such dialogue a transformed reality can further a transformative hope which can then blossom. Romero (2014) goes on to affirm that a crucial aspect of educational sovereignty is critical compassion, but one in which embodies liberation, empowerment, and humanisation. He states that within teaching praxis there must be a centring of hopes, dreams fears, and needs of all students, as well the makeup of the community that educators serve.

Cammarota and Romero (2006) through their research affirm that critical compassion elevates voices within the art of teaching that have been historically silenced and rendered invisible. It consists of a trilogy of educational practices that comprised of critical pedagogy, compassionate student/teacher relationships, and social justice content. They recommend that to facilitate critical compassionate intellectualism a social justice perspective guide all educational practices. Romero, Arce, and Cammarota (2009) concur that in realising critical compassion there is a need to highlight how the exclusion of racismisation process in the historical and social reality of the US is a mistake with profound implications. By students being mindful of agents of socialisation they are provided with an active connection to enable them in creating knowledge in-between the past, present and future, and assisted in providing what gives meaning to their lived experiences within a sociality reality.

We advance the conversation and call for action on the preparation of teacher credential programs to incorporate humanising (Orozco, 2025), and self-reflexive methodologies that assist future educators in uncovering their prejudices, traumas, and stereotypes (Bartolome, 2004; Graziano, 2008; Licona, 2004). To counter social reproduction within the art of teaching, those who teach must revisit their early socialisation. This calls for an interrogation of traditional socialisation, which is not limited to legacies of religion, family, immigration/migration histories, and education. It also implicates unpacking the trauma associated with the realities of our human experience. Through what Méndez-Negrete (2013) calls pedagogical *conocimientos,* teachers engage self and other in interaction, as they participate in a collaborate and collective process of knowledge creation as an interactional self-reflexive process of reciprocity.

Conocimiento is an epistemological, methodological, and theoretical approach to learning/teaching and a way to enact relationships with self/other. *Conocimiento* relies on

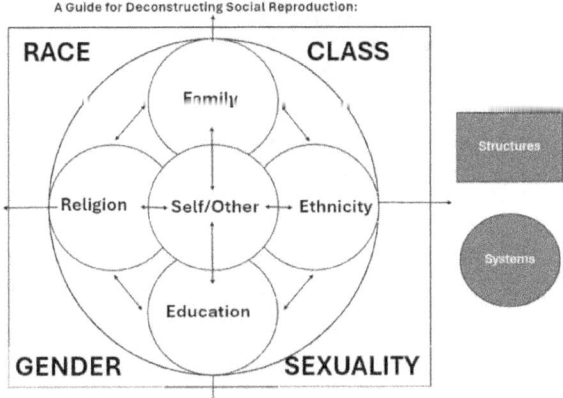

Figure 4.1 A guide for deconstructing social reproduction: pedagogical *conocimientos* in the context of teacher preparation.

Source: reproduced with permission from Jaime-Diaz and Mendez-Négrete (2021)

collaborative, reflexive, and critical spaces in the creation of knowledge. *Conocimiento* as a foundation for learning and teaching (Sanchez, Jaime-Diaz & Méndez-Negrete, 2022), whereby:

- There are no right or wrong answers, focus must be on what you know and have experienced.
- Every person carries knowledge and is not an "empty vessel" to be filled by those who have power or are perceived as the ones carrying the knowledge.
- Our emotions, past historical, personal, and family traumas may facilitate or impede learning as we unearth past hurts and violence to our psychological, spiritual, physical, and emotional selves.
- Through *conocimiento*, learners/teachers gain confidence in challenging power structures and their institutional practices.
- Teacher/learners engage in the creation of knowledge as a subject of the world whose agency creates possibilities or self and others.
- Oral and family histories are central to the excavation and retrieval of learner/teacher experiential knowledge.
- Through relational reciprocity in the examination of experience, *conocimiento* centres and honours dialogical voices embedded in trust.
- Learners/teachers recognise the value of their participation in the creation of knowledge. When and if learners opt out or "pass", they will have the option to share their thoughts, feelings, and reflections at another point.
- Information retrieved from *conocimiento* packets is utilised to create essays, videos, musical anthologies, artifacts, archives, and other creative projects.
- *Conocimiento* creates heightened awareness, critical empathy, and compassion.

REFLECTIVE ACTIVITY: NAVIGATING CRITICAL COMPASSION IN TEACHER PREPARATION

Part one: Explore the flows and frames model of compassionate leadership described in Chapter 1. Which flows of compassion do you rely on most in your current practice? Write 3-4 sentences about why those flows are most relevant in your setting.

Part Two: This chapter adopts cultural-historical and structural-political frames for exploring compassionate leadership. In what way could the values of *cariño, respeto,* and *confianza* enhance the existing flows of compassion you rely on as a leader?

Summary

Critical pedagogical approaches must be considered in the implementation of non-exploitive culturally relevant pedagogies rooted in languages, cultures, and epistemologies that value and honour counter-lessons of survival and resilience, because it affirms cultural dignity and integrity (Sánchez & Ek, 2013). Clearly, when working with marginalised communities and students of colour, the creation of such unconventional spaces is needed within structures of schooling.

With pedagogical *conocimientos*, future teacher preparation must incorporate a self-reflexive methodology whereby a teacher/learner approach foments understanding about us and others, in which teachers are immersed (Jaime-Diaz & Méndez-Negrete, 2021). The art of teaching must engage critical compassion, empathy, *respeto, confianza,* as paths to bridge difference toward critical consciousness (Jaime-Diaz & Méndez-Negrete, 2020). Race, racialised social class, gender, and sexuality, among other interstitial spaces (Jaime-Diaz, Ramos & Méndez-Negrete, 2020), must become central in the preparation of those who desire to create a human connection in the schooling of others.

Further Reading

Jaime-Diaz, J. & Combs, M. C. (2025). Teaching to labour & social reproduction: Pedagogical relics of the factory model in 21st century structures of schooling. *Journal for Critical Education Policy Studies JCEPS,* 22(3), 181-215.
Social reproduction theory is invaluable for providing insight into social stratification through schooling, particularly social ideologies from the past are transmitted through pedagogical labour. The authors suggest teacher preparation programs engage teacher candidates about the history of factory model schooling and normalised inequities that such a model continues to reproduce.
Jaime-Diaz, J. & Méndez-Negrete, J. (2021). A guide for deconstructing social reproduction: Pedagogical *conocimientos* in the context of teacher preparation. In M. J. Hernández-Serrano (Ed), *Teacher Education in The 21st Century: Emerging Skills For a Changing World,* 293-312. IntechOpen.
With changing student demographics in the 21st century, a pressing need exists for teacher programs to develop innovative pedagogies. This requires *pláticando* or actively communicating, listening to, and validating student experiences through pedagogical *conocimientos*. Educators must engage a critical compassion to act for the common good, in partnership with learners.

Mendez-Negrete, J. (2013). Pedagogical conocimientos: Self and other in interaction. *Rio Bravo: A Journal of the Borderlands*, 226-250.

Pedagogical conocimientos illustrates critical praxis and self-reflection as teaching/learning approach for coming to knowledge about the Self in relationship with others, through a conocimiento guide designed for the activity. Raised awareness moves into consciousness in relationship to the material, social, cultural, and spiritual forces that frame our coming to self-knowledge

Romero, A. Arce, S. & Cammarota, J. (2009). A barrio pedagogy: Identity, intellectualism, activism, and academic achievement through the evolution of critically compassionate intellectualism. *Race Ethnicity and Education*, 12(2), 217-233.

Critically compassionate intellectualism requires a dialogic approach to pedagogy that reveals counternarratives within the US education system, challenging the dehumanising master narrative of difference. As teaching practices evolve, diverse social and educational transformations will emerge, fostering a holistic international community committed to social justice for the common good.

References

Anyon, J. (1980). Social class and the hidden curriculum of work. *Journal of education, 162 (1)*, 67-92.
Anyon, J. (1997). *Ghetto schooling: A political economy of urban educational reform*. Teachers College Press.
Anyon, J. (2005). *Radical possibilities: Public policy, urban education, and a new social movement*. Routledge.
Anyon, J. (2011). *Marx and education*. Routledge.
Arum, R., Beattie, I., & Ford, K. (2021). *The structure of schooling: Readings in the sociology of education* (3rd ed.). Sage Publications.
Ball, S. (2013). *Foucault, power and education*. Routledge.
Bartolome, L. I. (2004). Critical pedagogy and teacher education: Radicalizing prospective teachers. *Teacher education quarterly*, 31(1), 97-122.
Belkhir. (2001). Marxism without apologies: Integrating race, gender, class; a working class approach. *Race, Gender & Class*, 8(2), 142-171.
Bowles, S, & Gintis, H. (2011). *Schooling in capitalist America: Educational reform and the contradictions of economic life*. Haymarket Books.
Bowles, S. Gintis, H. & Meyer, P. (2015). The long shadow of work. In Arum, B. & Beattie, I. R. (3rd Ed), *The structure of schooling: Readings in the sociology of education* (pp. 101-115). Sage Publications.
Brookfield, S. D. (2004). *The power of critical theory: Liberating adult learning and teaching*. Jossey-Bass.
Cammarota, J., & Romero, A. (2006). A critically compassionate intellectualism for Latina/o students: Raising voices above the silencing in our schools. *Multicultural Education*, 14(2), 16-23.
Carignan, N. Sanders, M. & Pourdavood, R. G. (2005). Racism and ethnocentrism: Social representations of preservice teachers in the context of multi-and intercultural education. *International Journal of Qualitative Methods*, 4(3), 1-19.
Carpenter, S., & Mojab, S. (2022). Marxist feminism and education: Gender, race, and class. In A. Maisuria (Ed), *Encyclopedia of Marxism and education* (pp. 453-466). Brill.
Carpenter, S., & Mojab, S. (2023). The class in race, gender, and learning. In In (R. Hall, I. Accioloy & K. Szadkowski Eds.), *The Palgrave international handbook of Marxism and education* (pp. 93-110). Springer International Publishing.
Castagno, A. E. (2014). *Educated in Whiteness: Good intentions and diversity in schools*. University of Minnesota Press.
Codiroli Mcmaster, N., & Cook, R. (2019). The contribution of intersectionality to quantitative research into educational inequalities. *Review of Education*, 7(2), 271-292.
Combs, M.C. DaSilva Iddings, A.C. & Moll, L.C. (2014). 21st Century linguistic apartheid: English language learners in Arizona public schools. In P. W. Orelus (Ed.), *Affirming language diversity in schools and society: Beyond linguistic Apartheid* (pp. 23-34). Routledge.
Crenshaw, K. (2019). "Difference" through intersectionality. In S. Arya & A Singh Rathore (Eds), *Dalit feminist theory* (pp. 139-149). Routledge India.

Cresswell, J. (2016). Disengagement, pedagogical Eros and (the undoing of?) dialogic pedagogy. *Dialogic Pedagogy: An International Online Journal, 4*.

Creswell, J., W. (2007). *Qualitative inquiry & research design: Choosing among five approaches*. Thousand Oaks, CA: Sage Publications.

Dafermos, M. (2023). The neoliberal transformation of university and restructuring of academic labour. *Journal for Critical Education Policy Studies (JCEPS), 21*(1).

Davis, A. Y. (1983). *Women, race, & class*. Vintage.

Dewberry, G. R., Redmon, C. F. & Larrington, M. W. (2006). *Vigilancia High School: Looking back 1955-1970. Michoco,* The Place of the Small Spring: *Vigilancia* High School Alumni Association.

Elenes, C. A. (2003). Reclaiming the borderlands: Chicana/o identity, difference, and critical pedagogy. In Darder, A. Baltodano, M. & Torres, R.D. (Ed), *The critical pedagogy reader* (pp. 191-210). Routledge.

Fierros, C. O., & Bernal, D. D. (2016). Vamos a platicar: The contours of pláticas as Chicana/Latina feminist methodology. *Chicana/Latina Studies, 15*(2), 98-121.

Foucault, M. (1977). *Discipline & punish: The birth of the prison*. Random House Publishing.

Freire, P. (2000). *Pedagogy of the oppressed*. Bloomsbury Publishing.

Freire, P. (2005). *Teachers as cultural workers: Letters to those who dare to teach*. Westview Press.

Freire, P. & Macedo, D. (2005). *Literacy: Reading the word and the world*. Taylor & Francis.

Giroux, H. (1992). Literacy, pedagogy, and the politics of difference. *College Literature, 19*(1), 1-11.

Gonzalez, J. C. (2012). Teaching from a critical perspective/enseñando de una perspectiva critica: Conceptualization, reflection, and application of Chicana/o pedagogy. *The International Journal of Critical Pedagogy, 4*(1), 18-34.

Graziano, K. J. (2008). Walk the talk: Connecting critical pedagogy and practice in teacher education. *Teaching Education, 19*(2), 153-163.

Griffin, E. (2013). *Liberty's dawn: a people's history of the Industrial Revolution*. Yale University Press.

Gutiérrez, J. A. (1998). *The making of a Chicano militant: Lessons from Cristal*. University of Wisconsin Press.

Halinan, M.T. (2000). Tracking from theory to practice. In Arum, B. & Beattie, I. R. (Ed), *The structure of schooling: Readings in the sociology of education* (pp. 218-224). Mayfield Publishing Company.

Healey, J. F. & O'Brien, E. (2022). *Race, ethnicity, gender & class: The sociology of group conflict and change*. Sage Publications.

Hesse-Beiber. S. N. & Leavy, P. et al. (2006). *Emergent methods in social research*. Sage Publications Inc.

Hesse-Biber, S. N. & Leavy, P. (2011). *The practice of qualitative research*. Sage Publications.

Hill Collins, P. (2017). On violence, intersectionality and transversal politics. *Ethnic and Racial Studies, 40*(9), 1460-1473.

Illich, I. (1970). *Deschooling society*. Marion Boyars.

Jaime-Diaz, J. (2019). Take a Little Trip on the AZ Side: Examining a pedagogy of surveillance within the structure of schooling. *Ethnic Studies Review, 42*(1), 83-94.

Jaime-Diaz, J., & Combs, M. C. (2025). Teaching to labour and social reproduction: Pedagogical relics of the factory model in 21st century structures of schooling. *Journal for Critical Education Policy Studies (JCEPS), 22*(3), 181-215.

Jaime-Diaz, J. & Méndez-Negrete, J. (2020). Racialized social class pedagogical praxis: Critical compassion, *cariño, respeto* and *confianza*. *Association of Mexican American Educators Journal, 14(1),* 49-70.

Jaime-Diaz, J. & Méndez-Negrete, J. (2021). A guide for deconstructing social reproduction: Pedagogical *conocimientos* in the context of teacher preparation. In M. J. Hernández-Serrano (Ed), *Teacher Education in The 21st Century: Emerging Skills For a Changing World* (pp. 293-312). IntechOpen.

Jaime-Diaz, J. Ramos, D.C. & Méndez-Negrete, J. (2020). Slipping into irrelevance: Pedagogical *conocimientos* in the preparation for teachers to contest ideological tracking. *Journal of Latinos and Education, 19(3),* 1-14.

King, Jr., M. L. (1963). *Letter from a Birmingham Jail*. The Martin Luther King Jr. Research and Education Institute. https://kinginstitute.stanford.edu/letter-birmingham-jail Accessed 17 January 2025

Kozol, J. (2012). *Savage inequalities: Children in America's schools*. Broadway Books.

Leonardo, Z. & Porter, R. K. (2010). Pedagogy of fear: Toward a Fanonian theory of "safety" in race dialogue. *Race, Ethnicity, and Education*, 13(2), 139-157.

Licona, M.M. (2004). Deconstructing oppressor ideology in teacher preparation. *International Journal of Learning*, 11.

Linley, J. L. (2017). Teaching to deconstruct whiteness in higher education. *Whiteness and Education*, 1(1), 40-59.

Lynch, M. E. (2018). The hidden nature of Whiteness in education: Creating active allies in White teachers. *Journal of Educational Supervision*, 1(1), 2.

Marshall, C. & Rossman, G. B. (2016). *Designing qualitative research*. Sage publications.

Marx, K. & Engels, F. (1999). *The communist manifesto*. Bedford/St. Martin's.

McIntyre, E. Rosebery, A. S. & González, N. (Eds.). (2001). *Classroom diversity: Connecting curriculum to students' lives* (Vol. 88). Heinemann.

McLaren, P. (1995). *Critical pedagogy and predatory culture: Oppositional politics in a postmodern era*. Psychology Press.

McLaren, P. (2005). *Capitalists and conquerors: A critical pedagogy against empire*. Rowman & Littlefield.

Méndez-Negrete, J. (2006). *Las hijas de Juan: Daughters betrayed*. Duke University Press.

Mendez-Negrete, J. (2013). Pedagogical conocimientos: Self and other in interaction. *Rio Bravo: A Journal of the Borderlands*, 226-250.

Méndez-Negrete, J. (2013). Expressive creativity: Narrative text and creative cultural expressions as a healing praxis. *Journal of Creativity in Mental Health*, 8(3), 314-325.

Méndez-Negrete, J. (2015). *A life on hold: Living with schizophrenia*. University of New Mexico Press.

Méndez-Negrete, J. & Rodriguez y Gibson, E. (2014). Word that matters: Tending to Chicana/Latina Studies as home. *Chicana/Latina Studies*, 13(2), 20.

Oakes, J. (2005). *Keeping track: How schools structure inequality*. Yale University Press.

Oakes, J. Lipton, M. Anderson, L. & Stillman, J. (2018). *Teaching to change the world*. Routledge.

Orosco, J. A. (2016). *Toppling the melting pot: Immigration and multiculturalism in American pragmatism*. Indiana University Press.

Orozco, R. (2019a). The method of avoidance: Niceness as whiteness in segregated Chicanx schools. *Whiteness and Education*, 4(2), 128-145.

Orozco, R. A. (2019b). White innocence as an investigative frame in a schooling context. *Critical Studies in Education*, 60(4), 426-442.

Orozco, R. (2025). Surveying Student/Intern Teachers for Their Development of Equity Literacy via Indigenous Epistemology. *Educational Researcher*, 54(1), 1-6.

Orozco, R. & Jaime Diaz, J. (2016). "Suited to Their Needs": White Innocence as a Vestige of Segregation. *Multicultural Perspectives*, 18(3), 127-133.

Orozco, R. A., & López, F. (2015). Impacts of Arizona's SB 1070 on Mexican American students' stress, school attachment, and grades. *education policy analysis archives*, 23(42), 1-23.

Ovando, C. J. & Combs, M. C. (2018). *Bilingual and ESL classrooms: Teaching in multicultural contexts*. Rowman & Littlefield.

Pavlidis, P. (2023). Teachers' work as a form of intellectual activity in conditions of their proletarianisation. *Journal for Critical Education Policy Studies*, 20(3) 1-30.

Rabois, I. (2016). *Compassionate critical thinking: How mindfulness, creativity, empathy, and Socratic questioning can transform teaching*. Rowman & Littlefield.

Rector-Aranda, A. (2017). *Critically compassionate intellectualism in teacher education: Making meaning of a practitioner and participatory action research inquiry* (Doctoral Dissertation, University of Cincinnati). www.proquest.com/openview/cca0102a878da97732f04776b56926eb/1?pq-origsite=gscholar&cbl=18750 Accessed 15 January 2025

Rector-Aranda, A. (2019a). Critically compassionate intellectualism in teacher education: The contributions of relational-cultural theory. *Journal of Teacher Education*, 70(4), 388-400.

Rector-Aranda, A. (2019b). Student responses to critically compassionate intellectualism In teacher education for social justice. In (A.E. Lopez & E.L. Olan Eds.) *Transformative Pedagogies for Teacher Education: Critical Action, Agency and Dialogue in Teaching and Learning Contexts*, 133-152. Information Age Publishing.

Reed, J. (2007). *Appreciative inquiry: Research for change*. Sage Publications.

Richards, L. (2014). *Handling qualitative data: A practical guide*. Sage Publications.

Romero, A. F. (2008). *Towards a critically compassionate intellectualism model of transformative education: Love, hope, identity, and organic intellectualism through the convergence of critical race theory, critical pedagogy, and authentic caring.* (Doctoral Dissertation, The University of Arizona). www.proquest.com/openview/c9dde097598443a8e85c3f920c699e64/1?pq-origsite=gscholar&cbl=18750 Accessed 17 January 2025

Romero, A. F. (2014). Critically compassionate intellectualism. In (J. Cammarota & A. Romero Eds.) *Raza Studies: The Public Option for Educational Revolution*, 14-39. University of Arizona Press.

Romero, A., & Arce, M. S. (2009). Culture as a resource: Critically compassionate intellectualism and its struggle against racism, fascism, and intellectual apartheid in Arizona. *Hamline Journal of Public Law and Policy*, 31(1), 179-217.

Romero, A. Arce, S. & Cammarota, J. (2009). A barrio pedagogy: Identity, intellectualism, activism, and academic achievement through the evolution of critically compassionate intellectualism. *Race Ethnicity and Education*, 12(2), 217-233.

Saldaña, J. (2009). *The coding manual for qualitative researchers*. Sage Publications.

Sánchez, P. & Ek, L. (2013). Cultivando la siguiente generación: Future directions in Chicana/Latina feminist pedagogies. *Journal of Latino/Latin American Studies*, 5(3), 181-187.

Sanchez, V. G., Jaime-Diaz, J. & Méndez-Negrete, J. (2022). Self/Other, Other/Self: Conocimiento as a Pedagogical Praxis. In *NACCS Annual Conference Proceedings*. 8.

Seidman, I. (2006). *Interviewing as qualitative research: A guide for researchers in education and the social sciences*. Teachers College Press.

Sleeter, C. E. (2017). Critical race theory and the whiteness of teacher education. *Urban Education*, 52(2), 155-169.

Spring, J. (2016). *Deculturalization and the struggle for equality: A brief history of the education of dominated cultures in the United States*. Routledge.

Stetsenko, A. (2023). Marxism in an Activist Key: Educational Implications of an Activist-Transformative Philosophy. In R. Hall, I. Accioloy & K. Szadkowski (Eds.), *The Palgrave International Handbook of Marxism and Education* (pp. 581-599). Springer International Publishing.

Ter Borg, M. B. (1988). The problem of nihilism: a sociological approach. *Sociological Analysis*, 49(1), 1-16.

Torres, C. A. (2009). *Globalizations and education: Collected essays on class, race, gender, and the state*. Teachers College Press.

Tyack, D, & Hansot, E. (2000). The Rising Tide of Coeducation in High School. In Arum, B. & Beattie, I. R. (Ed), *The structure of schooling: Readings in the sociology of education* (pp. 121-132). Mayfield Publishing Company.

Valdés, G. (1996). *Con Respeto. Bridging the distances between culturally diverse families and schools: An ethnographic portrait*. Teachers College Press.

Valenzuela, A. (1999). *Subtractive Schooling: US-Mexican Youth and the Politics of Caring*. State University of New York Press.

West, C. (2003). Race Matters. In Marable, M. & Mullings, L. (Ed), *Let nobody turn us around: Voices of resistance, reform and renewal: An African American anthology* (pp. 594-601). Rowman & Littlefield.

Willis, P. E. (1977). *Learning to labor: How working class kids get working class jobs*. Columbia University Press.

Yosso, T. J. (2005). Whose culture has capital? A critical race theory discussion of community cultural wealth. *Race ethnicity and education*, 8(1), 69-91.

5

Leading with Compassion or Control? Coaching Lessons from a Confucian Perspective

Hongguo Wei, Shaobing Li, and Amer Mohammad

CHAPTER AIMS

By the end of this chapter readers will be able to:

- Understand how Confucian cultural values underpin both compassionate and authoritarian leadership styles in Southeast Asian organisational contexts.
- Critically evaluate the dynamic tensions between compassion and authoritarianism through a Confucian yin-yang lens and their implications for managerial coaching.
- Apply the yin-yang structured compassion coaching framework to enhance employee outcomes such as wellbeing, performance, and career development.

Introduction

Managerial coaching, defined as "a supervisor/manager serving as a facilitator of learning by enacting behaviors that enable employees to learn and develop work-related skills and abilities" (Ellinger et al., 2011, p. 68), has been embraced by many organisations globally. According to the British Council, when managers have effective coaching skills, employees are 40% more engaged and 20% less likely to turnover (Corporate English Solutions, 2023). Effective managerial coaching also affects sales representative employees' performance (Proença, 2023).

Managerial coaching enhances employee performance, engagement and retention, learning, resilience, and wellbeing (Hui et al., 2021; Li et al., 2022; Nyfoudi et al., 2023; Ribeiro et al., 2021). Scholars have advanced managerial coaching research from different aspects such as its dimensions, indicators, and styles of managerial coaching (Hosseini et al., 2023; Hui et al., 2013; Smith et al., 2021). For instance, Smith and coauthors (2021) identify five dimensions of managerial coaching skills (open communication, team support, feedback, goal-setting, and empowerment) and empirically test that managerial coaching significantly impacts employees' personal learning and organisational commitment. Hosseini et al. (2023) find that managerial coaching indicators such as knowledge, ethics, and leadership enhance productivity and talent development. Hui et al. (2013) find that leaders with guidance and facilitation coaching styles provide different levels of direction and empowering to followers.

Despite the importance of managerial coaching and scholarly efforts in Southeast Asia to investigate its impacts on employee performance, commitment, creativity, and employee wellbeing, only limited attention has been paid to understand the impacts of managerial coaching from an indigenous cultural perspective. A few studies were conducted either with an indigenous sample (Hui et al., 2021 with a sample from Hong Kong), or testing the moderation of indigenous value orientation of the subordinates (Chinese traditionality; see Zhao & Liu, 2020). Yet, no research has examined how indigenous leadership behaviours cultivated by the Confucian culture impact managerial coaching and the outcomes. Of the few studies examining the impact of managerial coaching by relating to national culture, they mostly investigate the moderation of uncertainty avoidance (Bozer & Delegach, 2019), collectivism (Ye et al., 2016), and Chinese traditionality (Zhao & Liu, 2020), which lack a systematic examination of managerial coaching by relating to the indigenous Confucian cultural context and specific leadership behaviours. The purpose of this chapter is to explore the propriate managerial coaching practices for Confucian leadership behaviours that facilitate positive employee outcomes and provide practical guidance for organisational leaders' managerial coaching in Southeast Asia.

A Cultural Perspective to Managerial Coaching

Managerial Coaching and the Impacts of National Cultures

With more organisations investing in employee training and development, managerial coaching becomes more prevalent to fulfil this need. Managers are expected to clearly communicate expectations and goals with their employees, conduct regular performance appraisal to support employee task completion and learning, and provide learning and career development opportunities (Ellinger et al., 2003; Heslin et al., 2006).

Due to the manager's job role and obligations, their coaching practice to employees is likely to differ from professional external coaches who closely follow the guidelines of the International Coaching Federation. Most coaching research and practice share a common prototypical definition of coaching as facilitative, empowering, and developmental (Hamlin, Ellinger, & Beattie, 2008; Ellinger & Bostrom, 1999). However, leaders also use a more directive style (Yun, Faraj, & Sims, 2005) that involves leaders inform, assess, and advise the followers (Beattie, 2002). Hui et al. (2013) combine the two approaches and develop two types of managerial coaching, guidance and facilitation coaching, and each enhances different forms of task performance.

Despite scholarly efforts to identify the components of managerial coaching and empirically test its impacts on employee attitudes, behaviours, and wellbeing (Carvalho et al., 2022; Hui et al., 2013), relatively little is known of how managerial coaching should be practiced in Confucian cultural contexts where leaders lead with both compassion and authoritarianism. Such knowledge would also be applicable to other cultural contexts where leaders may wish to adopt both a compassionate and authoritarian approach. Additionally, scholars have advocated for examining the moderating impacts of cultural values on managerial coaching such as in Mainland China (Zhao & Liu, 2020) and Hong Kong (Hui et al., 2021). As such, it is essential to explore managerial coaching in Southeast Asia by relating to Confucian culture values.

Different coaching styles or behaviours may have culturally specific applications and benefits. For instance, in high power distance and hierarchical culture such as Southeast Asia, individuals obey their leaders and expectations and thus prefer to follow a structured approach rather than engage in open-ended dialogue for self-exploration. Directive coaching or guidance coaching from the leader can be more effective (Hui et al., 2013). Yet, in cultures with low power distance and less hierarchy, employees may enjoy self-exploration. Hence, facilitation coaching may be more beneficial for employees' learning and development.

Cultural values also impact leaders' managerial coaching practices. For instance, leaders in American and German cultures prefer direct communication while those in Japanese and Chinese cultures embrace indirect communication (Chmielecki & Contreras-Loera, 2020). In Western cultures, direct criticism is usually accepted as beneficial and necessary to change. On the other hand, most Asian cultures perceive direct criticism as disrespectful and can damage relationships (Chmielecki & Contreras-Loera, 2020). With this in mind, we will explore how Confucian cultural values shape business leaders' managerial coaching in Southeast Asia.

ON CULTURAL FOUNDATIONS OF LEADERSHIP

- How do your own cultural values shape how you lead or coach others in your school or setting?
- In what ways do you see elements of both compassion and control in your leadership style?

Confucian-Based Compassionate and Authoritarian Leadership in Southeast Asia

Theoretical Foundations

Confucian cultural values such as compassion (*ren*), righteousness (*yi*), propriety (*li*), wisdom (*zhi*), as well as filial piety (*xiao*) have long impacted organisational practices and leadership behaviours (*Mencius*, 6A). Scholars have conducted indigenous research and identified that leaders in Confucian-cultural contexts exhibit paternalistic leadership behaviours, with the simultaneous demonstration of authoritarianism and compassion[1] (Farh & Cheng, 2000). In this chapter, we focus on examining two types of Confucian leadership (compassionate and authoritarian leadership) and their cultural foundation embedded.

Compassion and Self-Cultivation

Confucian thoughts of *ren* nicely delineate the idea of compassion, showing *affection and care* to those who are close to oneself. Yet, to be a compassionate leader, one needs to build a self-cultivation system that serves as the foundation of compassion. Confucius clearly presents that five virtues: *courtesy, generosity of soul, good faith, earnestness* and *clemency*, drive the growth of compassion (*Analects*, 17). A nurturing system built on these virtues supports the development of one's moral growth and authenticity. A study by Wei, Zhu, and Li (2016) indicates that Chinese executive leaders' compassionate actions following the five virtues and sustained by self-cultivation positively affect employee commitment, wellbeing, and creativity.

Hierarchy and Authority

Confucian culture emphasises hierarchy and respect for authority. Confucianism believes that social stability stems from clearly defined roles and the implementation of obligations within a hierarchy (Ip, 2009). The well-known "three guidelines" of ruler guides subject, father guides son, and husband guides wife, as well as the "five cardinal relationships" of emperor-officials, father-son, older brother-younger brother, husband-wife, and between friends, present the social hierarchical relationships and roles of entities. From the leadership perspective, this hierarchical value highlights *control, discipline,* and *obedience*. The hierarchical structure has guided organisational and leadership practices in Southeast Asia. While the leader has the obligation to lead and guide others, the subordinate should obey and be loyal to the leader (Nangalia & Nangalia, 2010). An empirical study by Ma and Tsui (2015) shows that in a high-power distance Confucian society, employees in Chinese organisations accept authoritarian leadership because they see this type of leadership behaviour as a legitimate exercise of their moral authority. Similarly, managers in Singapore use an authoritarian approach to retain organisational harmony (Tan & Chee, 2005).

Filial Piety and Reciprocity

The Confucian concept of filial piety (*xiao*) sets the foundation of social order, emphasising obedience, respect, and care for one's parents and the seniors. However, over the years, its impact has been extended beyond the family domain to the organisational context. Paternalistic leadership in Confucian cultures indicates both strictness and kindness to their employees (Farh & Cheng, 2000). Likewise, employees often perceive obedience to their leaders as a filial duty; also, they should express gratitude to their leaders as a reciprocate as they do to the familial bonds (Peng et al., 2018).

Collectivism and Harmony

Confucian virtues of compassion (*ren*) and propriety (*li*) place group and collective needs above those of individuals. People in Confucian cultures are encouraged to maintain harmony through peace, respectful behaviour, and non-confrontation (Hwang, 2000). Collective goals and harmony can be achieved by disciplined coordination and empathy.

The concept of harmony enables the coexistence of compassion and authoritarianism from leaders in a Confucian culture.

Tensions between compassion and authoritarianism from a Confucian yin-yang perspective

Indigenous organisational researchers have carefully considered how Confucian cultural values shape leadership practices. Farh and Cheng (2000) conceptualise paternalistic leadership as an indigenous leadership style in Confucian cultural contexts with authoritarian and benevolent leadership components. In this section, we will discuss the tensions between authoritarian and compassionate leadership by referring to their cultural foundation.

Based on the Confucian yin-yang philosophy, authoritarianism and compassion embody a dialectical tension that is rooted in the expected role of leaders, as both a strict parent-like enforcer of orders and a caring, compassionate guardian. Authoritarian leadership embodies Confucian values on hierarchy, obedience, and righteousness that are needed to maintain control and discipline. Similarly, other Confucian notions such as *li* (propriety) and *xiao* (filial piety) that call for rituals and conduct also support hierarchy, obedience, and respect for authority. On the contrary, compassionate leadership reflects Confucian virtue of *ren* that is needed to facilitate loyalty and trust. As Confucius mentioned, an ideal ruler rules with compassion and people's wellbeing in mind (*Analects*, 2.1). When working with a compassionate leader, as a reciprocity, employees have the obligation to be obedient to the leader. The co-existence of authoritarianism and compassion creates an inherent tension, with authoritarianism emphasising *control*, *order*, and *hierarchy*, whereas compassion focusing on *affection*, *care*, *support*, and *empathy*. This tension can be perfectly illustrated with the yin-yang philosophy. The dominance, control, structure, and assertiveness indicated in authoritarianism are aligned with yang, while the nurturing, adaptability, and softness are aligned with yin (Graham, 1986).

A balance between yin and yang is essential for ensuring harmony and stability for leadership and organisational management (Liu & An, 2021). Following the Confucian dialectics of yin and yang, a balance between compassion and authoritarianism is necessary for effective leadership because overly exaggeration of one of them may lead to management issues. For instance, excessive compassion may weaken the leader's authority in the hierarchical system, while too much authoritarianism could lead to tyranny and undermine employees' trust of the leader. Hence, the compassionate and authoritarian lens of leadership in Confucian cultures co-exist and complement each other in shaping leadership effectiveness and employee behaviours.

Despite the tension and mutual dependence between yin and yang, they are not static but dynamic and adaptive with the change of circumstances (Fang, 2012). Accordingly, authoritarianism and compassion continuously adapt to varying contexts and situations. In the Confucian cultural contexts where *li* (righteousness) and *ren* (compassion) are valued, leaders adapt between strict control and empathetic support according to situational needs (Zhang, 2002). For instance, in the face of organisational change and crisis, a leader is likely to increase yang; direction, structure, and guidance to ensure efficiency and discipline.

Yet, in times of stability and growth, a leader will shift to demonstrate more compassion, care, and support to foster trust, employee learning, and employee wellbeing. The dynamic approach to authoritarian and compassionate leadership allows leaders to adapt to situational changes to retain organisational harmony and sustainable development (Farh & Cheng, 2000).

> **ON YIN-YANG BALANCE**
> - When have you leaned too far into structure and control in your role? What was the impact?
> - Where might you need to introduce more compassionate flexibility in your interactions with staff or pupils?

Compassionate and Authoritarian Leadership and Employee Outcomes

The dialectical tensions between authoritarianism and compassion in Confucian cultures are reflected through their varying impacts on employee behaviours at work. Concerning the goal of managerial coaching, we will focus on employee outcomes variables relating to their task performance, extra-role performance behaviours, wellbeing, and career development.

Research suggests that authoritarian leadership is associated with negative impacts on employee wellbeing, such as increased stress (Zhang & Xie, 2017), enhanced emotional exhaustion and burnout (Harms et al., 2018), decreased job satisfaction (Schmid et al., 2019). Authoritarian leadership also suppresses extra-role behaviours such as OCB, helping behaviour, and voicing behaviour. Aryee et al. (2007) found that authoritarian leadership has a negative impact on employee OCB because employees feel little psychological safety or intrinsic motivation to exceed their role expectations. On the contrary, compassionate leadership is associated with positive effects on employee wellbeing, such as greater emotional resilience (Dutton et al., 2014), higher job satisfaction, and more positive affect (Lilius et al., 2011). This type of leadership behaviour is particular important in high-collectivist cultures where authority and control are valued because it fosters care and support for employee wellbeing (Farh et al., 2007).

Regarding the relationship between authoritarian leadership and task performance, there have been some interesting findings. Chen et al. (2014) suggests that authoritarian leadership leads with direction and controlling and thus reduces ambiguity and increases compliance, which increases employee task performance in the short-term. However, this type of behaviour may reduce employee task performance in the long run because it reduces intrinsic motivation. In addition, scholars argue that the impact of authoritarian leadership on employee outcomes may vary by industry. Authoritarian leadership can lead to high task performance for industries that require strict rule-following such as manufacturing and military (Wu et al., 2010). It also improves task performance during high-pressure situations such as meeting deadlines (Farh et al., 2006). Yet, in knowledge-intensive industries that require adaptability, authoritarian leadership is harmful (Huang et al., 2015). On the contrary, compassionate leadership has been found to facilitate task performance by increasing employee intrinsic motivation.

Authoritarian leadership also discourages employee learning and skill development because they focus on control, obedience, and discipline, which prevent employees from knowledge sharing and open dialogue (Chan, 2014), and independent decision-making (Kim & Beehr, 2021). On the contrary, compassionate leadership facilitates higher learning orientation (Hannah et al., 2011) and employee growth (Boyatzis et al., 2006).

Given the tensions between Confucian-based authoritarian and compassionate leadership and their complex impacts on employee outcomes, we argue that corresponding managerial coaching behaviours will be needed to counterbalance the negative impacts and facilitate the positive impacts on employee outcomes at work. In this next section, we will propose how the managerial coaching practices deriving from the Confucian cultural values facilitate positive impacts of authoritarianism and compassion on employee outcomes.

Confucian Leadership and Yin-Yang Structured Compassion Coaching

Based on above analyses of the tensions between compassionate and authoritarian leadership, we aim to develop a conceptual framework illustrating the managerial coaching practices aligned with the two types of leadership behaviours and address their tensions for better employee outcomes in this section. Given the dialectical, contradictory, complement, and dynamic nature of the tensions between compassionate and authoritarian leadership, we propose that managerial coaching practices based on the Confucian yin-yang philosophy will be essential and thorough. In alignment with the various tensions between these two types of Confucian leadership, we propose a yin-yang structured compassion coaching framework, including four types of managerial coaching practices, and will explain their behavioural indications and impacts on employee outcomes. Figure 1 presents our framework and key components.

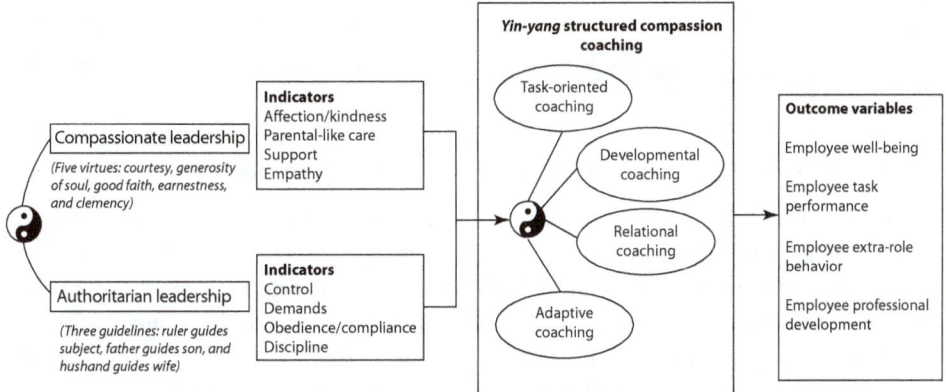

Figure 5.1 A framework of Confucian leadership and yin-yang structured compassion coaching.

> **ON COACHING STYLES**
> - Which coaching style, task-oriented, developmental, relational, or adaptive, feels most natural to you? Why?
> - Which coaching approach do you use least? What holds you back from using it more?

Task-Oriented Coaching Based on Authoritarianism and Yang

Task-oriented coaching focuses on task completion and improving work efficiency by providing clear directions, directive feedback, structured training, and measured performance standards. It is similar to directive coaching or guidance coaching (Hui et al., 2013). The leader provides specific directions, clear expectations, and closely monitors the progress and provides feedback. This style focuses on immediate performance improvement and efficiency. It is highly effective in the need for fast decision making and compliance, such as in the armed forces or emergency squads, in times of crisis management or organisational change. Task-oriented coaching indicates the essence of yang, structure, order, and compliance. This type of behaviour is aligned with authoritarian leadership that emphasises control, direction, and order in achieving work efficiency. However, it may suppress creativity and personal growth if overused (Pizzolitto et al., 2023); hence, it does not facilitate independent thinking or allows for autonomy in decision-making, and will not benefit employee career development or conduct of extra-role behaviours.

Developmental Coaching Based on Compassion and Yin

Developmental coaching focuses on employee learning, career development, and wellbeing. Leaders with development coaching empathises with their employees by learning about their needs, aspirations and challenges. They provide personalised support and care to support employees address problems and achieve career growth. Developmental coaching indicates the essence of *yin;* nurturing and care. Studies show that compassion and care foster positive coaching outcomes, such as increased job satisfaction and commitment. As such, this type of coaching behaviours is likely to enhance employee career development, wellbeing, and extra-role/in-role performance.

Relational Coaching Built on the Balance between Yin and Yang

Relational coaching highlights mutual respect and interdependence between the leader and the employee by establishing trust-based relationships (Critchley, 2010). Given the co-creation nature of this type of coaching, both the leader's expectations and the employee's needs are considered and openly communicated in this process. Relational coaching is aligned with a balanced view of yin-yang, that is, valuing both structures and compassionate support. This type of coaching behaviour is likely to benefit employee task performance and wellbeing.

Adaptive Coaching Built on the Dynamic Relationship between Yin and Yang

Adaptive coaching highlights how leaders adapt their coaching styles based on cultural expectations, organisational situations, and employees' needs (Bacon & Spear, 2003). Leaders with adaptive coaching may conduct a combination of different coaching behaviours such as directive, developmental, or facilitative behaviours, depending on the circumstances. This type of coaching caters to employees' needs and thus is likely to activate employees' extra-role behaviours and enhance their task performance.

> **REFLECTIVE ACTIVITY: BALANCING COMPASSION AND CONTROL IN LEADERSHIP**
>
> In this activity you will examine how cultural values, power dynamics, and relational coaching strategies presented in this chapter influence compassionate leadership in practice, using the flows and frames model of compassionate leadership presented in Chapter 1 (and in Figure 5.2).
>
>
>
> Figure 5.2 The flows and frames model of compassionate leadership.

Firstly, looking at the model, identify which flows of compassion are most challenged when balancing compassionate and authoritarian approaches. Why is this the case and where does the tension arise in your leadership practice?

Based on the ideas in this chapter that compassionate and authoritarian leadership is not as opposites, but as interdependent, each necessary at different moments, note a variety of strategies you could use to balance these in the flows you have identified.

Case Study: Compassionate and Authoritarian Leadership with Yin-Yang Structured Compassion Coaching

Mr Lee, a senior executive at a multinational manufacturing firm in Singapore, embodies a leadership style deeply influenced by Confucian cultural values. He sometimes adopts more authoritarian approach, enforcing discipline, efficiency, and high standards, ensuring that employees meet expectations. However, he also demonstrates compassionate leadership, mentoring, personal development, and employee care, which are essential for employees' long-term motivation and loyalty.

Mr Lee realises that these two types of leadership behaviours contradict each other, but both of them are important depending on the situation. He wants to implement managerial coaching to support his subordinates' career development and task completion. Yet, he is frustrated with what to do in his managerial coaching.

Given the tensions observed in his leadership, we propose that the yin-yang structured compassion coaching is likely to lead to positive outcomes. We will analyse how an integrated coaching model based on the four approaches in Figure 1 facilitates better employee outcomes.

First, following task-oriented coaching, Mr Lee should set clear and strict performance standards, provide directive feedback on employee errors and inefficiencies, provide structured training to enhance employee technical or soft skills, and monitor their performance with timely evaluations and goal alignment. With these coaching practices, employees are likely to experience improved task performance.

Second, following developmental coaching, Mr Lee should understand individual employee strengths and career aspirations, and offer personalised support for their skill and career growth. He should also encourage employees to solve problems and sharpen their skills. These developmental coaching practices are likely to facilitate employees' learning and motivation for career growth.

Third, following relational coaching, Mr Lee should work on relationship building with employees with mutual respect and trust. Mr Lee can still express strict expectations but do so with compassion and support. Mr Lee should recognise employees' achievements and efforts and reward them correspondingly. This is likely to increase employee commitment and extra-role citizenship behaviours at work.

Further, following adaptive coaching, Mr Lee should adjust his coaching style based on circumstances (e.g. employee competence, needs, and cultural expectations). Mr Lee may adopt a shift of various coaching styles such as directive, facilitate, or autonomous coaching. This is likely to help build employee confidence and support their career growth.

The above-mentioned coaching approach by Mr Lee exemplifies the yin-yang balance in Confucian leadership, where authoritarianism provides structure and compassion fosters engagement. By shifting between task-oriented, developmental, relational, and adaptive coaching, Mr Lee can successfully navigate the tensions between authoritarianism (yang) and compassion (yin). He can also ensure high employee task and extra-role performance while nurturing employees' wellbeing and career development.

Summary

This chapter has explored how Confucian culture-based compassionate and authoritarian leadership styles impact managerial coaching practice and employee outcomes in Southeast Asia. The yin-yang philosophical structure provides a framework for the interplay between compassion (yin) and authoritarianism (yang), supporting a harmonious and adaptable managerial coaching philosophy. The suggested yin-yang structured compassion coaching model integrates task-centred, developmental, relational, and adaptive forms of coaching techniques, enabling managers to meet diverse employee needs while addressing multifaceted cultural expectations.

Key recommendations for managers and leaders include developing self-awareness of their leadership styles, aligning coaching practices with both cultural values and individual employee needs, and dynamically adapting approaches based on specific situational conditions. By embracing the *yin-yang* philosophy, leaders can leverage the strengths of both empathetic and authoritarian styles. This enhances employee performance, wellbeing, and long-term development.

Note

1 Compassion and benevolence are used interchangeably in the context where Confucian value of ren is mentioned. We will use compassion consistently in this paper but it can mean both compassion and benevolence.

Further Reading

Fang, T. (2012). Yin yang: A new perspective on culture. *Management and Organization Review*, 8(1), 25-50.

This chapter offers an integrative approach to yin-yang as a cultural framework to interpret paradox and dualities in management. It is appropriate in viewing the theoretical foundation of the proposed coaching framework in this chapter.

Boyatzis, R. E., Smith, M. L., & Blaize, N. (2006). Developing sustainable leaders through coaching and compassion. *Academy of Management Learning & Education*, 5(1), 8-24.

This reading explores how compassionate leadership and coaching drive long-term organisational development. It provides substantive theoretical support for the benefits of developmental coaching.

Farh, J. L., & Cheng, B. S. (2000). A cultural analysis of paternalistic leadership in Chinese organizations. In Li, J. T., Tsui, A. S., & Weldon, E. *Management and organizations in the Chinese context* (pp. 84-127). London: Palgrave Macmillan UK.

This chapter defines paternalistic leadership and details how compassion and authoritarianism coexist in Confucian contexts, which is fundamental to understand the cultural background for the discussed leadership styles.

Critchley, B. (2010). Relational coaching: Taking the coaching high road. *Journal of Management Development*, 29(10), 851-863.

This article explains the importance of balancing relational dynamics in coaching, supporting a transformative, authentic approach to the coach-client relationship that is aligned with the yin-yang framework.

References

Aryee, S., Chen, Z. X., Sun, L. Y., & Debrah, Y. A. (2007). Antecedents and outcomes of abusive supervision: test of a trickle-down model. *Journal of Applied Psychology*, 92(1), 191-201.

Bacon, T. R., & Spear, K. I (2003). *Adaptive coaching: The art and practice of a client-centered approach to performance improvement*. Davies-Black Publishing.

Beattie, R. S. (2002). *Developmental managers: Line managers as facilitators of workplace learning in voluntary organisations*. University of Glasgow.

Beattie, R. S., Kim, S., Hagen, M. S., Egan, T. M., Ellinger, A. D., & Hamlin, R. G. (2014). Managerial coaching: A review of the empirical literature and development of a model to guide future practice. *Advances in Developing Human Resources*, 16(2), 184-201.

Boyatzis, R. E., Smith, M. L., & Blaize, N. (2006). Developing sustainable leaders through coaching and compassion. *Academy of Management Learning & Education*, 5(1), 8-24.

Bozer, G., & Delegach, M. (2019). Bringing context to workplace coaching: A theoretical framework based on uncertainty avoidance and regulatory focus. *Human Resource Development Review*, 18(3), 367-390.

Carvalho, C., Carvalho, F. K., & Carvalho, S. (2022). Managerial coaching: where are we now and where should we go in the future?. *Development and Learning in Organizations*, 36(1), 4-7.

Chan, S. C. (2014). Paternalistic leadership and employee voice: Does information sharing matter? *Human Relations*, 67(6), 667-693.

Chen, X. P., Eberly, M. B., Chiang, T. J., Farh, J. L., & Cheng, B. S. (2014). Affective trust in Chinese leaders: Linking paternalistic leadership to employee performance. *Journal of Management*, 40(3), 796-819.

Chmielecki, M., & Contreras-Loera, M. (2020). Leadership coaching across cultures. *Journal of Intercultural Management*, 12(1), 78-91.

Coimbra, J., & Proença, T. (2023). Managerial coaching and sales performance: the influence of salesforce approaches and organisational demands. *International Journal of Productivity and Performance Management*, 72(10), 3076-3094.

Corporate English Solutions. (2023). Why developing a coaching management style is essential for managers. https://corporate.britishcouncil.org/insights/why-developing-coaching-management-style-essential-managers

Critchley, B. (2010). Relational coaching: Taking the coaching high road. *Journal of Management Development*, 29(10), 851-863.

Dutton, J. E., Workman, K. M., & Hardin, A. E. (2014). Compassion at work. *Annu. Rev. Organ. Psychol. Organ. Behav.*, 1(1), 277-304.

Ellinger, A. D., & Bostrom, R. P. (1999). Managerial coaching behaviors in learning organizations. *Journal of Management Development*, 18(9), 752-771.

Ellinger, A. D., Ellinger, A. E., & Keller, S. B. (2003). Supervisory coaching behavior, employee satisfaction, and warehouse employee performance: A dyadic perspective in the distribution industry. *Human Resource Development Quarterly*, 14(4), 435-458.

Ellinger, A. D., Ellinger, A. E., Bachrach, D. G., Wang, Y. L., & Elmadağ Baş, A. B. (2011). Organizational investments in social capital, managerial coaching, and employee work-related performance. *Management Learning*, 42(1), 67-85.

Fang, T. (2012). Yin Yang: A new perspective on culture. *Management and Organization Review*, 8(1), 25-50.

Farh, J. L., & Cheng, B. S. (2000). A cultural analysis of paternalistic leadership in Chinese organizations. In J. T. Li, A. S. Tsui, & E. Weldon (Eds.), *Management and organizations in the Chinese context* (pp. 84-127). Palgrave Macmillan UK.

Farh, J. L., Cheng, B. S., Chou, L. F., & Chu, X. P. (2006). Authority and benevolence: Employees' responses to paternalistic leadership in China. In A. S. Tsui, Y. Bian, & L. Cheng (Eds.), *China's domestic private firms: Multidisciplinary perspectives on management and performance* (pp. 230-260). M. E. Sharpe.

Farh, J. L., Hackett, R. D., & Liang, J. (2007). Individual-level cultural values as moderators of perceived organizational support-employee outcome relationships in China: Comparing the effects of power distance and traditionality. *Academy of Management Journal*, 50(3), 715-729.

Graham, A. C. (1986). *Yin-yang and the nature of correlative thinking* (Vol. 6). Institute of East Asian Philosophies.

Hamlin, R. G., Ellinger, A. D., & Beattie, R. S. (2008). The emergent 'coaching industry': A wake-up call for HRD professionals. *Human Resource Development International*, 11(3), 287-305.

Hannah, S. T., Avolio, B. J., & Walumbwa, F. O. (2011). Relationships between authentic leadership, moral courage, and ethical and pro-social behaviors. *Business Ethics Quarterly*, 21(4), 555-578.

Harms, P. D., Wood, D., Landay, K., Lester, P. B., & Lester, G. V. (2018). Autocratic leaders and authoritarian followers revisited: A review and agenda for the future. *The Leadership Quarterly*, 29(1), 105-122.

Heslin, P. A., Vandewalle, D. O. N., & Latham, G. P. (2006). Keen to help? Managers' implicit person theories and their subsequent employee coaching. *Personnel Psychology*, 59(4), 871-902.

Hosseini, S. M., Rahimi, F., & Mousavi, S. A. (2023). Identifying the indicators of managerial coaching in service organizations. *Journal of Public Administration*, 15(2), 245-267.

Huang, X., Xu, E., Chiu, W., Lam, C., & Farh, J. L. (2015). When authoritarian leaders outperform transformational leaders: Firm performance in a harsh economic environment. *Academy of Management Discoveries*, 1(2), 180-200.

Hui, R. T. Y., Sue-Chan, C., & Wood, R. E. (2021). Performing versus adapting: how leader's coaching style matters in Hong Kong. *The International Journal of Human Resource Management*, 32(20), 4163-4189.

Hui, R. T. Y., Sue-Chan, C., & Wood, R. E. (2013). The contrasting effects of coaching style on task performance: The mediating roles of subjective task complexity and self-set goal. *Human Resource Development Quarterly*, 24(4), 429-458.

Hwang, K. K. (2000). Chinese relationalism: Theoretical construction and methodological considerations. *Journal for the Theory of Social Behaviour*, 30(2), 155-178.

Ip, P. K. (2009). Is Confucianism good for business ethics in China?. *Journal of Business Ethics*, 88, 463-476.

Kim, M., & Beehr, T. A. (2021). The power of empowering leadership: Allowing and encouraging followers to take charge of their own jobs. *The International Journal of Human Resource Management*, 32(9), 1865-1898.

Li, Q., She, Z., & Gu, J. (2022). Managerial coaching and employee knowledge sharing: A daily diary study. *Journal of Occupational and Organizational Psychology*, 95(4), 821-845.

Lilius, J. M., Worline, M. C., Dutton, J. E., Kanov, J. M., & Maitlis, S. (2011). Understanding compassion capability. *Human Relations*, 64(7), 873-899.

Liu, G., & An, R. (2021). Applying a yin-yang perspective to the theory of paradox: a review of Chinese management. *Psychology Research and Behavior Management*, 1591-1601.

Ma, L., & Tsui, A. S. (2015). Traditional Chinese philosophies and contemporary leadership. *The Leadership Quarterly*, 26(1), 13-24.

Nangalia, L., & Nangalia, A. (2010). The coach in Asian Society: Impact of social hierarchy on the coaching relationship. *International Journal of Evidence Based Coaching & Mentoring*, 8(1), 51.

Nyfoudi, M., Shipton, H., Theodorakopoulos, N., & Budhwar, P. (2023). Managerial coaching skill and team performance: how does the relationship work and under what conditions?. *Human Resource Management Journal*, 33(2), 328-345.

Pellegrini, E. K., & Scandura, T. A. (2008). Paternalistic leadership: A review and agenda for future research. *Journal of Management*, 34(3), 566-593.

Peng, C., Nelissen, R. M., & Zeelenberg, M. (2018). Reconsidering the roles of gratitude and indebtedness in social exchange. *Cognition and Emotion*, 32(4), 760-772.

Pizzolitto, E., Verna, I., & Venditti, M. (2023). Authoritarian leadership styles and performance: a systematic literature review and research agenda. *Management Review Quarterly*, 73(2), 841-871.

Ribeiro, N., Nguyen, T., Duarte, A. P., Torres de Oliveira, R., & Faustino, C. (2021). How managerial coaching promotes employees' affective commitment and individual performance. *International Journal of Productivity and Performance Management*, 70(8), 2163-2181.

Schmid, E. A., Pircher Verdorfer, A., & Peus, C. (2019). Shedding light on leaders' self-interest: Theory and measurement of exploitative leadership. *Journal of Management*, 45(4), 1401-1433.

Smith, J., Johnson, K., & Lee, M. (2021). Managerial coaching skills: Impact on personal learning and organizational commitment in a US tech firm. *Journal of Organizational Development*, 38(4), 123-140.

Tan, H. H., & Chee, D. (2005). Understanding interpersonal trust in a Confucian-influenced society: An exploratory study. *International Journal of Cross-Cultural Management, 5*(2), 197-212.

Wei, H., Zhu, Y., & Li, S. (2016). Top executive leaders' compassionate actions: An integrative framework of compassion incorporating a Confucian perspective. *Asia Pacific Journal of Management, 33*, 767-787.

Wu, J. B., Tsui, A. S., & Kinicki, A. J. (2010). Consequences of differentiated leadership in groups. *Academy of Management Journal, 53*(1), 90-106.

Ye, R., Wang, X. H., Wendt, J. H., Wu, J., & Euwema, M. C. (2016). Gender and managerial coaching across cultures: female managers are coaching more. *The International Journal of Human Resource Management, 27*(16), 1791-1812.

Yun, S., Faraj, S., & Sims Jr, H. P. (2005). Contingent leadership and effectiveness of trauma resuscitation teams. *Journal of Applied Psychology, 90*(6), 1288.

Zhao, H., & Liu, W. (2020). Managerial coaching and subordinates' workplace well-being: A moderated mediation study. *Human Resource Management Journal, 30*(2), 293-311.

Zhang, D. (2002). *Key concepts in Chinese philosophy*. Yale University Press.

Zhang, Y., & Xie, Y. H. (2017). Authoritarian leadership and extra-role behaviors: a role-perception perspective. *Management and Organization Review, 13*(1), 147-166.

6

Compassionate Leadership through Self-Cognition

Insights from Moral Education in Kazakhstan

Aigerim Mynbayeva, Anzhelika Karabutova, and Gainiya Tazhina

> **CHAPTER AIMS**
>
> By the end of this chapter, readers will be able to:
>
> - Understand the historical development and conceptual foundations of spiritual and moral education (SME) globally and within Kazakhstan, including the evolution of the subject of "self-cognition".
> - Analyse how the methods of the self-cognition subject, such as storytelling, reflection, positive mindset, and creative activities, can contribute to the development of compassionate leadership in school communities.
> - Evaluate teachers' perspectives on the relationship between spiritual and moral education and compassionate leadership, and consider practical strategies for applying these concepts in contemporary educational settings.

Introduction

The report *Looking Ahead Towards 2050* by the UNESCO International Commission on the Futures of Education proposes rethinking pedagogical approaches and developing a renewed pedagogy of cooperation and solidarity. This new definition of educational goals is associated with implementing a lifelong learning right, uniting people through "around collective endeavours and provide the knowledge, science, and innovation needed to shape sustainable futures for all anchored in social, economic, and environmental justice" (UNESCO, 2021, p. 12).

The report's key points include not only the development of cooperation and solidarity pedagogy but also emphasise curricula for ecological, intercultural, and interdisciplinary learning. These approaches expand students' access to knowledge and their ability to achieve by fostering critical thinking and practical application of knowledge. At the same time, teaching acts as a collective activity of teachers in knowledge production and social transformation. The role of schools as protected educational facilities supporting social integration, equality, and individual and collective wellbeing is strengthened. The result

DOI: 10.4324/9781003466031-8

of such approaches will lead to the expansion of educational opportunities across an individual's lifespan.

The "Pedagogy of Cooperation and Solidarity" (UNESCO, 2021), as we understand it, can draw on the experience of spiritual and moral education worldwide. This pedagogy appeals to values such as peace, cooperation, justice, non-violence, respect for individuals, other people and cultures, and love. These values are foundational for compassionate leadership in individuals and organisations.

> **THE "SELF-COGNITION" SUBJECT**
>
> *Self-cognition* is a school subject from Kazakhstan that helps children explore who they are and how they relate to others. Through storytelling, reflection, and creative activities, students learn key life values like truth, love, peace, right action, and non-violence. The goal is to nurture kind, thoughtful, and compassionate individuals who lead with empathy and care.
>
>
>
> *Figure 6.1* Values of the self-cognition subject curriculum.

In Kazakhstan, over 34 years of independence, there has been significant experience in implementing the self-cognition curriculum. The goal of this subject and curriculum is to unlock human potential and foster the harmonious development of physical, mental, spiritual, social, and creative capacities. The subject "self-cognition" was taught in Kazakhstan from 2010 to 2022, delivered once a week to students in grades 1 through 11. It was one of the foundational subjects for developing children's spiritual and moral qualities, aimed at instilling values such as truth, love, righteous behaviour (duty), inner peace (peace), and non-violence in students' behaviour (Mukazhanova & Omarova, 2013). According to the subject's curriculum, these values were interpreted as:

- **Truth:** is what remains unchanged, the fundamental principle of life: spirituality pervading all creation, the essence inherent in the entire universe. There is only one absolute Truth, which is the source of all others. When one finds it, their actions align with it. It is not subject to changes in time, past, present, or future.
- **Righteous behaviour:** is behaviour aligned with duty and obligations, where actions are guided by the inner voice of conscience.
- **Love:** whether pure, unselfish, or unconditional love, is the energy that creates and powers life. Love is understood as the positive energy of a human, which can be shared with others. For example, a parent embracing her child gives them the energy of love.
- **Inner peace:** is represented as perfect peace of mind, the underlying nature of a person.
- **Non-violence:** is seen as causing no harm to anyone, neither by thought, word, nor action (Programma duhovno-nravstvennogo obrazovaniya, 2018).

Since 2022, the curriculum has transitioned from being mandatory to elective. Today, progressive teaching methods are used in extracurricular activities with students, class hours (advisory period), and events. For example, they are applied in the anti-bullying Dos bolayik ("Let's Be Friends") programme (Programma profilaktiki, 2024).

The Self-Cognition Subject Project

This section explores our research into how Kazakhstan's self-cognition subject serves as a foundation for promoting compassionate leadership within schools. Through historical analysis and teacher perspectives, the research examined how spiritual and moral education can shape leadership practices rooted in empathy, reflection, and core human values.

Research Objectives

The central research objective for the project was to summarise the experience of spiritual and moral education by conceptualising the self-cognition subject for developing and implementing the concept of compassionate leadership in Kazakhstani schools.

Research Questions

1. What is the historical foundation of spiritual and moral education for developing and implementing the concept of compassionate leadership in the school education system?

2. Which methods of the self-cognition subject can be used, and how, to implement the concept of compensatory leadership in Kazakhstani schools?
3. What is teachers' assessment of the potential for spiritual and moral education and the ideas for compensatory leadership in Kazakhstan?

Research Design and Methods

In the theoretical part of the research, we will present the stages of spiritual and moral education development worldwide. We will demonstrate the potential of teaching the self-cognition subject in Kazakhstan for identifying elements of compassionate leadership implementation in schools. This will provide an overview, synthesising the history and current state of spiritual-moral education in Kazakhstan. Methods include analysis, historical-retrospective and historical-systemic approaches, and periodisation.

Spiritual and moral education can become an actual resource and foundation for implementing compassionate leadership concepts in school communities. The golden rule of morality; "Do (not) unto others as you would (not) have them do unto you", lays the groundwork for engaged behaviour toward others.

In the second part, we will present survey results on the continuity of spiritual and moral education values and compassionate leadership. We will analyse the possibilities of applying storytelling, positive mindset, reflection, and coaching methods to develop compassionate leadership in school practice.

These methods were applied in self-awareness studies. A questionnaire was developed, and an online survey was conducted among 34 teachers, primarily former self-cognition teachers. The questionnaire covered three blocks: Organisations applying compassionate leadership, target groups of leadership models, and the relationship between spiritual-moral education, self-cognition methodologies, and compassionate leadership. Analysis employed quantitative and qualitative methods.

WHAT IS PERIODISATION?

Periodisation is a way of breaking down history into meaningful chunks to help us understand how ideas or practices have changed over time.

According to Tumak (2016), this can be done in three levels:

- **Epoch:** the broadest time frame (like the Middle Ages or Modern Era).
- **Period:** a section within an epoch (such as the Renaissance within the Modern Era).
- **Stage:** specific phases or developments within a period.

This approach helps researchers map the evolution of spiritual and moral education across different historical contexts.

Compassionate Leadership Conceptualisation

As noted by Beiley and West (2022), compassionate leadership, as a personal quality and leadership style, is associated with building relationships through attentive listening, understanding, and empathy toward others. It involves supporting individuals, enabling those we interact with to feel safe, valued, and respected: "so they can unlock their potential and do their best work" (p. 1). Describing this leadership phenomenon, the authors propose the following behavioural models in a community: attending, understanding, empathising, and helping.

Compassionate leadership will help create a safe environment in the education system for children, as mandated by the *Pedagogy of Cooperation and Solidarity*. Such leadership will enable the implementation of humanistic psychology and pedagogy principles. Its behavioural models foster a favourable and comfortable psychological and social environment in schools, creating an engaged space for students and staff development. Therefore, implementing compassionate leadership strategies in school communities will contribute to spiritual and moral education, serving as a positive example for student upbringing. This is especially significant in the context of inclusive education implementing in schools and universities.

The Concept of "Spiritual and Moral Education" and Its Development Stages in Global Education and Kazakhstan

The concept of "spiritual and moral education" consists of three key words, spirituality, morality, and education. "Education" (in Russian: *obrazovanie*) originates from the word "image" (*'obraz'*). Thus, to understand the essence of "spiritual and moral education," we must examine how the image of spirituality and morality is formed in the learner's consciousness. For example, Amonashvili (2002) develops the idea of nurturing a student's inner potential, in which "the image of the Creator is embedded"(p.5). This emphasises the subjective nature of education. Amonashvili (2002) reveals the essence of education as unlocking the "Image of the Creator"; inner qualities, potential, and personality as part of a higher purpose.

According to Seitheshev (2008), the "image" in education is a holistic perception of spiritual and moral values, integrating cognitive, emotional, and spiritual-moral components. It helps to form a well-rounded personality, ensuring inner harmony and moral self-determination. The goal of education is to develop a harmonious whole personality capable for building a dignified life. Thus, for both Amonashvili (2002) and Seitheshev (2008), the "image" plays a key role in education. The image connects knowledge with personal experience and emotions, serving as a guide for moral behaviour applicable in life. Table 6.1 compares the concepts of "spirituality" and "morality" to highlight their synergistic effect in education.

According to Stepin (2006), the development of science, and the ways we understand knowledge, can be divided into four key stages: pre-classical, classical, non-classical, and post-non-classical. Each stage reflects a different worldview, from early religious and philosophical thinking, through scientific rationalism, to more modern approaches that

Table 6.1 Explanation of the concepts "spirituality" and "morality" and their synergy.

Criteria	Spirituality	Morality	Synergy of spirituality and morality as the basis for spiritual and moral education
Definition	"Spirituality" is an ontological given, characterising the human essence, their inner world and values, promoting self-improvement, spiritual-moral growth, and harmony with oneself and the world.	Morality is a special form of social consciousness and a type of social relations. It is a set of behavioural rules and norms toward others and society, based on unwavering adherence to universal, humanistic principles (Russian Language Dictionary, 1986)	The synergy of spirituality and morality represents their harmonious interaction, where spiritual principles and moral values mutually reinforce each other. This fosters personal development, societal progress, and human advancement. When these aspects interact, spirituality becomes the foundation for moral guidelines.
Core components	Universal human values, ideals, self-improvement striving for spiritual-moral growth, harmony with oneself and the world.	Rules and norms, adherence to inner principles, humanism.	The more universal human values are emphasised, the stronger the conviction in one's inner principles, humanism, and the correctness of actions.
Focus	The inner world of a person, their spiritual development.	Moral behaviour is aligned with ethical norms and societal standards.	Moral norms of behaviour, aligned with the inner world, enhance spiritual development.
Goal	To recognise the human essence, pursue self-improvement, spiritual-moral growth, and harmony with oneself and the world.	To follow rules and norms of behaviour toward others and society, adhering to universal humanistic principles.	Developing a harmonious personality with a holistic worldview, combining spiritual and moral guidelines.
Methods	Reflection, positive mindset, storytelling	Conviction, positive moral examples, societal laws, exercises, Socratic dialogue.	Educational and upbringing programmes, extracurricular activities aimed at developing spiritual and moral qualities.
Connection to society	Finding inner balance with oneself and others, serving society.	Regulating interpersonal relations and behaviour in a moral context.	Includes nurturing values that harmoniously connect spiritual development with moral norms.

recognise complexity, uncertainty, and the role of the individual in shaping knowledge. We can identify different historical periods in how spiritual and moral education (SME) has developed around the world. These periods reflect changing beliefs about human nature, learning, and the role of values in education across time.

1st Stage of SME Development: Pre-Classical Period

The first stage of SME is associated with the pre-classical period of science development. It is characterised by mythological and theological concepts (early antiquity, the Middle Ages, the search for absolute truth, observation and reflection, and the method of analogies). The core of spirituality is the Spirit represented in Christianity as the "Holy Spirit," in Buddhism as the "Supreme Mind," and in Islam as the "Essence of Divinity". Spirituality influences all aspects of human life including their views, behaviour, values, and worldview. At this stage, spirituality is presented as a state of the soul striving to unite with the Spirit, the Supreme Mind, or the Absolute, manifesting its divine essence, thus, its foundation is immaterial. The theological approach (methodology of theological cognition) is linked to the religious paradigm of explaining human spiritual nature, which is not accepted by atheistic or secular societies.

The central focus of spiritual and moral education (SME) is the development of the person as a conscious being, someone who recognises their spiritual origins and their connection to a higher principle, whether described as the Spirit, the Supreme Mind, or the Absolute. Across history, many influential thinkers have explored what this means for education.

For Socrates, spiritual and moral growth is nurtured through *dialogue,* a shared search for universal values like truth and justice. Plato builds on this by describing education as a means to achieve goodness, truth, justice, and harmony, framing these ideals within his concept of the *ideal state*. Aristotle adds to this tradition with his notion of *virtue ethics*, where education supports the development of both reason and character through practical action.

In the Islamic philosophical tradition, Abu Nasr al-Farabi views education as a path to personal perfection, emphasising the harmony between reason and spirituality in his vision of *The Virtuous City*. Similarly, Yusuf Balasaguni defines the purpose of education as the pursuit of happiness, articulated in his work *Kutadgu Bilig*.

Other thinkers also highlight the deep connection between education and moral development: Seneca emphasises the role of reason in achieving happiness through virtue; Augustine of Hippo sees education as a journey of inner transformation; and Thomas Aquinas frames the educational goal as attaining the highest good and social harmony.

Together, these perspectives reflect a shared understanding across cultures and eras that education is not only about knowledge but about nurturing the inner life of the learner, guiding them toward moral insight, self-awareness, and compassionate action.

> **KAZAKHSTAN'S SPIRITUAL HERITAGE**
>
> The spiritual and moral education traditions of Kazakhstan are deeply influenced by the works of local thinkers such as Abu Nasr Al-Farabi, Yusuf Balasaguni, M. Kh. Dulati, and others.
>
> Rooted in philosophy, Islamic philosophy and ethical teachings, their ideas focus on the harmony between soul and society, and the pursuit of a moral life through reason and spiritual practice.
>
> Kazakh thinkers-poets and storytellers (in Kazakh *Akyn*) contributing to this stage include:
>
> - Asan-Kaygy: human existence, harmony, and the pursuit of happiness.
> - Dospambet-zhirau: moral responsibility and the righteous path.
> - Shalkiiz-zhirau: spiritual purity and personal responsibility in child-rearing.
> - Shal-akin: truth, beauty, and justice as moral foundations.
> - Bukhar-zhirau: enlightenment, dignity, and respect for tradition.
>
> The legacy of these thinkers continues to shape educational values in Kazakhstan today, particularly through the emphasis on virtue, ethical living, and the search for higher truth.

In summary, the concept of spiritual and moral education within a theological context focuses on the assimilation of spiritual and moral values through religious teachings. Human nature was also regarded as a spiritual substance. The role of the individual was to develop the ability for exegesis, the interpretation of sacred texts. Within this theological approach, methods such as analogy and reflection, commonly used in antiquity and the Middle Ages, were employed to explore divine principles through symbols, metaphors, and comparisons drawn from various philosophical and religious traditions.

2nd Stage of SME Development: Classical Period

The second stage of spiritual and moral education (SME) is associated with the classical period of scientific rationality. The main methodological approaches during this stage were deterministic, mechanistic, empirical, and rationalistic. Philosophers, humanist educators, poets, and thinkers of this period advocated for humanistic education grounded in the study of classical literature, philosophy, rhetoric, and history. Spirituality was viewed through the lens of reason and scientific objectivity. In the context of this classical stage, spirituality was considered an epiphenomenon, a byproduct of reason, brain function, and the social environment. The scientific approach suggested that spirituality developed through the interaction of biological, psychological, and social factors. The focus of SME at this stage was the human being as a biosocial entity, regarded as lacking inherent spiritual potential. Knowledge about human beings and their spiritual lives was pursued through observation, experimentation, and scientific research.

KEY THINKERS OF THE CLASSICAL STAGE IN SPIRITUAL AND MORAL EDUCATION

During the classical period, approaches to spiritual and moral education were often shaped by philosophers, humanist educators, working in contrast to theological models. These thinkers emphasised reason, scientific inquiry, and human potential as central to moral development. Some philosophers and early scientists were public figures, and remained religious people, and were even religious figures.

Some of the influential voices from this period include:

- Erasmus of Rotterdam: virtues and moral improvement.
- Michel de Montaigne: critical thinking and self-reflection.
- Francis Bacon: empirical methods and experimentation.
- René Descartes: the role of reason and types of cognition (theoretical, empirical, intuitive).
- Thomas Hobbes: authoritarian style of education.
- Baruch Spinoza: humans as part of nature; activity as existence.
- John Locke: personal example, emotional regulation, and good habits.
- Gottfried Wilhelm Leibniz: logical thinking and harmony.
- Immanuel Kant: theory of ethics, categorical imperative, principles of moral behaviour.
- Johann Fichte: subjective idealism and the role of self-awareness.
- Jan Amos Comenius: cardinal values and didactic principles.
- Robert Boyle: scientific education and pedagogy.
- Feofan Prokopovich: moral values in education.
- Mikhail Lomonosov: development of character, consciousness, and moral values.
- Johann Heinrich Pestalozzi: education through hands-on learning and moral values.
- Johann Herbart: formation of a virtuous person, theory of ethics and aesthetics, moral education.

Other significant contributors to this stage include:

- Karl Marx: labour and social relations as key factors in human development.
- Friedrich Engels: collective education and moral progress as drivers of social justice.

Together, these thinkers highlight the classical period's emphasis on reason, ethics, and the shaping of character through education.

Kazakh thinkers-enlightener (first scientists):

- Ybyrai Altynsarin: education as the footing for societal development, systematic education, the formation of an open learning system.
- Abai Kunanbayev: spiritual development, the concept of "Tolyq Adam" [Complete Human], moral, ethical values and behaviour.

- Shokan Valikhanov: synthesis of Eastern and Western cultures, reflections on human nature, traditions, and cultural identity.
- Shakarim Kudaiberdiev: synthesis of philosophy, the idea of personal freedom, the search for truth.

Within Kazakhstan, influential thinkers such as Shokan Valikhanov, Ybyrai Altynsarin, Abai Kunanbayev, and Shakarim Kudaiberdiev became representatives of the classical stage. Their work explored the blending of Eastern and Western cultural traditions, the pursuit of truth, and the spiritual development of the individual, shaping new approaches to education that emphasise self-awareness and cultural identity.

In summary, the image of SME was presented as the development of individual reason, self-awareness, and building the ability to adhere to moral laws and ethical principles based on human experience. The methods of SME included empirical methods accessible to sensory perception, objective research methods, analysis of cause-and-effect relationships, experimentation, and the object's mathematical modeling.

3rd Stage of SME Development: Non-Classical Period

The third stage in the development of spiritual and moral education (SME) aligns with what is known as the non-classical period of scientific rationality. This stage is characterised by a move away from fixed, linear models of knowledge toward an understanding of complexity, relativism, and the interconnectedness of systems. It acknowledges uncertainty, structural diversity, and the evolving nature of human experience.

In this period, education is seen not simply as the transfer of knowledge, but as a process that recognises the multifaceted nature of the individual, encompassing biological, psychological, social, and cultural dimensions. The focus shifts toward the development of the *whole person*, integrating emotional, intellectual, and moral growth.

KEY THINKERS AND IDEAS

A wide range of philosophers, psychologists and educators contributed to this stage, emphasising practical learning, moral development, and the importance of personal experience. Notable contributors include:

- Carl Jung: the importance of integrating contradictions in consciousness for personal growth, revealing the integrity of one's being, archetypes.
- Rudolf Steiner: anthroposophy and the Waldorf educational approach.
- Leo Tolstoy: the power of personal example and inner freedom in education.
- P.F. Kapterev: personal growth and self-development as educational aims.
- Antoine de Saint-Exupéry: the search for meaning, inner harmony, and value in life.

- Hermann Nichtenberg: integration of science, art, and philosophy; moral freedom and spiritual engagement.
- Konstantin Ushinsky: free education, the role of the family, and personalised approaches to moral learning.
- Anton Makarenko: stages of collective development and the formative role of labour in education.
- Maria Montessori: educational anthropology, sensitive education, free education, space theory.

Kazakh enlighteners:

- Zhussupbek Aimautov: human development through subjective experience.
- Magzhan Zhumabayev: personal freedom and dreams for the nation's future.
- Sultan-Makhmut Toraygyrov: higher love, unity of faiths, and social justice.
- Mirjaqyp Dulatov: progress and reflections on the future, and other.

At the heart of this stage is the sociocentric view of human development – the belief that individuals are shaped by their social environment, including class, culture, and economic structures. This view emphasises the collective over the individual, often subordinating personal spiritual aspirations to broader societal interests. Cognition and learning within this framework are seen as both empirical and theoretically grounded, drawing on historical-cultural and dialectical methods to understand how education can nurture moral and social consciousness.

The image of the learner in this stage is that of a bio-psycho-socio-cultural being, a holistic individual whose development is guided not by spiritual essence alone, but by the interplay of moral principles and social context. The aim of spiritual and moral education in the non-classical period is therefore to foster the integration of all aspects of the self, supporting the growth of individuals as engaged, ethical participants within their communities.

4th Stage of SME Development: Post-Non-Classical Period

The fourth stage in the development of spiritual and moral education (SME) reflects the rise of humanistic psychology and the growing recognition of the unique, complex nature of each individual. Moving beyond earlier tensions between spiritual and material worldviews, this stage embraces an integrative approach – one that sees the person as a whole being, combining physical, emotional, mental, and spiritual dimensions.

Thinkers at this stage emphasise personal growth, self-awareness, and the nurturing of human potential. This stage also sees the influence of transpersonal psychology, which explores higher levels of consciousness and spiritual experience, deepening our understanding of the spiritual dimensions of human development.

> **KEY THINKERS AND APPROACHES ACROSS CONTEXTS**
>
> A wide network of philosophers, educators, and psychologists have contributed to shaping the post-non-classical understanding of SME, including:
>
> Western Scholars:
>
> - Martin Heidegger: being-in-the-world, existential freedom, authenticity.
> - Edgar Morin: complexity, integration, and transdisciplinarity.
> - Paulo Freire: critical pedagogy, self-knowledge, and reflection.
> - Jean-François Lyotard: postmodernism and the questioning of universal truths.
> - Abraham Maslow: personality theory should include the potential for growth, theory of motivation and self-actualisation of personality.
> - Carl Rogers: Self-actualising tendency, client-centred approach, mental health.
> - Viktor Frankl: meaning of life as the central motivational force of a person, logotherapy.
> - Lawrence Kohlberg: stages of moral development, Hans's dilemmas, moral education.
>
> Kazakh researchers and educators:
>
> - Tolegen Tazhibayev: anthropocentrism and humanism.
> - Kubigul Zharykbayev: synthesis of traditional and modern approaches to education, ethnopedagogical ideas of personality education.
> - Aida Beisenbayeva: humanistic approach to teaching and upbringing.
> - Makpal Dzhandrina: psychological and pedagogical assistance in personality development in the context of SME.

At the heart of SME during this period is the focus on personal growth, grounded in the principles of humanistic education. The approach emphasises emotional engagement, the development of self-awareness, moral reflection, and ethical action, all supported by experiential learning. Educational methods encourage learners to engage actively with their own development through approaches such as moral role-modelling, learning through activity and participation, and emotional engagement with feelings and experiences. Reflection on moral and ethical dilemmas is a central part of this process, alongside cooperative learning through shared projects and meaningful work, promoting responsibility, empathy, and self-knowledge.

One of the key features of the post-non-classical approach is the move toward integrating the spiritual and material dimensions of life, rather than viewing them as opposing forces. Scholars like Merab Mamardashvili, A. Nysanbayev, G. Solovyov, and A. Radugin emphasise that true human development involves a synthesis of these elements, achieving freedom, responsibility, and moral consciousness through their union. As Mamardashvili argued, personal freedom and responsibility are impossible without integrating both spiritual and material experiences. This vision calls for a balance between ethical reflection, spiritual awareness, intellectual development, and social engagement.

The Experience of the "Self-Cognition" Subject for Spiritual and Moral Education and Extracurricular Development

In Kazakhstan, spiritual and moral education holds an important place. Since 2010, it has been implemented within the framework of the National Program "Self-Cognition", focusing on personality development through the awareness of moral and spiritual guidelines. To understand self-cognition within SME, it is essential to consider the subject as a secular teaching based on universal and national values within a cultural-historical approach emphasising not religious dogmas but the search for the Self through philosophical, ethical, and existential teachings (Mukazhanova & Omarova, 2013; Arinova, 2016; Arinova, Moldassan, & Arinova, 2020). The highest expression of both morality and spirituality is the aspiration toward the "Spiritual Self," an ideal that inspires individuals to live accordingly to the highest spiritual and moral values.

"Self-cognition" as a subject is interdisciplinary, integral, and synergetic. The didactic foundations regulating the content selection of the self-cognition subject are as follows:

- The goal of SME, aimed at unlocking human potential and the harmonious development of their physical, mental, spiritual, social, and creative capacities.
- The goal of the self-cognition subject, focused on fostering intellectual, communicative, reflective, and spiritual cultures in schoolchildren (Mukazhanova & Omarova, 2013).

The curriculum synthesises directions of both spiritual-moral development and personal self-development of the child. Self-cognition in the context of SME is interpreted as an integral part of raising a harmonious personality. Through self-knowledge, individuals become aware of their values, moral guidelines, and spiritual nature. Different approaches

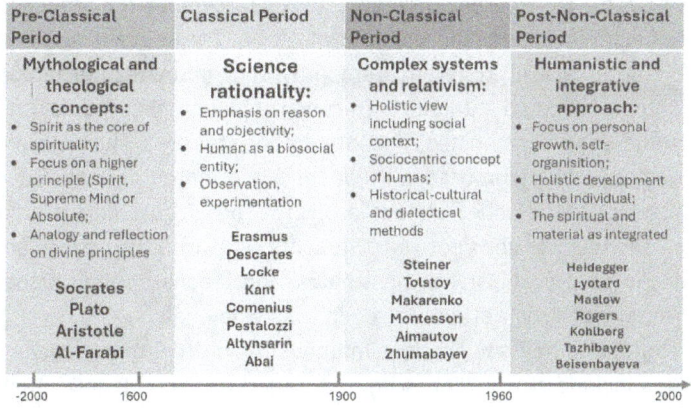

Figure 6.2 Historical timeline.

emphasise various aspects of self-cognition starting from moral maturity and personal responsibility towards spiritual maturity and understanding one's role in society.

The lesson structure is innovative, featuring the following elements:

- Positive attitude: the lesson's quote, which is a positive statement with accompanying discussion.
- Storytelling.
- Group work.
- Creative tasks.
- Group singing.
- A minute of silence to conclude.

Methodologically, when telling stories, students try to identify values such as truth, love, righteous behaviour (duty), inner peace (peace), and non-violence in the actions of the main characters, the benefits of activities, actions, and behaviour for others which can later be projected onto their own actions. Table 6.2 compares the structure of a traditional combined lesson (commonly used in our schools and post-Soviet states) and a self-cognition lesson.

Analysis of the self-cognition teaching experience indicates the priority of value-semantic content in education focusing on modern pedagogical and psychological theories and technologies. In this case, it is important to have faith in humanity, in its humanistic potential and positive essence.

Kazakstan's modern digital society is often referred to as a "knowledge society". This era is marked by "knowledge spillover" and "knowledge diffusion" (Spankulova, 2020), where teaching methods and ideas can be adapted to new fields of activity and contexts.

Teaching methodologies for self-cognition are used by teachers in implementing the Dos bolayik programme. These methods include storytelling, identifying values in children's actions, positive attitude, and group singing. The programme teaches students moral values for cooperation and kindness while also serving as an anti-bullying programme for Kazakh schools. The Dos bolayik programme, developed by the National Scientific and Practical Institute for Child Well-being "Orken," was approved by the order of the Republic of Kazakhstan Ministry of Education on March 1, 2024. The programme aims to develop students' socio-emotional skills (tolerance, empathy, etc.), improve interpersonal and intergroup relationships, and equip students with constructive conflict resolution skills. It also seeks to reduce aggressive and hostile reactions among students. The programme is implemented by engaging students in grades 1-11 in socially oriented project activities through class hours and practical activities at each project stage (Programma profilaktiki, 2024). Each grade includes four sessions per year. Students reflect on their experiences, observe positive changes in relationships with classmates, and teachers monitor the progress of social projects in terms of their effectiveness in achieving goals.

Thus, the programme actively employs methods of spiritual-moral education and self-awareness. These include storytelling, with discussions and the identification of universal human values in the actions and stories of characters, deeds for the good of others, and

Table 6.2 Comparison of combined lesson and self-cognition lesson structures.

Comparison criteria	Combined lesson	Lesson on "self-cognition"
Lesson structure	Greeting Introduction Home assignment review Questions handling Delivery of new material Consolidation of knowledge, skills and competencies Hand out homework assignments and conclusion	Greeting Positive thinking Home assignment review Quote of the lesson Conversation, storytelling Creative teamwork Singing together Giving home assignment and conclusion Final element of the lesson – a moment for peacefulness
Lesson objective	Has the following lesson objectives: communicating new knowledge; consolidation; applying knowledge and skills; generalising and systemising knowledge; checking and correcting knowledge and skills.	Has the only lesson objective – identifying universal human values in learners
Analysis	Analysis: • focus on didactic task. • focus on knowledge; more frequent reproductive student activity; etc.	Analysis: • identifying universal values and storyline, i.e. focus on personality development. • focus on value-sematic development of each student. • outcomes – spiritual and moral education, unity of thoughts, words and actions, value-based approach to the world.
Advantages	Advantages: • Structured knowledge, skills and competencies, system of knowledge; • logical design of knowledge; • discipline; teacher- and learning-oriented education; • focus on cognitive abilities.	Advantages: • Faith in humanistic principles; realisation of social constructivism, pedagogy of existentialism, environmental pedagogy, "living the moment"; • storytelling strategy (parables), showing videos; • practising relaxing techniques, • purification of mind, development of intuitive reasoning; • possibility to employ coaching practices, strong open questions, the Wizard's, the Wise Elder's, the Friend's coaching tones; outcome frames, etc.

(Continued)

Table 6.2 (Continued)

Comparison criteria	Combined lesson	Lesson on "self-cognition"
Risks	• consolidation of thinking reproductive way; • passive attitude of some students	• depends on teacher's personality – his/her spiritual culture, pedagogical and psychological background, knowledge and competencies, pedagogical creativeness; • technical classroom equipment; • artificially favourable school environment may decrease students' adaptability to outside the school real-life competitive community.

Source: Mynbayeva, et al. (2016)

moral examples. Methods of positive mindset, coaching techniques, creative group and individual activities, art-based methods, collaborative singing, and project-based methods are also used. These methods help create a favourable classroom atmosphere and extend it to the broader school community.

Results of Kazakhstani Teachers' Survey

The practical part of the study involved 34 teachers. They answered a questionnaire on compassionate leadership in relation to spiritual-moral education. All participants consented to take part in the study. 97.1% of respondents had previously taught self-cognition courses.

The questionnaire comprised 12 questions divided into three sections. The first block focused on understanding the target audience of compassionate leadership and the organisations applying its concepts and strategies. The second block examined how and which models of compassionate leadership are implemented in Kazakhstani schools. The third block explored the continuity between spiritual-moral education, self-cognition methodologies, and the development of compassionate leadership in children. The study identified the ideas and methods through which compassionate leadership can be transmitted to the school community, according to teachers. Participants could select multiple answers.

First Block

Most teachers, 88.2% (30 out of 34), believe that the concept of compassionate leadership is applied in educational institutions; 76.5% (26), in family and domestic relationships; and 29.4% (10), in healthcare settings. This suggests teachers find compassionate leadership principles to be closely aligned with their work. This can be explained by teachers' constant care for children as part of their developmental role.

Teachers believe compassionate leadership primarily targets students and children with special educational needs. It is then addressed to parents and educators. 85.3% of respondents (29 teachers) stated that strategies for such leadership are implemented by

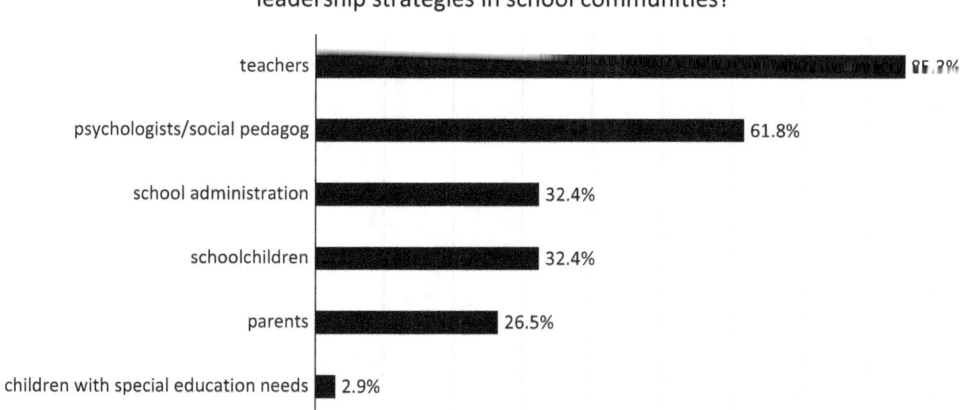

Figure 6.3 Teachers' assessment of who employs compassionate leadership strategies in school communities (%).

teachers, while 61.8% (21) attributed this role to psychologists and social educators. Only 32.4% believed that school administration and students also use these strategies, and 26.5% mentioned parents.

The findings suggest that teachers view compassionate leadership as closely aligned with their role, particularly in supporting students and children with special educational needs. Compassionate leadership is seen as primarily teacher-led, with less involvement from administrators, parents, or students. This highlights both the centrality of care in teaching and a potential gap in shared leadership across the wider school community.

Second Block

67.6% of teachers believe that compassionate leadership models are fully implemented in Kazakhstani schools, while 23.5% consider they are partially applied. The most used models by teachers are attention and assistance (70.6%; 24 respondents), followed by empathy (52.9%; 18 respondents) and understanding (50%; 17 respondents). Teachers also suggested additional compassionate behaviour models: empathy, "cultivating universal values as a need to help others," "mutual respect," "building a culture of kindness in teams and classrooms," "not only being a compassionate leader but inspiring others, teachers, parents, students, to participate, support, and care for one another," "mercy," "kindness toward others," "safe environments free of fear and judgment," "acceptance of differences," "honesty and humanity, leaders can also be vulnerable".

Third Block

94.1% of respondents believe spiritual-moral education and compassionate leadership are closely interconnected. Teachers stated that "both share a common foundation," "aim to

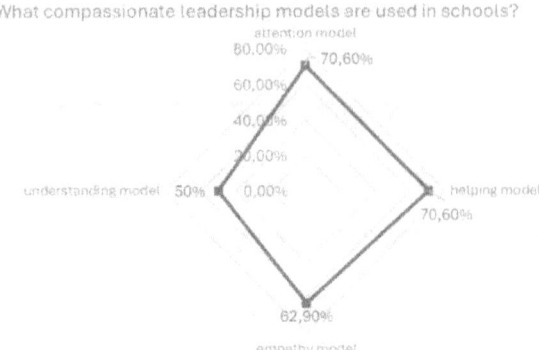

Figure 6.4 Teachers' assessment of which compassionate leadership models are used in schools.

shape deeply conscious, responsible, and internally stable individuals oriented toward goodness, service, and respect for others," and "focus on qualities like compassion, empathy, responsibility, and ecological spirituality". One teacher (R16) provided a detailed response:

Spiritual-moral education and compassionate leadership are connected through:

1. Empathy and compassion: understanding and supporting others.
2. Honesty and sincerity: he importance of trust and openness.
3. Respect: recognising every person's worth.
4. Responsibility for others: caring for community well-being.
5. Peacemaking: resolving conflicts peacefully.
6. Inner harmony: developing personal balance and mutual understanding.

These responses align with the six qualities of compassionate leadership outlined by Ramachandran et al. (2024): Empathy; openness and communication; physical, mental health, and wellbeing; inclusiveness; integrity; respect and dignity.

To foster compassionate leadership in students, teachers recommend methods of self-cognition such as positive mindset and reflection (76.5%; 26 respondents), storytelling (52.9%; 17 respondents), and creative activities. They also propose volunteer projects, coaching methods, charity initiatives in upper grades, and leading by example.

REFLECTIVE ACTIVITY: MAPPING COMPASSIONATE LEADERSHIP IN YOUR SCHOOL COMMUNITY

Purpose

This activity invites readers to reflect on how compassionate leadership is currently practiced in their own educational context and consider ways to expand its reach across the whole school community (Sewell, 2022).

Instructions

1. Think about your school or educational setting.
    a. Who do you believe demonstrates compassionate leadership?
    b. Who are the main recipients of this leadership (e.g. students with SEND, parents, colleagues)?
2. Draw a simple map or diagram of your school community. Include groups such as:
    a. Teachers
    b. School leadership/administration
    c. Students
    d. Parents and families
    e. Psychologists/social educators
    f. Other key stakeholders
3. On your map, indicate:
    a. Where compassionate leadership is most visible.
    b. Where it might be less present or absent.
4. Reflect and write:
    a. What strategies from the self-cognition approach (e.g. storytelling, reflection, positive mindset, creative activities, leading by example) could help strengthen compassionate leadership where it is currently lacking?
    b. What small action could you take to foster a more compassionate culture within one of these groups?

Conclusion

This chapter synthesises the experience of spiritual-moral education through the lens of self-cognition courses to identify pathways for implementing compassionate leadership in Kazakhstani schools. It highlights the potential of spiritual-moral education and its methods to cultivate values aligned with compassionate leadership. Teachers advocate storytelling, reflection, creative activities, art-based methods, and personal example as key strategies. Indeed, spiritual-moral education and compassionate leadership share roots in universal values; goodness, justice, empathy, communication, responsibility, humanity, and mercy. Compassionate leadership aligns with the essence of spirituality and morality.

By reviewing the history of spiritual-moral education and analysing the implementation of self-cognition courses in Kazakhstan, we have indicated the sustained ideas and methods for nurturing compassionate leadership in school communities. Further research could explore compassionate pedagogy to preserve physical and mental health, improve school climate (Killingback et al., 2025), and validate the Compassionate Leadership Behavior Index (Folger, 2025) among Kazakhstani teachers in Kazakh and Russian.

References

Amonashvili, Sh. (2002). Shkola zhizni [School of life]. *Raritet*, 80. [In Russian]

Arinova, B. A. (2016). Рухани-адамгершілік білім беру бағдарламасының ҚР жалпы білім беру жүйесіне ендірілуін құрылымдық– функционалды талдау [Structural and functional analysis of the implementation of the spiritual and moral education program in the general education system of the Republic of Kazakhstan]. *Journal of Educational Sciences, 42*(2). извлечено от https://bulletin-pedagogic-sc.kaznu.kz/index.php/1-ped/article/view/59. [In Kazakh]

Arinova, B., Moldassan, K., & Arinova, N. (2020). Soderzhatel'naya struktura predmeta "Samopoznaniye" v usloviyakh obnovlennogo soderzhaniya obrazovaniy [The substantive structure of the subject "self-cognition" in the context of the updated content of education]. *Journal of Educational Sciences, 65*(4), 4-11. https://doi.org/10.26577/JES.2020.v65.i4.01

Beiley, S., & West, M. A. (2022). What is compassionate leadership? www.kingsfund.org.uk/insight-and-analysis/long-reads/what-is-compassionate-leadership#introduction

Folger, T. D. (2025). Measuring compassionate leadership in education: a validation study. *International Journal of Leadership in Education*, online ahead of print.

Killingback, C., Tomlinson, A., & Stern, J. (2025). Compassionate pedagogy in higher education: A scoping review. *Journal of University Teaching and Learning Practice, 22*(1), 1-32.

Mukazhanova, R. A., & Omarova, G. A. (2013). *Metodika prepodavaniya samopoznaniya v shkole* [Self-cognition teaching methods for schools: Teacher's guide]. Bobek NSPWC.

Mynbayeva, A., Anarbek, N., & Yeseeva, M. (2016). Education and spirituality in Kazakhstan: "Self-cognition" metadiscipline features and methods of teaching. *The European Proceedings of Social & Behavioural Sciences, 8*, 154-161.

Programma duhovno-nravstvennogo obrazovaniya "Samopoznanie" [Program of moral and spiritual education "Self-Cognition"]. (2018). Ministry of Education and Science of the Republic of Kazakhstan. September 29, 2018. Astana. [In Russian]

Programma profilaktiki travli (bullinga) obuchayushchikhsya v organizatsiyakh obrazovaniya "DosbolLIKE". [Program for the prevention of bullying of students in educational organizations "DosbolLIKE"]. (2024). НАО ННПИБД "Өркен. https://orken-instituty.kz/ru/akciya-dosbollajk. [In Russian]

Ramachandran, S., Balasubramanian, S., James, W. F., & Al Masaeid, T. (2024). Whither compassionate leadership? A systematic review. *Management Review Quarterly, 74*(3), 1473-1557.

Russian Language Dictionary. (1986). *Russian language dictionary*, vol. II. Institute of Russian Language, USSR Academy of Sciences.

Seitheshev, A. (2008). Sovremennye problemy vospitaniya i puti ih resheniya [Modern problems of education and ways of their solution]. *Mysl, 1*, 26-33. [In Russian]

Sewell, A. (2022). *Diverse voices in educational practice: A workbook for promoting pupil, parent and professional voice.* Routledge.

Spankulova, L. S. (2020). *Diffuziya innovatsiy i peretoki znaniy v regionakh Kazakhstana* [Diffusion of innovations and knowledge flows in the regions of Kazakhstan]. Almaty.

Stepin, V. S. (2006). *Filosofiya nauki: Obshie problemy* [Philosophy of science: General problems]. Gardariki.

Tumak, O. (2016). Критерії визначення етапів розвитку методики навчання англійської мови в закладах освіти Буковини (кінець XIX–початок XX століть). Наукові записки Тернопільського національного педагогічного університету імені Володимира Гнатюка. Серія: педагогіка, (4), 233-239. (In Ukrainian) [Tumak, O. (2016). Criteria for determining the stages of development of English language teaching methods in educational institutions of Bukovyna (late 19th-early 20th centuries). *Scientific notes of Ternopil National Pedagogical University named after Volodymyr Hnatyuk. Series: Pedagogy*, (4), 233-239. [In Ukrainian]

UNESCO. (2021). *Reimagining our futures together: a new social contract for education; executive summary.* https://unesdoc.unesco.org/ark:/48223/pf0000379707.locale=en.

PART III
Contextualising Compassionate Leadership in Practice

7

Nurturing Compassion in the Early Years

Foundations for Professional Practice

Angela Hodgkins

> **CHAPTER AIMS**
>
> By the end of the chapter, readers will be able to:
>
> - Define and explore compassion and associated terms within an early years context.
> - Debate ideas about professional love.
> - Evaluate the need for compassion with young children, families, colleagues, and self in an early years context.

Introduction

In this chapter, compassion within the context of early years education and care (ECEC) will be explored. The overriding view of this chapter is that compassion is the most important quality for early years practitioners. In research with nursery workers, care/compassion was the top response to the question "What constitutes professionalism in early years education and care?" coming before 20 other traits, including expertise, knowledge, organisation, and commitment (Osgood, 2010). Compassion in early years settings is crucial, not just in relationships with young children, but with parents/ carers and work colleagues too. It is a caring professional's "active desire to alleviate the suffering of others" (Kleineidam & Fischbach, 2023, p. 4). Although compassion and empathy are different concepts, they are closely related, so empathy, and other associated concepts (for example heartful practice and professional love) are also discussed in this chapter. The chapter draws upon examples of compassionate practice by early years practitioners, taken from a substantive research investigation focussing on empathy within their practice (Hodgkins, 2024).

Compassion

The *Oxford English Dictionary* defines compassion as "sympathetic pity and concern for the sufferings or misfortunes of others". In a seminal text on human emotion, Lazarus (1991) adds to this, defining it as "being moved by another's suffering and wanting to help" (p. 289). This is a more helpful definition for the context of the early years, as practitioners are in a position to help, to take action and to alleviate suffering. Compassion underpins the building of social relationships, so is essential when building relationships with young children and for teaching children to demonstrate compassion for others. We rarely remember the exact words that people say to us at times of need, but we do remember how we were treated and how we were made to feel. In Buddhism, the Buddha taught people that showing compassion to others is something everyone can do, even if they find other parts of his teaching difficult to follow. The 14th Dalai Lama said, "I believe that at every level of society, the key to a happier world is the growth of compassion" (India Today, 2021).

Compassion is necessary because suffering is part of the human condition; no one goes through life without experiencing it. It is not always possible to avoid these experiences, so reacting with a "culture of compassion" (Lipponen, Rajala, & Hilppö, 2018) is essential. Even for babies and young children, there is unavoidable hurt and pain. The youngest babies will signal feeling uncomfortable when wet or sore and needing a nappy change, for example. All children are hurt physically at some point, by falling while mastering learning to walk and run, or from minor accidents while playing. Skinned knees and bumped heads are all normal aspects of childhood. But pain and hurt can be emotional too; babies become emotionally distressed when separated from their main caregiver. There is even some research suggesting that newborn babies can experience emotional trauma following a difficult birth (Becker, 2016). As children get older, they may be hurt through being excluded by other children. Table 7.1 identifies some of the social and emotional stages of development and associated potential origins of hurt and pain in babies and young children.

Of course, the amount of hurt or pain that children experience is variable, and we are all too aware of the suffering of children who are unreasonably chastised or abused. As early years practitioners and teachers, we are in a position to identify such hurt and to take action to make a difference to the child. Working compassionately with children in a child protection context is explored later in this chapter. Vuorinen, Pessi, and Uusitalo (2021), writing about compassion in kindergarten in Finland, refer to compassion as "noticing, feeling and acting to alleviate suffering in others". This is important in determining the stages of compassion. To be compassionate, we first have to notice that someone is suffering, and then we need to be able to feel the emotion ourselves, in order to want to help. Feeling the emotion of others is a feature of empathy.

Empathy

The words empathy and compassion are often used as synonyms of each other, yet they are different. Empathy is notoriously difficult to define, as it is understood in various ways in different disciplines, for example, in developmental psychology, neuroscience, and social psychology. A leading writer on empathy, Hoffman (2000, p. 30), affirms, "the more I study empathy, the more complex it becomes". However, most people would identify it as the ability to understand something from someone else's point of view; to *walk in their shoes* or *see the world through their eyes*. Empathy, therefore, is a precursor to compassion; we must understand suffering from someone else's point of view to be motivated to take action and help. Morgan (2017) suggests that "compassion should be thought of as a component of this larger concept of empathy" (p. 1). For example, suppose a new baby comes into your

Table 7.1 Potential causes of hurt in the early years.

Age	Potential causes of hurt
From birth to 2 months	Reacts to discomfort and pain with cries
From 6 months	Becomes upset when separated from their main caregiver
9 months	Develops a fear of strangers
9 months	May cry when their caregiver leaves the room
From 1 year	May develop new fears and phobias, may be fearful of new situations
1 year–18 months	Can become upset when demands are not met, or when adults give limitations
From 18 months	Can become upset if they are not the centre of attention, frustrated when they are not able to communicate (often referred to as temper tantrums)
18 months–3 years	Difficulties in learning to share and take turns with others
2–3 years	Feels hurt when told off or disciplined
2–3 years	May need a security object and become very upset when it is not with them
From 3 years	May become upset about major changes in their routine
3–4 years	Confuses reality and make-believe, so may become afraid and begin to have nightmares

nursery and is crying for their parent. In that case, it is by trying to put yourself in the baby's position and understanding how upset they must be at seeing their parent leave that makes us want to help the baby. If we were unable to understand why they are upset, if we did not feel empathy, we would be less likely to want to show compassion by stepping in to help. Therefore, compassion is not the same as empathy, it is a *result* of empathy.

Singer and Klimecki (2014) wrote about empathy and compassion and identified two possible reactions to another person's suffering. Figure 7.1 gives an example of this from an early years perspective.

As Figure 7.1 shows, empathy can lead to compassion or empathic distress, depending on whether the empathiser is able to take compassionate action. There is evidence that acting to relieve hurt in others and taking compassionate action also affects our own mood; we feel better when we can help others (Hoffman, 2000). This is why we feel slightly better about suffering when giving charity money. But there may be times, in early years practice, when it is not possible to take compassionate action due to barriers such as setting policies and procedures. For example, you may know that a child wants to be held and carried but work in a setting that discourages this. Feeling empathy for the child and inability to take action can lead to the empathic distress described in Figure 7.1. In empathic distress, the emotion is internalised.

Scenario: You are working in a nursery class at a Primary School. It is the first few weeks of the new school year, and you have several new children starting school. One child is struggling with separation from her mother and is crying incessantly when left in your class in the mornings.	
Empathy	
You feel empathy for the child, who has not attended any sort of pre-school setting before. You can understand how scary it must be for the child to be separated from her mother for the first time. There are two possible ways of reacting to the situation:	
Compassion	Empathic Distress
You may feel positive feelings of warmth toward the child, which makes you want to help and make her feel better and cope better with the situation. You may also feel compassion for the child's parents which makes you want to improve the situation for them too, so you act.	You may feel very frustrated and stressed about the situation in the classroom. You think about all that you must do and wonder how on earth you will manage. You may get a headache, and you may try to find someone else to deal with the child, avoiding emotional distress.

Figure 7.1 Empathy and compassion.

Source: adapted from Singer and Klimecki (2014)

Galetz (2019, p. 453) agrees that "one must have empathy before one can have compassion". Empathy is an innate skill, every person having "a brain primed for empathy" (Manassis, 2017). However, empathy develops throughout childhood (Decety, 2010), and there is evidence that empathy is a teachable skill that can be further developed (Konow Lund et al., 2018) through experience, reflective practice, or training (Jasper, 2005). There are many different stages and types of empathy described in the literature. Belzung (2014) describes the development of empathy over time in three stages (see Table 7.2). An additional stage has been added to Belzung's idea, stage 4: "intuitive empathy" (Hodgkins, 2024), based on findings from the empathy research.

Heartful Practice

Dachyshyn (2015) writes about "mindful, heartful and ecological practice" (p. 32) in the early years, reflecting on wisdom from indigenous people around the world to return to living in the moment and connecting with others. She advocates *being with* children rather than *doing to* children. In New Zealand, Dachyshyn studied Māori people's values and beliefs and identified themes that relate to compassionate care:

- *Whanauntanga* (relationships): Relationships with others and with the Earth are central; Nature and people are interconnected, so we must care for both; Everything we do affects others.
- *Rangatiratanga* (self-determination): Everyone's decision-making and choices must be respected and valued; Everyone has power, agency and free will.
- *Manaakitanga* (ethos of care): It is everyone's responsibility to care for others.
- *Kotahitanga* (unity and bonding):We gain strength from unity with others; We are enhanced by shared experiences with children, families, colleagues and communities.
- *Pumanawatanga* (a beating heart): As we accept and know others, we create a community where all people, ideas, joys and sorrows and valued, accepted and treated with gracious kindness.

Table 7.2 Stages of empathy.

Stage		Definition	Examples
Stage 1	Emotional contagion	This basic response is both unconscious and primitive.	A person yawns, and other people nearby yawn too. A baby in a nursery starts to cry and other babies join in and cry too.
Stage 2	Emotional contagion with concern	Emotional contagion plus the capacity to be worried by another person and to want to help.	A child falls and starts to cry. Another child is concerned about her and goes to try and help. A baby is distressed, so a practitioner goes to comfort him.
Stage 3	To put oneself in another person's position	The ability to put oneself "in someone else's shoes" and understand their feelings.	Listening to a friend talking about her marriage breakup and trying to understand how she must feel. Going to help an unbalanced elderly person to cross the road, even though you are in a rush.
Stage 4	Intuitive empathy	Ascertaining someone's emotions intuitively, emotions that the person themselves may not be aware.	Observing the non-verbal signs that a child is likely to become upset and intervening to prevent distress. Being aware that something is wrong with another person, without them having to say anything.

Source: adapted from Belzung (2014) and Hodgkins (2024)

The term "gracious kindness" describes compassion beautifully. Dachyshyn also worked in Africa and studied the values and beliefs of the Ismaili religion in Tanzania. The values of Zakah (charity) and Nazrana (offering) were of the utmost importance to the Ismaili people. Commitment to country, community and charity were key, through the offering of time and knowledge. The Ismaili people believed that tiny actions can change the world for the better. Dachyshyn advocated taking the values from both groups of indigenous people and using this "old wisdom" as an antidote to many of the world's twenty-first-century problems, for example its obsession with policies, testing and evidence-based practice. The image below shows the three guiding principles of this approach.

The principles of "mindful" practice echo the core conditions outlined by Rogers (1959), emphasising a non-judgmental approach, openness, trust, and compassion, which is fostered through empathy (Singer & Klimecki, 2014). Despite the prevalent constraints imposed by government policies and the emphasis on evidence-gathering in early years practice worldwide, contemporary approaches such as "planning in the moment" (Ephgrave, 2018) offer a degree of flexibility to cater to children's individual interests and personalities. The necessity to continually evolve and adapt the environment and available resources becomes apparent when prioritising child-led approaches, alongside the cultivation of full awareness and presence.

The "ecological" principles articulated by Dachyshyn (2015) should serve as the foundation for early years practice, considering that understanding the diverse world is integral to the Early Years Foundation Stage (EYFS) guidance. These principles are not novel concepts, as highlighted by Dr Diane Boyd, sustainability advisor to the Department for Education (DfE), who points out that key figures such as Froebel, Montessori, Owen, and Steiner advocated for social justice, equality, and the empowerment of all children, especially the disadvantaged and girls (Boyd et al., 2021). These pioneers recognised the environment as a valuable resource and understood the interconnectedness between the child and their world"

> **REFLECTIVE ACTIVITY**
>
> Look at the "heartful" section of Figure 7.2 and try to give an example (in Table 7.3) of each of the points.
>
> - How difficult was the exercise?
> - Were any of the points difficult to answer? Why?
> - Can you identify one action for yourself, based on the exercise?

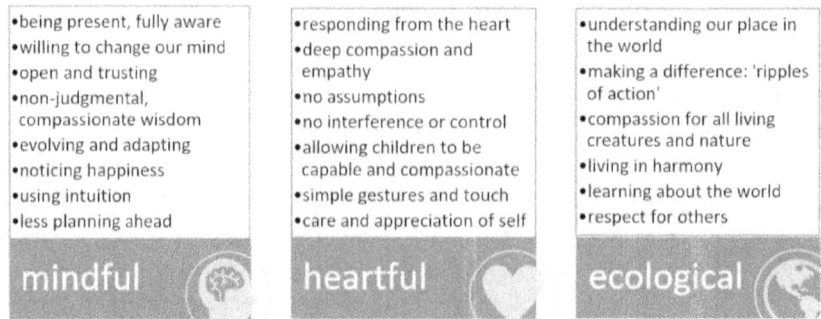

Figure 7.2 Dimensions of mindful, heartful, and ecological orientations for compassionate and sustainable living.

Table 7.3 Example prompts.

Give an example of a time when you ...	
Responded to a child or parent/ carer "from the heart"	
Showed deep compassion and empathy	
Made certain that you were not making assumptions	
Allowed children to play without interfering or controlling their play	
Enabled a child to feel capable and competent	
Used a gesture or touch to make a child feel valued	
Cared for your own wellbeing and appreciated yourself	

Compassionate interactions with children

In this section, the concepts of compassion previously explored are applied to routines and practices in early years contexts. Care routines are paramount as they are an integral aspect of daily interactions with young children, presenting invaluable opportunities for fostering relationships and providing compassionate care.

Care Routines

All children should be treated with care and compassion, but working with babies, who are dependent on adults for much of their care, demands careful sensitivity. Each child's individual needs must be respected, and children encouraged to do as much as they can for themselves to promote independence and self-confidence. Working in partnership with parents and carers is essential in tailoring care to the individual child, with an appreciation that parents and carers know their child best. In all aspects of intimate care (nappy changing, dressing and undressing and toileting), practice must ensure dignity for the child in order to meet the safeguarding and welfare requirements of the EYFS and the Disability Discrimination Act (2004) which states that no child should be excluded from a setting due to not yet being toilet trained. Nappy changing should be a positive experience for the child, so it is important that members of staff are calm and kind and that they do not make negative comments about the contents of nappies. Nappy changing can be a great opportunity for building a relationship with the child and spending some time talking, playing or singing with the child, making the child feel relaxed. Toilet (or "potty") training should be seen as an important self-care skill which children will develop at their own pace. Partnership with parents is crucial to ensure consistency of messages at home and at the setting. Allowing children as much choice and control over the process as possible will make the process easier. New guidance for early years settings from ERIC, the children's bowel and bladder charity, provides a model policy with the objective, "potty training is a positive experience; the family and child should feel supported throughout" (ERIC, 2019, p. 1).

Food is another aspect of practice that can be potentially stressful but that can also be a good opportunity for quality time and compassionate attention. Key workers should coordinate feeding routines for the children they know well, and communication with parents and carers is again crucial. In an early years setting, it is important that children are not rushed and that mealtimes are as pleasant as possible. Helping very young children to identify when they are hungry and full, offering different foods and allowing plenty of time to eat will help to promote healthy eating habits. Food should never be used as a punishment or a reward. Food and emotion can be closely connected and there is evidence that stress and negative emotion affect children's eating (Moss, Conner, & O'Connor, 2021). Therefore, in a compassionate environment which has children's best interests at heart, it is important not to battle with a child over food but to make mealtimes pleasant, unhurried social activities. Clark (2023) calls this approach "slow pedagogy", which she describes as, "an unhurried approach that aims to be more conscious of the relationship with time and its impact on both young children and practitioners. It is about valuing the present moment and being attentive to children's pace, rhythm and interests." A project based on this philosophy, entitled "Marvellous Mealtimes" (Patterson, 2022), was adopted in Falkirk, Scotland. Practitioners working on the project found that their small changes made a big difference, "for example, buying jugs and serving tongs that were easier for the children to handle themselves" (Patterson, 2022, p. 101). The approach is about stepping back and encouraging independence. The practitioners found that this approach had an unexpected positive effect on children's behaviour.

Transitions and Attachment

Transitions and changes are a part of everyday life, and for a child they are likely to stressful. At times, for some children, they can be overwhelming. Some transitions can seem relatively trivial, for example, moving from one activity to another, or moving to a new group or table. Other transitions are major milestones, for example starting school or moving to a new school. All children are different, and some will worry about the smallest changes, so it is important to be aware of how challenging transitions can be and to identify ways of supporting children with compassion. Figure 7.3 identifies factors which can affect young children's transitions. If a child has a special educational need, or speaks English as an additional language, for example, transitions may require much more compassionate consideration and preparation. Working with very young children who are starting nursery or primary school for the first time requires a caring, welcoming attitude, as children's emotions can be intense and overwhelming for them (Datler, Datler, & Funder, 2010). What young children need, at times of transition and uncertainty, is structure and routine. There

Health needs or disability Children who have a known disability, special educational need or health needs will need additional support with transitions. They are particularly vulnerable to change.		**Under-developed executive functioning skills** Executive function refers to a group of skills we use to execute a task, stay focused, and keep organised. It includes a working memory, mental flexibility and self-control. Ages 3-5 are a time of rapid skills development. These skills are essential in 'school readiness'. Premature and summer born children may not have developed these skills to the extent of other children.

Attachment problems	**Previous experiences**	**Language differences**
It is well known that children need a secure relationship with a caregiver. Children who do not have this may present disruptive behaviour, withdrawal, or anxiety. Transitions can be extremely difficult for a child with an attachment disorder.	If the child has no past experience of being separated from their parent(s) or if they have had too much change or loss in their lives so far, this may make transitions difficult.	Not being able to communicate and, therefore, not being able to make oneself heard and understood, can be very scary for a child. Children for whom English is not their first language, and children with speech and communication difficulties are likely to find transitions extremely challenging.

Figure 7.3 Factors affecting young children's transitions.

is security in knowing what is going to happen, which helps children feel calmer. Frequent verbal reminders of what is happening next are helpful. Visual timetables and cue cards can be especially useful for younger children, those unable to read written English and children who have difficulty in processing information.

Transitional objects can be very helpful for children at times of transition. Winnicott (1989) coined the term "transitional objects" to describe items to which young children develop deep, persistent attachments. These objects tend to be blankets, soft toys, pieces of cloth, etc., which remind the child of home and act as a bridge between home and school. Cottis (2017, p. 21) explains that "the object can become a carrier for the essence of the relationship itself, helping a person move between states, especially states of separation, distress or confusion". Some early years settings and schools do not allow objects from home to be brought in, purportedly in case they get lost or damaged, but it is worth remembering how important such objects are to the child, to choose to be compassionate and try to allow this where possible.

In the majority of cases, the transition from nursery to school, and then from class to class each year, are major transitions for children. An exception is Steiner education, which advocates vertical groupings where children stay with the same teacher and children throughout the nursery and school. There are isolated instances of Foundation Stage Units (O'Connor, 2017) which integrate nursery and reception classes in school, but this is unusual. In the empathy research (Hodgkins, 2024), it was evident that early years practitioners understand the problematic nature of transitions and they manage these with empathy and compassion. The following two diary entries give an example of such compassion, Harriet describes her interactions with one of her key children, a toddler in her first full week of nursery. The following comments are on day 1 and day 4:

> She was struggling with understanding why people were going. I feel she may have felt a loss of attachment … being "left".
>
> (Harriet)

> The child was more "prepared" on the Wednesday, more aware of what will happen and that I am there to comfort her and for support.
>
> *(Harriet)*

These entries show that Harriet has ensured that the child is aware of the routine and is comfortable in the knowledge that she will be comforted by her keyworker. There is evidence that practitioners empathise with children at times of transition and understand the emotion felt, as this diary entry demonstrates:

> If there's a child who's really struggling with separation from their parents and they're really upset it used to get to me a lot and I'd get really upset about it.
>
> *(Mel)*

Mel is clearly experiencing affective empathy, as she is becoming upset herself. As she explains later, in the past she has been very upset about the situation. However, as she became more experienced in her role, she saw that showing compassion for the child resulted in comfort and ultimately the building of a new attachment figure at the nursery.

Professional Love

When working with young children, practitioners are "in loco parentis", they have the responsibility of a parent while the child's parent is not there. Many practitioners believe that this means they should provide hugs and physical comfort for children as a parent would. Page (2018), who devised the phrase "professional love", conducted research to find out whether parents wanted practitioners in early years settings to *love* their babies and found the answer to be an overwhelming "yes". As early years professionals, we build close emotional attachments with children, and this is both important and mutually rewarding. The love we have for the children in our care is not a replacement for the child's parents" love, but it complements the love within the home; the child's emotional needs still need to be met within the setting. As Davis (2021), a supporter of professional love explains:

> If they fall over, they might need a cuddle and their tears wiped away, if they're tired and struggling to give in to sleep, they might need to be held and rocked or if a child is missing their family, some kind, gentle words and a sit on a lap can offer comfort and reassurance.

In Maslow's (1962) hierarchy of needs, love is described as a basic need. Although people generally see love as being identified only in the third level of Maslow's hierarchy (love and belonging), he believed that love is a basic need that drives all human development: "We must understand love; we must be able to teach it, to create it, to predict it, or else the world is lost to hostility and to suspicion" (Maslow, 1962, p. 236).

The "L" Word

In English, the word "love" has many meanings, one having sexual connotations, which may explain why its use is sometimes seen as controversial in early years practice. While researching practitioners' views for this chapter, it has become evident that some settings have rules for staff for the use of the word "love". One practitioner told me that if a child says, "I love you" to a staff member, the appropriate response is to say something like "thank you, that's lovely" or "and I love being with all of you children too". In some settings, saying "I love you too" to a child is clearly frowned upon, but what message does avoiding the word *love* give to a child? Hearing "I love you" reciprocated is very positive; it lets children know that the adults around them are there for them and it validates their feelings. In Page's (2018) research, 47% of practitioners said they would respond to a child saying "I love you" by saying "I love you" back to the child. Page's participants gave reasons for responding in another way (for example, "and I love spending time with you too") including worry about the child's parents thinking they have overstepped a boundary, not feeling comfortable saying the words in general, or safeguarding concerns. Much of the anxiety about using the word *love* is around child protection and wanting to protect oneself from potential allegations of abuse.

Safeguarding

Close relationships with other people's children can be complicated and concerns about being accused of inappropriate behaviour can be a barrier to loving practice. Although it is known that touch is vital for young children, some settings are very cautious and produce strict guidelines for staff. In a profession where safeguarding children is our highest priority, defensiveness and over-cautiousness are understandable. However, being touched is a right; Professor McGlone from the Fit and Healthy Childhood All-Party Parliamentary Group says, "My view is that *not* touching children is a form of abuse … touch is a necessity as much as food. What we are doing is removing an essential experience for young children" (cited in Goddard, 2020). Giving hugs and using touch to build secure attachments are important features of "professionally loving practice" (Purcell, Page, & Reid, 2022).

Touch

The value of touch in interactions with babies and toddlers is well documented, but Svinth's research (2018, p. 933) showed that with older children, too, "nurturing touch has the potential to transform children's well-being and participation." Physical touch which is gentle and loving increases levels of oxytocin (the "love" hormone) and reduces cortisol (the stress hormone). It can also increase dopamine (the reward hormone), help to release serotonin (for happiness and wellbeing), and lower our heart rate (Coffey, 2020). Bergnehr and Cekaite (2018) identified five functions of touch (Figure 7.4), all of which were seen in their observational research with 1–5-year-olds in a Swedish nursery.

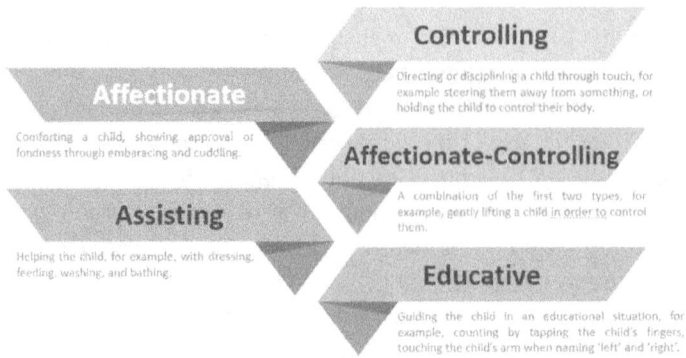

Figure 7.4 Five types of touch.

Of the five types of touch detailed above, "assisting touches" and "educative touches" are the most widely used in the day-to-day life of the early years setting. Affectionate touches are important for young children to feel approval and fondness, and this can be even more important at times when a child needs comfort in times of distress. Consideration of *controlling* touches includes balancing the needs and rights of the child with protection and safety. A controlling touch where a child is lifted away from something they are doing may seem appropriate but when an adult decides where to place a child and uses their strength and stature to physically move a child, care should be taken to ensure that doing so is in the child's best interest (Bergnehr & Cekaite, 2018). Affectionate-controlling touches are preferable to controlling a child's body, if the child needs to be *controlled*.

It is worth pointing out, too, that some children do not like to be touched. This can be due to personal preference and personality or it can be due to sensory sensitivity, an extreme version of which is "tactile defensiveness", a presentation sometimes seen in children with special educational needs. For children with tactile defensiveness, a gentle touch can feel like a spider crawling over the skin and causes the child to go into "fight or flight" mode (Kranowitz, 2006). A further reason for children avoiding touch is past experience of trauma. Therefore, it is wise (and respectful) to ask a child for permission to touch them, for example, "can I help you wash your hands?" or "can I give you a pat on the back?" It is important, too, to teach children about appropriate touch. The NSPCC's (2023) underwear rule, "PANTS" (Figure 7.5), is a great resource for helping young children to keep themselves safe from inappropriate touches.

Consistently giving to others is a form of emotional labour (Hochschild, 2013) which can lead to exhaustion and depression if we feel drained and unappreciated ourselves. The Buddha once said, "if your compassion does not include yourself, it is incomplete." Interactions with children can be emotionally draining for practitioners and, in some cases, can lead to "compassion fatigue" (Taggart, 2016). This has been exacerbated in recent years due to the demands of working at the time of the COVID-19 pandemic (Nelinger et al., 2021).

Figure 7.5 PANTS.

Source: NSPCC (2023)

Compassionate Interactions with Families

Working in partnership with parents and carers is a fundamental characteristic of early years practice, so every early years setting should have a policy which sets out their principles and objectives. Research has identified that, "regardless of the quality of settings, the most important predictor of children's future outcomes is the quality of the home learning environment" (Birth to 5 Matters, 2021). Therefore, children are likely to have the best prospects when practitioners and parents work together in an inclusive and trusting relationship. As Vygotsky (1978) noted, the parent is the child's first educator, so should be valued and included as such. Solvason, Cliffe, and Bailey (2019, p. 201) point out:

> If we have a genuine respect for the parents we work with as the child's first educator, we should be prepared to act on the advice that they offer. We should value the role that parents play in their child's development during their many hours in the home environment, and not presume that their role is a supporting act for us as educators.

Compassion for parents and carers must include empathy and taking the time to get to know individuals so that we appreciate their views and don't make assumptions. Often, there is an assumption that parents and carers can "control, organise and prioritise their own time and activities" (Wilson & Gross, 2018, p. 322), which may not be the case. It would be easy to assume that the family who never come to open days or parents" evenings are not interested in their child's education. However, there is a multitude of barriers to engagement, for example, working hours, anxiety, a chaotic lifestyle or language barriers. It is always important to remember that "what teachers and other practitioners see of parents/carers is just a small part of what is going on in their lives" (Hodgkins, 2024, p. 53). Finding the time to talk to parents can be difficult but should be prioritised for the children's sake, as the relationship is so important. Showing compassion and understanding with parents and carers will likely encourage open conversations built on trust. Rather than only talking to parents and carers when there is a problem, it is important to share good news, achievements, and stories about the child's day.

Case Study: Empathy Research

Here are two examples of good practice from participants in the empathy research (Hodgkins, 2024). The first is from George, who is the deputy manager of a private day nursery. In this excerpt, he describes a time when he phoned a parent to reassure her that her child had settled. When she had left the nursery earlier, both she and her toddler were upset about being separated. George demonstrates his knowledge of the parent's life, his empathy for her situation, and his compassionate actions:

> It can mean a lot … she's a single parent still living with her own parents, she wants to try and be independent, but she can', so with all that going on that phone call I gave her was important. OK, my day is going to be OK because my child is fine. For some parents, when their child is their literal world, if they don't hear they're OK it can ruin everything for them.
>
> (Hodgkins, 2024, p. 162)

In the second example, Jake, who manages a small rural kindergarten, explains his response to an anxious parent:

> I reminded the parent of all the great work they are doing … I know parents are very anxious … I reassured them that it was perfectly normal … I think it is important to care and be kind if you can … by showing empathy, you are kind of saying we're here when you need us… if the parents are happy, the children are going to be happy and confident, and we're happy because the children are happy.
>
> (Hodgkins, 2024, p. 161)

Research by Faulkner et al. (2016) suggests that working with parents and carers is one of the biggest stressors in the early years profession. There are times when practitioners need to have difficult conversations. An example of this is talking to parents and carers about potential SEN diagnoses. Practitioners in the early years may be the first people to highlight a potential developmental delay or difficulty, and communicating this to the child's parents or carers demands extreme care and compassion. Any discussion concerning a problem with a child's development is likely to be met with an emotional response. Solvason and Proctor (2021, p. 472) explain that "all parent partnerships can be fragile when there are conflicting views about what is in the best interest of the child, but where children with SEN are concerned, emotions are frequently heightened." Parents and carers may feel denial, guilt, sadness, and even "emotional turmoil" (Solvason & Proctor, 2021, p. 470), which needs to be anticipated and managed with care. In the research by Hodgkins (2024, p. 160), Joel, a manager of a day nursery, describes a time when he had to have such a conversation:

I felt a sense of responsibility to convey accurate information and was worried about how the parent may respond to hearing their child has a developmental delay. I felt sorry for the parent as they tried to make sense of this interaction.

It is clear that Joel feels both empathy and compassion for the parent, and he is demonstrating thoughtfulness in preparing accurate information likely to be easily understood by a parent experiencing an emotional response.

REFLECTIVE ACTIVITY

The three examples above by George, Jake, and Joel demonstrate compassion for the parents and carers of the children in their care. Using the examples and the section of this chapter on "compassionate interactions with families", write some good practice points as a guide for early years practitioners, consider how these could be systemically embedded by leaders.

Table 7.4 Good practice points.

Good practice in compassionate work with families
1.
2.
3.
4.
5.
6.

Compassion within the Early Years Team

Compassionately working with others leads to understanding and mutual support. If we consider Maslow's (1962) hierarchy of human needs, we see that safety and security are of great consequence; thus, being in a secure team is essential. Just like the children we care for, adults, too, need to feel emotionally secure and psychologically safe. For this to happen, team members need to know each other. Purvanova (2013, p. 299) says, "one of the most basic human needs is the need to be understood, to receive acknowledgment of one's unique qualities and characteristics, to be humanized".

It is important to get to know other team members, to understand their individual qualities and needs, just as we would do with the children in our care. Just as we show empathy, congruence, and unconditional positive regard (Rogers, 1959) for children, this should also be afforded to the people we work alongside. Biggart et al. (2017) explains how important it is to get to know people holistically, too, just like we do with children, as factors affecting people outside the work setting will inevitably have an impact on people's work:

> Showing compassion and understanding for people's lives and feelings outside work was an important part of providing support as it could explain behaviour which was not related to the work itself, thus enabling supervisors and colleagues to understand and accommodate their interactions to take into account personal circumstances.
>
> *(Biggart et al., 2017, p. 124)*

Compassionate teams need compassionate leaders who lead by example and set the tone for the organisation. A good example of compassionate leadership comes from the prime minister of New Zealand, Jacinda Ardern, who famously said:

> One of the criticisms I've faced over the years is that I'm not aggressive enough or assertive enough, or maybe somehow, because I'm empathetic, it means I'm weak. I totally rebel against that. I refuse to believe that you cannot be both compassionate and strong.
>
> *(Jacinda Ardern, 2018, in Van Wart et al, 2022)*

Ardern's leadership has been praised worldwide by leaders and by her own team. However, as she says, leadership is hard. There are many difficult decisions to be made as a leader and tough feedback to give, so strength and compassion need to go hand in hand, which is no easy task. In the research by Hodgkins (2024), nursery managers Jake and Joel wrote in a reflective diary about their interactions with nursery staff. Jake evidently prioritises the emotional wellbeing of his staff team, writing, "It is difficult as we are all busy, but it is important to listen to the staff team and be there for them". This sort of emotional support is invaluable for staff members. Everyone needs to feel they are listened to and valued and that their wellbeing is important. The use of empathy to *tune into* people's feelings is a core skill needed by managers. In this next quote, manager Joel describes trying to "see the world through their eyes" (Rogers, 1959) when there is a problem. Joel says, "trying to dig to find the root cause of the problem with that member of staff. Every individual is slightly different so it's understanding their point of view." By understanding where the other person is coming from, Joel can then make a plan to support them. In this example, Joel was concerned about a staff member's lack of motivation. As motivation is closely linked with performance and there are so many individual differences (Chowdhury,

Alam, & Ahmed, 2014), it is important to ascertain what is likely to motivate someone to improve their outcomes and, in this case, in turn, improve outcomes for children and families. Another important point to consider is compassion for managers. In both cases, Jake and Joel spend much time and effort supporting their teams, but who supports the manager? Joel points this out in the research. "Being a manager is quite a lonely place to be". In support of this view, Elfer's (2012) research identified managers in early years settings feeling responsibility "akin to parental concern" (p. 134) for their staff. This additional layer of responsibility, in addition to responsibility for the children and families, can be overwhelming, and there is often no system of support for managers. A solution to this may be in finding ways for staff to recognise and show compassion for their manager as an integral part of the team.

REFLECTIVE ACTIVITY

Consider Table 7.5 and try to complete it for your setting. This would be a good activity to do as a staff team.

Table 7.5 Compassion in your setting.

	What do we do to show compassion?	What more could we do?
Staff team *Consider:* Language used Listening Judgement Encouragement Helping others Gratitude and appreciation Celebrating success When others are suffering When others make mistakes		
Managers *Consider:* Language used Listening Judgement Encouragement Gratitude & appreciation Celebrating success		

In the most successful teams, there will always be room for improvement. It is hoped that the exercise above will identify practices for the future which will result in a team with increased compassion for each other.

Summary

In this chapter, we have identified definitions of compassion within early years practice, with an acceptance that hurt and pain are an unavoidable part of the human condition. Compassion is closely related to empathy, but is not the same. In fact, compassion is an action resulting from empathy. Heartful practice, an approach that sees practitioners responding to children "from the heart" has also been explored.

Compassion should be integral in all interactions with children, in care routines with very young children, at times of transition, and when attachments are being developed. When thinking about demonstrating compassion with young children, the idea of "professional love" is one that describes the closeness of the relationship between practitioners and children. Love is a word with strong associations and safeguarding concerns, but in this chapter, we have explored the issue with an appreciation of what young children need; a close attachment with someone who cares for them. For young children, touch is important; hugs and skin contact are vital and should be an essential part of everyday practice.

A case study from Aadiya gives a wonderful description of compassion and individual support for children, based on knowing the child, his family, and his background well and not making assumptions. Aadiya's story shows how her own background has led to her view of compassionate care in her work in school. Aadiya follows the principles of the EYFS while tailoring care to children's individual needs.

Compassion in the early years should include more than compassion for the children in our care; understanding the child holistically is important so compassion needs to be extended to parents and families too. Compassion can have negative effects on oneself, so self-compassion and compassion for the staff team and managers are just as important in creating a supportive environment in which everyone feels cared for.

Further Reading

Elfer, P., Greenfield, S., Robson, S., Wilson, D., & Zachariou, A. (2018). Love, satisfaction and exhaustion in the nursery: methodological issues in evaluating the impact of work discussion groups in the nursery. Early Child Development and Care, 188(7), 892-904.

Peter Elfer is one of the most prolific writers about the emotion involved in working in the early years. In this article, Elfer and colleagues examine the multi-faceted role of the early years practitioner, which encompasses "love, satisfaction and exhaustion". In the article, the authors discuss the emotional impact of the work and suggest a way of allowing practitioners to manage these feelings within "work discussion groups".

Nelinger, A., Album, J., Haynes, A., & Rosan, C. (2021). Their *challenges are our challenges: A* summary report of the experiences facing nursery workers in the UK in 2020. London: Anna Freud. Retrieved from www.annafreud.org/resources/under-fives-wellbeing/their-challenges-are-our-challenges-report.

The Anna Freud centre is a world-leading mental health charity for children and families. Their website has a wide range of resources to support children's mental wellbeing. There is a library of resources, including the report shown above. This report gives a summary of the experiences of nursery workers during the COVID-19 pandemic. The report aims to highlight the need to support early years staff.

References

Becker (2016). Does birth trauma lead to psychological problems? Retrieved from www.beckerjustice.com/blog/does-birth-trauma-lead-to-psychological-problems (accessed 8 August 2023).

Belzung, C. (2014). Empathy. *Journal for Perspectives of Economic, Political, and Social Integration*, 19(1-2), 177-191.

Bergnehr, D. & Cekaite, A. (2018). Adult-initiated touch and its functions at a Swedish preschool: controlling, affectionate, assisting and educative haptic conduct. *International Journal of Early Years Education*, 26(3), 312-331.

Biggart, L., Ward, E., Cook, L., & Schofield, G. (2017). The team as a secure base: Promoting resilience and competence in child and family social work. *Children and Youth Services Review*, 83, 119-130.

Birth to 5 Matters. (2021). Non-statutory guidance for the Early Years Foundation Stage. Retrieved from https://birthto5matters.org.uk (accessed 21 February 2024).

Boyd, D., King, J., Mann, S., Neame, J, Scollan, A., & McLeod, N. (2021). An early childhood education for sustainability resource that embeds the Sustainable Development Goals and STEM into pedagogical practice. NCFE. Retrieved from www.ncfe.org.uk/media/xbcbjrfj/early-years-sustainability-resource.pdf (accessed 21 February 2024)

Chowdhury, M., Alam, Z., & Ahmed, S. (2014). Understanding employee motivation: the case of non-teaching staff of a public university, *British Journal of Marketing Studies*, 2(6), 17-24.

Clark A. (2023). *Slow knowledge and the unhurried child: Time for slow pedagogies in early childhood education*. Routledge.

Coffey, H. (2020). Affection deprivation: What happens to our bodies when we go without touch? *The Independent*, 8 May. Retrieved from www.independent.co.uk/life-style/touch-skin-hunger-hugs-coronavirus-lockdown-isolation-ctactile-afferent-nerve-a9501676.html (accessed 4 February 2024).

Cottis, T. (2017). "You can take it with you": transitions and transitional objects in psychotherapy with children who have learning disabilities. *British Journal of Psychotherapy*, 33(1), 17-30.

Dachyshyn, D. M. (2015). Being mindful, heartful, and ecological in early years care and education. *Contemporary Issues in Early Childhood*, 16 (1), 32-41.

Datler, W., Datler, M., & Funder, A. (2010). Struggling against a feeling of becoming lost: a young boy's painful transition to day care, *Infant Observation*, 13(1), 65-87.

Davis, E. (2021). Why children need professional love. Retrieved from www.famly.co/blog/professional-love-early-years (accessed 24 December 2023).

Decety, J. (2010). The neurodevelopment of empathy in humans. *Developmental Neuroscience*, 32(4), 257-267.

Elfer, P (2012). Emotion in nursery work: Work discussion as a model of critical professional reflection. *Early Years*, 32(2), 129-141.

Ephgrave, A. (2018). *Planning in the moment with young children: A practical guide for early years practitioners and parents*. Routledge.

ERIC. (2019). Let's go potty. Retrieved from https://eric.org.uk/potty-training/problems (accessed 4 February 2024).

Faulkner, M., Gerstenblatt, P., Lee, A., Vallejo, V., & Travis, D. (2016). Childcare providers: work stress and personal wellbeing. *Journal of Early Childhood Research*, 14(3), 280-293.

Galetz, E. (2019). The empathy-compassion matrix: Using a comparison concept analysis to identify care components. *Nursing Forum*, 54(3), 448-454.

Goddard, C. (2020). EYFS best practice in schools – Be in touch. *Nursery World*, 16 March. Retrieved from www.nurseryworld.co.uk/features/article/eyfs-best-practice-in-schools-be-in-touch (accessed 24 December 2023).

Great Britain. (2004). Disability Discrimination Act 2004: Chapter 14. The Stationery Office.

Hochschild, A. (2013). *The managed heart: Commercialization of human feeling*, 3rd edn. University of California Press.

Hodgkins, A. (2024). *Exploring early childhood practitioners' perceptions of empathic interactions with children and families*. PhD thesis. University of Worcester. Retrieved from https://eprints.worc.ac.uk/13525 (accessed 27 January 2024).

Hoffman, M. (2000). *Empathy and moral development*. Cambridge University Press.

India Today. (2021). *The purpose of life is to be happy* by His Holiness the Dalai Lama. Retrieved from www.dalailama.com/messages/transcripts-and-interviews/the-purpose-of-life-is-to-be-happy (accessed 28 December 2023).

Jasper, M. A. (2005). Using reflective writing within research. *Journal of Research in Nursing*, 10(3), 247-260.

Kleineidam, N. & Fischbach, A. (2023). Emotional labour job characteristics in compassion work – differentiating exposure, empathy, compassion, and distancing. *Work and Stress*, 37(4), 531-551.

Konow Lund, A., Heggestad, A., Nortvedt, P. & Christiansen, B. (2018). Developing mature empathy among first-year students: The learning potential of emotional experiences. *Nordic Journal of Nursing Research*, 38(3), 128-134.

Kranowitz, C. (2006). *The out-of-sync child: Recognizing and coping with sensory processing disorder*. Tarcher Perigee.

Lazarus, R. (1991). *Emotion and adaptation*. Oxford University Press.

Lipponen, L., Rajala, A. & Hilppö, J. (2018). *Compassion and emotional worlds in early childhood education: Early childhood education and change in diverse cultural contexts*. Routledge.

Manassis, K. (2017). *Developing empathy: a biopsychosocial approach to understanding compassion for therapists and parents*. Routledge.

Maslow, A. H. (1962). *Toward a psychology of being*. D. Van Nostrand Company.

Morgan, A. (2017). Against compassion: In defence of a "hybrid" concept of empathy. *Nursing Philosophy*, 18(3), 1-6.

Moss, R.H., Conner, M., & O'Connor, D. B. (2021). Exploring the effects of positive and negative emotions on eating behaviours in children and young adults. *Psychology, Health & Medicine*, 26(4), 457-466.

Nelinger, A., Album, J., Haynes, A., & Rosan, C. (2021). *Their challenges are our challenges – a summary report of the experiences facing nursery workers in the UK in 2020*. Anna Freud.

NSPCC (2023). PANTS (the underwear rule). Retrieved from www.nspcc.org.uk/keeping-children-safe/support-for-parents/pants-underwear-rule (accessed 23 December 2023)

O'Connor, A. (2017) EYFS best practice in schools: Foundation stage units.www.nurseryworld.co.uk/content/features/eyfs-best-practice-in-schools-foundation-stage-units-all-in-one

Osgood, J (2010). Reconstructing professionalism in ECEC: the case for the "critically reflective emotional professional. *Early Years*, 30(2), 119-133.

Page, J. (2018). Characterising the principles of professional love in early childhood care and education. *International Journal of Early Years Education*, 26(2), 125-141.

Patterson, C. (2022). Marvellous mealtimes at Bowhouse Early Learning and Childcare setting in Scotland. In L. Arnott & K. Wall (Eds.), *The theory and practice of voice in early childhood: An international exploration*. Routledge.

Purcell, M. E., Page, J., & Reid, J. (2022) Love in a time of colic: Mobilizing professional love in relationships with children and young people to promote their resilience and wellbeing. *Child & Youth Services*, 43(1), 3-27.

Purvanova, R. (2013). The role of feeling known for team member outcomes in project teams. *Small Group Research*, 44(3), 298-331.

Rogers, C (1959). A Client-centred/person-centred approach to therapy. In H. Kirschenbaum & V. Henderson (1990), *The Carl Rogers reader*, 135-152. Constable.

Singer, T. & Klimecki, O. (2014). Empathy and compassion. *Current Biology*, 24(18), 875-878.

Solvason, C., Cliffe, J. & Bailey, E. (2019). Breaking the silence: Providing authentic opportunities for parents to be heard. *Power and Education*, 11(2), 191-203.

Solvason, C. & Proctor, S. (2021). "You have to find the right words to be honest": nurturing relationships between teachers and parents of children with special educational needs. *Support for Learning*, 36(3), 470-485.

Svinth L. (2018). Being touched – the transformative potential of nurturing touch practices in relation to toddlers' learning and emotional well-being. *Early Child Development and Care*, 188(7), 924-936.

Taggart, G. (2016). Compassionate pedagogy: the ethics of care in early childhood professionalism. *European Early Childhood Education Research Journal*, 24 (2), 173-185

Van Wart, M., Macaulay, M. and Haberstroh, K. (2022). Jacinda Ardern's compassionate leadership: a case of social change leadership in action. *International Journal of Public Sector Management*, 35(6), 641-658.

Vuorinen, K., Pessi, A. & Uusitalo, L. (2021). Nourishing compassion in Finnish kindergarten head teachers: How character strength training influences teachers' other-oriented behavior. *Early Childhood Education Journal*, 49, 163-176.

Vygotsky, L. S. (1978). *Mind in society: The development of higher psychological processes*. Harvard University Press.

Wilson, D. & Gross, D. (2018). Parents' executive functioning and involvement in their child's education: An integrated literature review. *Journal of School Health*, 88(4), 322-329.

Winnicott, D. (1989). *Playing and reality*. Routledge.

8

Rethinking Relational Leadership
Compassion with and beyond the Human

Kay Sidebottom

> **CHAPTER AIMS**
>
> By the end of this chapter, readers will be able to:
>
> - Be introduced to posthuman and new materialist thinking, and understand how these philosophies can help us think differently about compassion.
> - Be able to consider new modes of caring that draw upon affirmative ethics.
> - Explore how human care and compassion are always-already entangled with the non-human.
> - Reflect on how notions of "kinship" can help broaden compassion to include more-than-human others.

Introduction

This chapter will introduce the reader to critical posthumanism as a tool for viewing compassion differently. Drawing on the philosophies of Braidotti, Deleuze and Guattari, and Spinoza, as well as Indigenous scholarship, and exploring practical processes based around affirmative ethics, this approach will be explained in an accessible way through examples and stories from professional practice. Affirmative ethics is based around the creation of "joyful encounters" which move people away from spaces of negativity and cynicism. It calls for a turn towards difference, rather than the flattening of it via uniformity, and a recognition that "We are in this [predicament] together, but we are not one and the same" (Braidotti, 2020). This philosophical approach is antithetical to the individualist, neo-liberal and meritocratic values often embedded in our education systems (as outlined in Chapter 1). As such, it offers a radical way to live and work while accepting that we are embedded in the very systems we attempt to resist.

> **WHAT IS CRITICAL POSTHUMANISM?**
>
> Critical posthumanism challenges the idea that humans are separate from, or superior to, other beings and systems. It invites us to rethink the human as always entangled

> with the non-human world, such as animals, technology, and the environment. Rather than focusing solely on individual agency or human-centred values, critical posthumanism emphasises relationships, interconnectedness, and shared responsibility across species and matter. It opens space for more ethical, inclusive, and sustainable ways of being in the world.

After a focus on human compassion and posthumanism's potential for its acceleration, the chapter will explore the extension of compassion to more-than-human others. Positioning Indigenous scholarship as central to these ideas, it will put to work the findings from a recent research project which found that processes of decentring, noticing, attuning to, creating with and learning from animals, insects and land can help to promote notions of kinship and learning to care differently.

Compassion through a Posthuman Lens

The word "compassion" has its roots in the Latin *com pati*, meaning "to suffer with". It is important to firstly explore my own understanding and interpretation of this term, given that compassion is often used synonymously with "care", "empathy", and so on; and also interpreted in various ways. For the purposes of this chapter, compassion (expressed in different terms by Spinoza; as misericordia in this instance) will draw from the definition in the philosopher's *Ethics*:

> xvii. Misericordia is love, in so far as it induces a man to feel pleasure at another's good fortune, and pain at another's evil fortune.
>
> (Spinoza, 2002, §3:24)

Compassion as *"love"* is key to the processes and examples explored in this chapter. Love, however, is a difficult word in education; too often associated with the erotic (in the West). As bell hooks states, "to speak of love in relation to teaching is already to engage a dialogue that is taboo" (2003, p. 127). Accepting compassion as a form of love however resonates in terms of the relationships many of us have with our students, and students have with each other. Despite the tendency within education to reify objectivity and encourage professional distancing, emotions such as love are always-already present in our classrooms. bell hooks further asserts that, "refusing to make a place for emotional feelings in the classroom does not change the reality that their presence overdetermines the conditions where love can occur" (p. 133). The love and desire for knowledge is, as Parker J. Palmer puts it, also closely connected to compassion because "the mind motivated by compassion reaches out to know as the heart reaches out to love. Here the act of knowing is an act of love, the act of entering and embracing the reality of the other, of allowing the other to enter and embrace our own" (Palmer, 1993, p. 8). "Knowing" here is not about the accumulation of knowledge (as seen in current curricula developments) but instead, the deep joy of learning and the way in which understanding (the world) can help us to overcome pain.

For Spinoza, a critical point about existence is that all entities aim to do things that increase their capacity to act and endure; that is, they have "connatus"; the desire to persist in their own being. This desire to grow should not be corrupted by "sad passions"; feelings of hatred or sadness towards others that limit this capacity. Spinoza is clear that by relating to others, feeling compassion and acting on it, and carrying out acts of care we can both improve our own capacity, and the capacity of others to feel love and joy. Compassion is therefore not about love as "lack" (as often described in contemporary discourse relating to romance, where objects of desire are unobtainable or rejecting) but love as plenitude, reciprocity and mutual growth.

This notion is more commonly known as "do unto others as you would have done unto you", or as Braidotti (2019) puts it, "The harm you do to others, is immediately reflected in the harm you do to yourself" (p. 169). Compassion therefore can be seen as love with action; feeling for another person's sadness and then helping them to enhance their own lives and restore themselves in a way that causes no harm or injury to others. The notion of noticing, feeling and then acting speaks to processes of relationality and mutual understanding; moving beyond simply "feeling for" (sympathy) or "feeling as" (empathy). For Spinoza, to act with compassion is entirely reasonable, because we must persist in our own being, and for us to do so, others must be able to do the same. Gaining reason, or knowledge, is therefore key to acting compassionately; and this can be done through educating ourselves, in communion with others.

However, compassion is often hard to enact within systems of power that constrain us to following particular processes and rules. When thinking about power, we are also constrained by language. In English, of course, there is only one word for it. French has two (*pouvoir* and *puissance*); other languages have many. Spinoza used the words *potestas* and *potentia* to form an important distinction between hierarchical, bureaucratic and political power (*potestas*) and natural, generative, relational power (*potentia*). Organisations are generally spaces of *potestas*; rigid, hard to change, and mired in complex processes ("politics-as-usual"). However, *potentia* power still emerges through the joyful connections and reimaginings made by like-minded souls and breaks through in leaderless movements like Black Lives Matter and Occupy. You will feel *potentia* energy in your body, in the moments you connect with someone interesting on social media; when you start a project with people outside your own usual working environment; or when you meet a new person and jump on the flow of energy you feel between yourselves. It is an activist power; rhizomatic in its messy serendipity, and often subversive. By recognising it, augmenting it, and sharing it, we can activate *potentia* energy and thus move from compassion to action.

Of course, we cannot work purely in spaces of *potentia* all the time. Rosi Braidotti recommends a life which attempts to balance the necessary realities of *potestas* with time spent in *potentia*. Thinking about our own balance of energy, and where we can find the joyful, *potentia*-full encounters that Spinoza believes are necessary for a fulfilled life, should be an important and regular reflection in terms of activating compassion.

The Challenge of Compassion in Contemporary Times

Within systems of "schooling-as-usual", as suggested previously, acting with compassion (or love-in-action) can be problematic. As Chatzidakis et al. (2020, p. 8) state: "Neoliberalism … has neither an effective practice of, nor a vocabulary for, care". Contemporary discourses of meritocracy, "grit", zero-tolerance and warm-strict behaviour management within education use the language of masculinity, strength and dominance. Increasingly, rigorous disciplinary and surveillance practices serve to further flatten difference and limit the ways in we can demonstrate compassion within the boundaries of fixed disciplinary systems. We are also facing the growth of algorithmic, instrumental care practices which are often linked to computerised systems which, while aiming to streamline support services, can depersonalise and de-individualise.

Limited understandings of "care" are based around the education of an "Vitruvian" autonomous rational human being; the "homo economicus" who acts in self-interest for the furthering of neo-liberal values (Attick, 2017). The posthuman thinking of Braidotti, which builds on Spinozan ethics, calls us to question what kind of humans we centre in education; to "mark the end of the self-reverential arrogance of a dominant Eurocentric notion of the human, and to open up new perspectives" (Braidotti & Hlavajova, 2018, p. 3). This move requires us to go beyond, or after humanism as we augment and reposition the voices of those overlooked and oppressed by Enlightenment ideas of "humanity, as exemplified by Homo Economicus or Da Vinci's Vitruvian Man. It poses a challenge to the deeply engrained legacy of humanism and strikes at the heart of our current predicament; that the refusal to admit so many people to the category of "human" has resulted in the horrors of slavery, eugenics, settler colonialism and many more injustices based around an assumed view of idealised "Man" (Wynter, in McKittrick, 2015).

VITRUVIAN HUMAN

The *Vitruvian* human refers to the idealised figure of the autonomous, rational, and able-bodied man, often traced to Leonardo da Vinci's famous drawing. This concept symbolises a human-centred worldview rooted in Enlightenment thinking, where the human is seen as separate from nature, universally rational, and in control of their environment.

HOMO ECONOMICUS

Homo economicus is a term used to describe a model of the human as a self-interested, rational actor who always makes decisions to maximise personal gain. Common in neoliberal and economic theory, this view reduces human behaviour to competition, efficiency, and profit, often neglecting emotion, ethics, and relationality.

Within education this reification of a certain type of human (white, male, able-bodied, neurotypical, European and so on) can manifest as ableism and inflexibility in teaching and assessment, meritocratic attitudes that suggest giving everyone the same opportunity will result in fair treatment, and the persistence of gender binary splits in practices such as school uniform enforcement and PE teaching. The second move in posthuman thinking is post-anthropocentrism; the decentring of the human and elevation of other species and ecological systems which have been relegated beneath "Man" in an exploitative and limiting hierarchy. This convergence of ideas, which are often dealt with separately, necessitates complex, non-binary responses to the questions of our times. In this way, scholars putting this theory to work in practice must hold together often competing interests of human and non-human entities, both decentring the human while paying attention to the ways in which humans themselves are not treated equally. In this way, understandings of care and compassion should necessarily extend to wider issues of planetary health and concern, given that our existence in bound up in the thriving of our more-than-human worldly companions.

Compassion in Teaching Practice

As suggested in the previous section, putting compassion as affirmative ethics to work in education requires a shift in terms of what we understand humanity to be. Posthuman thinking highlights the ways in which "human" has always been a problematic term; for too long, certain types of human being (i.e. ones most distant from the "Vitruvian Man" ideal of white, able-bodied, Western, perfection) have been elevated at the expense of minoritised humans who were perceived to be different and thus "less-than". Humans lacking these characteristics suffered, and continue to suffer oppression, discrimination and rights violations ranging from slavery, colonisation, eugenics and identity-based hate crime. Humanism thus has a troubled genealogy because we rarely ask what kind of humans the concepts are based around. Yet its legacy persists in the ages and stages standards of Piaget, the way in which lessons are designed for a particular normative kind of child, the reification of standard English in assessments, and many other hegemonic elements of the education system. While we may show empathy for those pupils or colleagues who are marginalised, "feeling for" is not enough. To act with compassion within problematic institutional arrangements also requires a shift to activism and a desire to enact change.

The Thinking Environment

One practice which enacts affirmative ethics is the "thinking environment" (Kline, 1999). Based around ten components which include attention, encouragement, difference and equity, the thinking environment works to augment individuals' potential to act and grow, while being relational in its emphasis on listening and appreciation. Practically, thinking environments in the classroom are based on the premise that individuals are able to show up exactly as they are; and that difference (be in terms of neurodiversity; ethnicity; gender; and so on) is not to be flattened or assimilated, but to be celebrated and affirmed. Part of this affirmation involves the practice of "thinking rounds"; gentle questions to check in and out of learning situations, in which every learner has the opportunity share their thoughts in turn. During thinking rounds, participants listen to each other with attention (a process which can take a little time to normalise) and are able to speak for as long as they need to, or pass if they would rather not speak. This process often enables quieter members of groups to participate and share their thoughts, as they know that they will not be interrupted. Paying attention to others, and using structured processes such paired talking to resolve conflict, further enhances community and shifts the focus from individual growth to relational spaces of care.

Restorative Practice

In a similar way, restorative practice, when enacted as intended (that is, not neo-liberalised and utilised as a tool to reinforce behaviour management practices), enables acts of compassion within communities, whereby restitution is key (Howard, 2009). Accounting for wrong-doing; taking responsibility; and restoring community through restorative acts, are essential components for the furthering of community relations. Punishment through penalties such as isolation or removal of privileges are seen as counterproductive, as they do not directly benefit the aggrieved party.

Alternative modes of community-building, as enacted in restorative practice, challenge the Western-centric understandings of man as liberal, autonomous individual. They allow for compassion to be shown and enacted otherwise; applied in context, with an emphasis on relationality. In a similar vein, and also grounded in Indigenous epistemology, Yunkaporta (2019) calls us to move from spaces of "safety" to spaces of protection. In teaching practice this means that we should not attempt to create learning spaces that are deemed psychologically "safe" (as who is to say what "safe" means for each individual?) but instead establish protective spaces whereby each person is responsible for caring for both themselves and each other. In practice, this involves creating group agreements in which students and teachers posit their desires and needs regarding comfort and wellbeing. These desires are shared and discussed at the outset of each learning experience and are reviewed during the course of study, with negotiation processes incorporated, should desires conflict. The ensuing agreement forms a bond which all parties sign up to and abide by; with everyone taking responsibility for protecting each other's needs in a process of love and care.

Case Studies: Compassion in Action

In the following two sections I explore further how compassion has been enacted in my practice through the sharing of two case studies. The first is centred about human-human interactions. In the second, I extend notions of care and compassion to more-than-human others.

Compassionate Teaching in Further and Adult Education

Working with mature students has always troubled the teacher-taught binary. Significant life experiences, and shared concerns as parents, carers or women in the mid-life (among many other things) has meant that hierarchies of knowledge and boundaries of care and compassion are often inverted and stretched. For a number of years, I worked within Adult and Community Education, and with International Students who do not in many ways fit the normative, middle-class, teenage student-standard in Further and Higher Education. Within formal systems, students" linear and outcome-based learning journeys suggest an "ending" (for example, when a result is gained) that conflicts with the idea of "extended relations" that Noddings (1984) deems essential for an ethics of educational care. This section explores the ways in which I worked together with mature, "non-traditional" students on an Education degree at a university in the north of England to unsettle well-established modes of educational practice, in a shared attempt to create care-ful, response-able relations within the classroom.

One key concept that I put to work here was Deleuze and Guattari's (1987) notion of the rhizome. In botanical terms, a rhizome is a kind of plant that has no fixed root systems, but a complex network of nodes, shoots and tendrils which span a wide area (such as bamboo or couch grass). Thinking with the rhizome reveals new modes of human and other-than-human relationality, making apparent a range of sustainable figurations which, in our case, extended beyond the walls of the classroom. Putting the concept of the rhizome to work and relating it to our own system of education helps us to think more widely about both relationships and the process of learning; as a rhizomatic lens reveals the way in which anything can be connected to any other thing at any point. It emphasises the point that much of learning, and the way in which people learn, cannot be controlled or predicted. Students will always have lives outside of the classroom, and do much of their thinking alone, in relation with friends and family, or in the company of companion species. Learning will happen on the bus, when a student realises something for the first time; in bed, reading at night; in a WhatsApp group with their peers; or by connecting an idea to a TV show or TikTok reel.

Higher Education for part-time students, in an era of above-inflation tuition fees, reduced employer support and other financial pressures, is not often seen as a viable option for those wanting to return to education. Since 2010, the number of part-time undergraduate entrants living in England has dropped dramatically; by 2015, student numbers had decreased by at least 45% at UK universities and FE colleges (Callender & Thompson, 2018). For those mature students that do enter the system, pressures of work, caring duties and complex relationships with education (due to past experiences) can render the transition stressful and dislocating. The Education degree in question here recruits students via a "widening participation" agenda, aimed at offering educational opportunities that may initially seem out of reach. As a result, students can feel out of place; imposter syndrome (Brookfield, 1995) looms large, and staffing levels may not be sufficient to offer the amount of individual support required.

Working and being together within a troubled higher education system in this context required me, as a programme manager, to reflect carefully on process of creating supportive environments which were conducive to learning. I firstly made a conscious move away from discourse concerning gratitude and indebtedness (which often manifest in adult education) to the language of mutual recognition and relationality, in order to resist academic capitalism in spite of our complex and embedded roles within it. Rosi Braidotti's approach of affirmative ethics offered a way in which I could work within the constraints of the neoliberal system to create educational spaces as "sites for prefigurative practice" (Suissa, 2014) through practices that included "emphasis on the collective; acceptance of relationality and of viral contaminations; concerted efforts at experimenting with and actualizing virtual options; and a new link between theory and practice, including a central role for creativity" (Braidotti, 2016, p. 26).

My affirmative standpoint, expressed and shared with students as an ethics of joy, identified "potentia" as a productive and distributed form of power (Braidotti, 2013) that overcomes "places of pain" and seeks agency where it can be found. It was on this basis that we proceeded to navigate our way rhizomatically through the system in a continual process of negotiation and re-negotiation; trying new configurations of teacher-student-community, which start from the basis that all human beings need to receive care and give care to others.

In my teaching practice, with its roots in the critical pedagogic practice of hooks, Freire and many others, I had long worked with the idea of radical hospitality; a process whereby educators continually invite students and their insights into the conversation, working from the assumption that they have "stories to tell" (Palmer, 1998, p. 4). Thinking with the rhizome (Deleuze & Guattari, 1987) I explored how the relational connections of radical hospitality get made and unmade during the teaching and module requirements. The word "hospitality" itself suggests compassion, warmth and generosity; it is a symbiotic process in which the host both nurtures others and receives sustenance, thereby establishing a mutually beneficial environment. Food may well be involved (and in our case, often was; time, and encouragement to eat was vital for busy student-parents who often had no break between work and lesson time).

Building on Palmer's work, I also embraced the idea of "relentless welcome" (Felten & Lambert, 2020), making the process of induction for new students not a time-limited event but a constant practice of reaffirming space together, checking-in with each other through "invitation" and community-building "thinking environment" questions at the start of every class. Differences such as those relating to culture, gender identity and neurodiversity were seen not as lack but as advantage to our thinking; making our being together not just a process of accommodation but a process of celebration.

A rhizomatic approach suggests that separations, such as those between home and work life, are artificial as the world does not exist of discrete, isolated objects; and realising that we are all part of multiplicities exposes complexity within our social systems, as in our ecological habitats. Thinking with the rhizome reveals that hospitality was not in fact limited to the classroom, but stretched beyond its walls, as for many students, as learning is an emergent, non-linear process that may take place in spaces outside the remit of the university. Spaces of "undercommons" (Harney & Moten, 2013) such as smoking areas, corridors, buses, kitchens, bedrooms and cafes are sites of teaching and learning, as rhizomatic understandings of the "community as the curriculum" (Cormier, 2008) show us where and when learning spills out into informal spaces. Our embracing of social media networks such as Twitter was further blurring the boundaries between the different facets of our identities (teacher-student-parent-employee and so on) and exposing the various ways in which we were connected, not only to each other, but to a wider community of thinkers. By establishing a range of Twitter hashtags, Facebook groups and community online open courses (COOCs) we had moved to an iterative space of public pedagogy, in which our hospitality extended outwards to include thinking companions across a variety of geographical, educational and social contexts.

This shift to viewing hospitality as a rhizomatic process, reliant on the nurturing of positive conditions for growth, encouraged us to see that the establishment of pro-social spaces over time was the responsibility of all. As a result, an ensuing focus on the development of extended peer cultures was added to the curriculum and this introduced an affirmative move away from the individualism and isolationary nature of the neo-liberal academy. This establishment of productive and supportive relations was vital in order to build communities that might then move into sustainable "constellations of practice" (Mycroft & Sidebottom, 2018) in online spaces such as social media platforms, or face to face in future work and community-based projects.

Several years since the first cohort graduated, we continue to come together nomadically and rhizomatically; gathering around shared drive and energy, often working on multiple projects, writing together or following different lines of thought at the same time. In this practice students are "re-creators of knowledge" and I am a "teacher-in-relation" (Noddings, 1984) as we formulate together a new, co-intentional reality. While these spaces, like rhizomatic plants, may have a limited lifespan, we see them as a continual practice of resistance and community-building. Even in fallow periods we know that, when conditions are right, we will re-emerge into the sunlight together and continue to "collectively imagine ways to move beyond boundaries, to transgress" (hooks, 1994, p. 207).

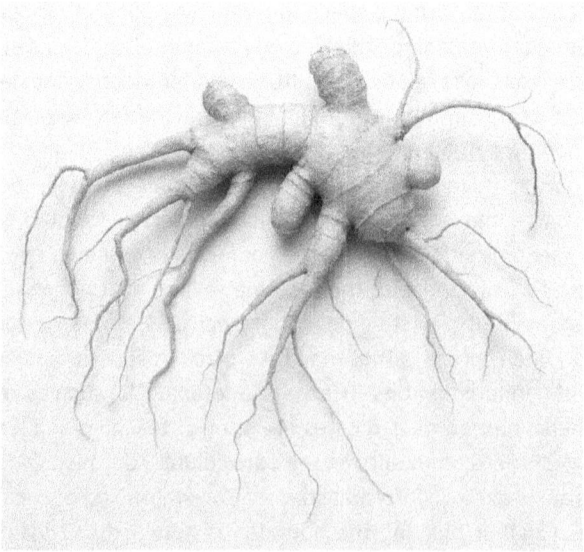

Figure 8.1 Example of a rhizomatic structure.

Compassion and the More-Than-Human

Spinoza's notion of affirmative ethics requires us to understand that, although we are differently configured, every element and being on earth comes from essentially the same matter. As such, compassion and care must be extended beyond the human to build relations with more-than-human others in order for us all to sustain and thrive on this planet. Compassion within education is rarely discussed in relation to non-human beings; and this human-centric paradigm can be hard to shift. However, it is arguably essential that we de-centre humans in the face of ensuing catastrophic environmental degradation.

In this case study I reflect on a project undertaken in 2021, in which a group of educators spent a weekend exploring what can be learnt when we view more-than-humans (such as trees, water, animals and plants) as teachers (Sidebottom and Mycroft, forthcoming). This project, which took place in the Yorkshire Dales, UK, took place shortly after Covid-enforced lockdown and was an opportunity to both de-centre ourselves but also regain a sense of community and belonging with each other. We began the project by extending compassion to other beings through seeing them as active participants in our research project. Acknowledging the ways in which more-than-humans are entangled in, and affect every activity, began for us as a process of noticing and attunement. A "place-acknowledgement" circle activity, in which we stood outside and gave thanks to the various elements and beings around us, felt strange initially but was vital in order to re-root us in the surrounding landscape.

During the course of the residential weekend we learnt about fungi, wrote poetry and created art, walked and sat outside, and each identified a "more-than-human" companion to learn from. Participants became intimate observers of moss, water, sheep and rocks; beginning to see and interact with them via processes of naming differently. The tendency in Western cultures is to taxonomise or categorise natural beings into classifications ("it's a birch tree!") and so on. However, Indigenous scholars such as Robin Wall Kimmerer (2013) suggest this process can objectify nature and distance us from it, harming relations through processes of "othering" and labelling. Instead, we addressed trees as "ancestors", drawing on Native American (Cree) traditions which see humans as younger relatives of species that have been on the planet for millennia. This shift in focus helped us to relate differently and acknowledge the relationality between plants and humans. In doing so, we began to attach and care in different ways; not through knowledge or information, but through the kinds of compassion we might actually feel for our (human) relatives (Sidebottom & Mycroft, forthcoming).

Donna Haraway (2016) suggests that we are always-already in relation with more-than-human companions, and that relationality requires vulnerability; a desire to "become-with" them. Compassion for the natural world, here, then requires us to give up something of ourselves; to deny ourselves as autonomous subjects and to fully acknowledge the "other-ness" of nature by noticing and becoming "response-able" to them. Wall Kimmerer (2020) suggests that we can draw on our feelings of vulnerability, created by climate doom, economic crisis and the fall-out of mass pandemic. Instead of becoming cynical or seeing to reassert authority and control, we should as ourselves the question: "Can we expand our own vulnerability to experience ecological compassion? How might we propel it, and what might it look like?" For the participants of our project, this vulnerability included humility in admitting that we have much to learn from the natural world and the holders of its knowledge, such as

Indigenous scholars. This extension of care and compassion to more-than-human companions also led us to relate to each other in more mindful ways; with the practices of noticing, paying attention, and naming differently applying to all our kin, regardless of species.

REFLECTIVE ACTIVITY: A POSTHUMAN REFLECTION WALK

This activity invites you to leave the classroom or office and take a reflective walk, alone or with other, in a natural or outdoor setting. Using prompts grounded in the flows of compassion (see Table 8.1) and the more-than-human perspectives of this chapter, you'll explore how compassion is not only something you "do" but something that emerges between you and the world. Bring a notebook or voice recorder if you'd like or just walk and reflect.

Table 8.1 Reflective prompts illustrating flows of compassion.

Flows of compassion	Prompts
Self-to-self	• As you walk, notice how your body responds to the environment. • In what ways does nature care for you today? • What does the ground beneath you say about how to lead gently, with presence?
Past-to-present	• What histories live in this landscape? • Can you sense traces of ancestral care, harm, cultivation, or erasure? • In what ways does this space carry memory, and how might that inform your own ethics of compassion?
Other-to-self	• Let a non-human being "speak" to you, perhaps the wind, a crow, a stone. • What might it be offering you? • What if this moment *is* a form of feedback?
Self-to-community	• As you walk, think about how your leadership ripples outward. • How do your actions affect others, human and non-human? • What *kind of ecosystem* do you help to shape through your leadership?
Beyond-the-human	• Stop at something more-than-human (a tree, a bird, a shadow). • How might this entity redefine what compassion means? • How do you receive care or co-create relationships with the non-human world?

Choose a location with elements of the natural or more-than-human world:

- A forest, field, park, river, coast, or garden.
- Even an urban green space or walking among old buildings and trees can work.

As you begin your walk, take a moment to pause. Breathe. Notice what's moving around you. Try to de-centre yourself. You are not the observer, you are part of the system. Use these prompts as you walk. These prompts align with the flows of compassion but ask you to experience them through ecological, embodied, and relational ways.

Summary

The processes and ideas mentioned in this chapter remind the reader of the need to reconnect to our own ethics, philosophies and values to build compassion on a foundation grounded in our own beliefs, not the ethical processes enforced by institutions who may not have ours, or our students" best interests at heart. Knowing what our beliefs and values actually are (in a world where the emphasis is on committing to external organisational or professional ethical standards) may necessitate a process of ongoing reflection; perhaps best done via study in communion with others.

Maintaining a focus on values is essential to ensure that ethics are continually lived, and emergent according to the various problematic situations in which teachers will inevitably find themselves. Acknowledging our own vulnerability and acting with humility; relating differently to the natural world; and seeing students (in all their different aspects) in terms of relationality and reciprocity are also some of the "turns" required for a culture of greater belonging and compassion. These processes naturally require introspection and reflection, which can be difficult in times of increased surveillance, unmanageable workloads and time pressures. However, drawing on affirmative ethics and "potentia" as joyful energy can help us to remain grounded and connected during difficult times. As Braidotti (2020, p. 4) explicates, This transformative force lies at the heart of affirmative ethics, which emphasises the boundless potential of all living beings, human and non-human, to form new, yet-to-be-discovered connections. It speaks to the idea of life as something created together, through shared experiences in a common world. What is truly limitless is not an abstract, idealised concept of Life, but the ongoing, grounded process of building a life in relationship with others.

As Smith et al. (2023, p. 3) state: "Care can be radicalized, localized, embodied, situated, relational, affirmative, nested in communities, with and between all people and matter and things in all spaces and places". Seeing compassion as something we are all responsible for creating, and can enact all the time, can liberate us from organisational and systemic constraints. This move towards affirmative ethics is arguably essential in these complex, troubled times in which "we are in this together, but we are not one and the same" (Braidotti, 2020).

Further Reading

Braidotti, R. (2019a) *Posthuman knowledge*. Polity Press.
Accessible introduction to posthuman thinking and affirmative ethics.
Kline, N. (1999). *Time to think*. Cassell.
Describes how to work in a thinking environment.
Yunkaporta, T. (2019) *Sand talk*. Text Publishing.
Exploration of Indigenous care ethics and practices in relation to culture and history.

References

Attick, D. (2017). Homo economicus at school: Neoliberal education and teacher as economic being. *Educational Studies*, 53(1), 37-48.
Braidotti, R. (2013). *The posthuman*. Polity Press.
Braidotti, R. (2016). Posthuman critical theory. In *Critical posthumanism and planetary futures*, 13-32. Springer.
Braidotti, R. (2019). *Posthuman knowledge*. Polity Press.
Braidotti, R. (2020). "We" are in this together, but we are not one and the same. *Bioethical Inquiry*, 17, pp.465-469.
Braidotti, R. & Hlavajova, M. (2018). *Posthuman glossary*. Bloomsbury Academic.
Brookfield, S. J. (1995). *Becoming a critically reflective teacher*. Jossey-Bass.
Callender, C. & Thompson, J. (2018). *The lost part-timers: The decline of parttime undergraduate higher education in England*. The Sutton Trust.
Chatzidakis, A., Hakim, J., Litter, J., & Rottenberg, C., & The Care Collective.(2020). *The care manifesto: The politics of interdependence*. Verso.
Cormier, D. (2008). Rhizomatic education: Community as curriculum. Retrieved from http://davecormier.com/edblog/2008/06/03/rhizomaticeducation-community-as-curriculum (accessed 14 December 2020).
Deleuze, G. & Guattari, F. (1987). *A thousand plateaus: Capitalism and schizophrenia*. Trans. B. Massumi. Bloomsbury Academic.
Felten, R. & Lambert, L. M. (2020). *Relationship-rich education: How human connections drive success in college*. John Hopkins University Press.
Haraway, D. (2016). *Staying with the trouble: Making kin in the Chthulucene*. Duke University Press.
Harney, S. & Moten, F. (2013). *The undercommons: Fugitive planning and black study*. Minor Compositions.
hooks, b. (1994). *Teaching to transgress: Education as the practice of freedom*. Routledge.
hooks, b. (2003). *Teaching community: A pedagogy of hope*. Routledge.
Howard, P. (2009). *Restorative practice in schools*. CfBT Educational Trust.
Kline, N. (1999). *Time to think*. Cassell.
McKittrick, K. (2015) *Sylvia Wynter: On being human as praxis*. Duke University Press.
Mycroft, L. & Sidebottom, K. (2018). Creating spaces to think. Retrieved from www.excellencegateway.org.uk/content/etf2872 (accessed 10 September 2020).
Noddings, N. (1984). *Caring: A feminine approach to ethics and moral education*. University of California Press.
Palmer, P. J. (1993). *To know as we are known: Education as a spiritual journey*. HarperCollins.
Palmer, P. J. (1998) *The courage to teach. Exploring the inner landscape of a teacher's life*. Jossey-Bass Publishers.
Sidebottom, K. & Mycroft, L. (forthcoming). [Birdsong]: Pedagogies of attunement and surrender with more-than-human teachers. *Australian Journal of Environmental Education*.
Smith, J. B., Klumbytė, G., Sidebottom, K., Dillard-Wright, J., Willis, E., Brown, B. B., & Hopkins-Walsh, J. (2023). We all care, ALL the time. *Nursing Inquiry*, e12572.
Spinoza, B. de. (2002) *Complete works*, trans. S. Shirley, ed. M. L. Morgan. Hackett.

Suissa, J. (2014). Towards an anarchist philosophy of education. In *New perspectives in philosophy of education*, 139-159. Bloomsbury Academic Press.
Wall Kimmerer, R. (2013). *Braiding sweetgrass*. Milkweed Editions.
Wall Kimmerer, R. & MacFarlane, R. (2020). Dandelions as global citizens: Robin Wall Kimmerer in conversation with Robert MacFarlane. *Emergence Magazine Podcast*, May.
Yunkaporta, T. (2019) *Sand talk*. Text Publishing.

9

Leading with Heart in Times of Crisis
Cultivating Teacher Resilience, Wellbeing, and Performance

Richard Marcel

CHAPTER AIMS

By the end of this chapter, readers will be able to:

1 Understand the significance of compassionate leadership in schools, particularly during crises, and its impact on teacher resilience, engagement, psychological wellbeing, and job performance.
2 Examine the psychological mechanisms; self-efficacy, positive emotions, and trust, that mediate and moderate the relationship between compassionate leadership and teachers' work attitudes and performance.
3 Apply evidence-based insights to develop and sustain practical strategies for cultivating compassionate leadership in schools, fostering a supportive, resilient, and high-performing work culture.

Introduction

Case Study: A Principal's Compassionate Leadership in Action

(Note: Names and details have been changed to preserve confidentiality.)

In March 2020, Dr Rebecca Thomas, Principal of Cambridge International School, Bengaluru, faced an unprecedented challenge. As schools shut down during the COVID-19 pandemic, she was thrust into a role that demanded more than academic oversight. This was a crisis that called for compassion.

The teachers were overwhelmed. Some lacked digital skills; others suffered personal losses. In her first virtual staff meeting, Rebecca didn't begin with instructions, but with a heartfelt: "How are you really doing?"

The responses were raw. A senior teacher admitted, "I feel like I'm drowning." Another shared that she'd recently lost her father. Rebecca listened. "You're not alone. We'll figure it out together." That moment shifted everything. Her leadership became a catalyst for resilience, connection, and collective strength.

Rebecca implemented several targeted strategies:

- **Emotional support**: Weekly check-ins, a no-emails-after-hours policy, and free counselling created space for wellbeing (Fredrickson, 2001).
- **Practical empowerment**: Peer mentoring for digital teaching, simplified lesson plans, and flexible expectations helped teachers regain control (Bandura, 1997).
- **Building trust**: Shared decision-making, celebrating small wins, and personal appreciation messages fostered a culture of recognition and inclusion.

By the time the school reopened, staff morale was stronger than ever. Teachers felt empowered, anxiety levels dropped, and engagement increased. Most importantly, trust in leadership soared. Rebecca's story proves that compassion is not soft leadership, it's strategic. Research confirms it builds resilience and sustains excellence (Luthans et al., 2007).

> **REFLECTIVE ACTIVITY**
>
> Recall a time when a leader's compassion changed your work experience:
>
> 1 What three ways could compassion enhance your current workplace?
> 2 In a crisis, what immediate actions would you take to support your team?

Theoretical Foundations and Conceptual Framework

This chapter draws on key psychological and organisational theories to explore how compassionate school leadership enhances teachers' work attitudes and job performance. The framework centres on trust, self-efficacy, and positive emotions as core mechanisms, with links to broader concepts such as resilience, psychological wellbeing, and work engagement.

- *Trust:* Trust is foundational to effective leadership. It enables open communication, collaboration, and psychological safety, critical conditions for teachers to thrive. In compassionate leadership, trust strengthens the impact of supportive actions; when teachers trust their leaders, they are more receptive, engaged, and resilient.
- *Self-efficacy:* Bandura's (1997) theory of self-efficacy highlights how belief in one's capabilities shapes motivation and perseverance. Compassionate leaders foster self-efficacy by providing emotional support, constructive feedback, and autonomy, enabling teachers to feel confident and capable, even under pressure.
- *Positive emotions:* Fredrickson's (2001) broaden-and-build theory explains how emotions like gratitude, joy, and hope expand cognitive flexibility and build psychological resources. Compassionate leadership creates the conditions for these emotions to flourish, fuelling creativity, resilience, and wellbeing.
- *Positive organisational behaviour and psychology:* Luthans (2002) and Seligman and Csikszentmihalyi (2000) emphasise strengths-based approaches to human functioning.

Compassionate leadership aligns with this by cultivating psychological capital, hope, optimism, and resilience, thereby supporting teacher satisfaction and performance.
- *Resilience and wellbeing:* Resilience enables teachers to adapt during adversity. Compassionate leadership supports this by providing consistent emotional and practical support (Masten, 2001). Similarly, Ryff and Keyes's (1995) multidimensional model of wellbeing shows how compassion enhances teachers' sense of purpose, growth, and connection.
- *Work engagement and job performance:* Engaged teachers are energised, dedicated, and absorbed in their work (Schaufeli et al., 2002). Compassionate leadership contributes to this state by meeting psychological needs and affirming teachers' value, improving job performance through empowerment rather than pressure (Campbell et al., 1993).

Conceptual Framework

This chapter proposes a conceptual model linking compassionate leadership to teacher work attitudes and job performance through two key mediators: self-efficacy and positive emotions. These factors fuel resilience, wellbeing, engagement, and professional growth. Trust acts as a moderator, amplifying the impact of compassion by shaping how support is received and internalised.

By integrating these perspectives, this framework offers a practical and research-informed pathway for understanding how compassionate leadership transforms educational environments, promoting not only performance, but also flourishing.

Key Mechanisms of Compassionate Leadership in Schools

Compassion: An Overview

Compassion has been a central theme in spiritual and philosophical traditions for centuries. Etymologically derived from the Latin *passio* (to suffer) and *com* (with/together), compassion literally means "to suffer with". It is closely associated with kindness, empathy, and care but is distinct in its action-oriented nature; compassion not only involves recognising suffering but also taking steps to alleviate it (Lilius et al., 2008; Shuck et al., 2019).

Compassion is defined as an empathetic response to another's suffering that motivates action to ease their distress (Lilius et al., 2008). Unlike empathy, which is a passive emotional state, compassion drives a proactive response to help those in need. Boyatzis et al. (2006) outline three core components of compassion: (1) understanding another's emotions, (2) caring deeply, and (3) a willingness to act in response. Similarly, Geshe Thupten Jinpa (2013) describes compassion as a multidimensional construct involving cognitive awareness of suffering, emotional resonance, a desire for relief, and the motivation to help.

In the workplace, compassion is increasingly recognised for its positive impact on organisational dynamics. Research suggests that compassionate workplaces foster positive emotions, reduce stress, and strengthen employee commitment and loyalty (Dutton et al., 2006; Lilius et al., 2008). Additionally, compassion enhances workplace relationships and improves employee performance, particularly in caregiving professions and emotionally demanding roles (Grant et al., 2008; O'Donohoe & Turley, 2006). As a growing field in organisational psychology, workplace compassion is proving to be a valuable factor in creating supportive, resilient, and high-performing work environments (Dutton et al., 2002, Frost et al., 2000).

Compassionate Leadership

The global leadership crisis, exacerbated by COVID-19, highlighted a lack of compassion in leadership across government, industry, and education. Employees increasingly expect leaders to demonstrate care and empathy, especially in challenging times. The Centre for Creative Leadership identified "compassion and sensitivity" as the fifth most important leadership skill among the top 20, yet many leaders lack proficiency in this area (Leslie, 2015). A study by Hougaard et al. (2018) found that while 91% of leaders believe compassion is essential, 80% struggle with how to practise it effectively.

Compassionate leadership is defined by a leader's ability to be present, recognise challenges, empathise, and offer support when possible. Such leaders prioritise the wellbeing of their teams and foster long-term, positive relationships. They lead with both heart and mind, demonstrating emotional intelligence and resilience. Compassionate leadership is not about seeking rewards but about creating a culture of trust, openness, and support (Boyatzis et al., 2006). Research confirms that compassion does not hinder productivity; rather, it enhances commitment, collaboration, and efficiency in the workplace (Frost, 1999; Dutton et al., 2002).

The Positive Impact of Compassionate Leadership on Organisations

Compassionate leadership plays a pivotal role in organisational success and employee wellbeing. By fostering a culture of kindness and care, leaders can enhance employee engagement, loyalty, and resilience (Dutton et al., 2002). Compassion has also been linked to faster recovery from stress and improved workplace relationships, particularly during crises (Frost et al., 2000; Dutton et al., 2006).

During difficult times, such as the COVID-19 pandemic, compassionate leadership became especially vital. Leaders who actively listened, empathised, and supported their employees helped foster a sense of safety and trust, boosting self-efficacy and positive emotions within teams. Research highlights that compassionate responses during crises contribute to organisational stability and high performance (Dutton et al., 2007). Beyond crisis management, compassionate leadership is equally valuable in day-to-day operations, shaping positive workplace cultures that enhance overall job satisfaction and wellbeing (Benevene et al., 2022). Ultimately, by integrating compassion into leadership practices, organisations create thriving, supportive, and high-performing workplaces.

Compassion in Schools

Compassion plays a vital role in schools, not only for students but also for teachers, who experience emotions as any human person does. Beyond their interactions with students, teachers also give and receive emotional support from colleagues. Research in organisational psychology confirms that workplace emotions significantly impact employee engagement, satisfaction, and performance (Brief & Weiss, 2002; Hareli & Rafaeli, 2008; Robinson et al., 2013). However, while compassion's role in organisational success is well-studied, its impact on teachers as compassion receivers remains underexplored.

Studies suggest that compassion enhances teachers' wellbeing, aligning with findings in other professions. When employees receive empathy, care, and support, they experience positive emotions, which reduce negative work attitudes and behaviours (Kahn, 1998; Hallowell, 1999; Dutton, 2003). While educational psychology has largely focused on compassionate teaching's effects on students' success and wellbeing, it has overlooked its impact on teachers' experiences (McCormick et al., 2013).

Since school principals significantly influence teachers' job satisfaction, engagement, and trust in the organisation (Bogler, 2001), examining the effects of compassionate leadership in schools is crucial. Drawing on organisational psychology, we contend that school principals' compassionate leadership fosters positive emotions and self-efficacy, which, in turn, enhance teachers' resilience, psychological wellbeing, work engagement, and job performance. Furthermore, compassionate leadership serves as a coping mechanism for teachers facing crises, helping them navigate stress and workplace pressures more effectively.

Ultimately, school principals' compassionate leadership not only enhances teachers' emotional and psychological wellbeing but also fosters a supportive and thriving school environment, benefiting both educators and students alike. More than just a leadership approach, compassionate leadership is essential for cultivating trust, fostering positive emotions and self-efficacy, promoting wellbeing and resilience, and inspiring engagement. Compassionate leaders enable teachers to flourish personally and professionally by prioritising empathy and support. Thus, we assert that the compassionate leadership of school principals positively influences teachers' work attitudes, including resilience, psychological wellbeing, work engagement, and job performance, ultimately fostering a more motivated, committed, and high-performing educational workforce.

Compassionate Leadership and Self-Efficacy

Compassionate leadership fosters an environment that nurtures self-efficacy, contributing to employees' wellbeing and performance. Compassionate leaders and principals instil hope and resilience by demonstrating care, understanding, and encouragement, helping employees and teachers bounce back from setbacks with greater confidence in their abilities.

Self-efficacy refers to an individual's belief in their capability to successfully complete tasks and achieve goals (Bandura, 1997). It significantly influences motivation, perception, and performance as employees who believe in their abilities are more likely to take on challenges and persist through difficulties (Bandura, 1997). In contrast, those with low self-efficacy often avoid challenges, struggle with setbacks, and experience higher levels of stress and negative emotions (Schwarzer & Hallum, 2008).

The Role of Compassionate Leadership in Building Self-Efficacy

Emerging research highlights the positive impact of compassionate leadership on self-efficacy. Leaders who demonstrate care and psychological safety enhance employees' confidence and ability to manage stress and uncertainty (Grant, 2008). Recent studies show that supervisor support fosters psychological safety, which in turn strengthens self-efficacy and resilience (Hebles et al., 2022; Zhou & Chen, 2021). When employees feel safe and supported, they are more willing to take risks, embrace challenges, and develop new skills, further increasing their self-efficacy and motivation.

In contrast, a lack of self-efficacy leads to avoidance behaviours, lack of commitment, and heightened stress. Employees who doubt their abilities tend to focus on obstacles rather than solutions, feel overwhelmed by challenges, and recover slowly from failure (Bandura, 1997; Jerusalem & Schwarzer, 1992). However, compassionate leaders can help mitigate these effects by providing emotional support, reducing burnout, and fostering an environment where employees feel valued and empowered (Oruh et al., 2021).

Compassionate Leadership and Teacher Self-Efficacy

For teachers, self-efficacy is a protective factor that helps them overcome adversity and professional challenges. Teachers with higher self-efficacy approach difficulties with confidence, remain engaged in their work, and view setbacks as opportunities for growth (Salanova et al., 2006). Compassionate school principals play a crucial role in enhancing teachers' self-efficacy by fostering a supportive work environment, offering constructive feedback, and equipping them with effective stress-management strategies (Eldor & Shoshani, 2016). By providing emotional support, recognition, and growth opportunities, compassionate principals help teachers build confidence in their abilities, leading to higher job satisfaction, resilience, and performance.

Thus, compassionate leadership among school principals significantly enhances teachers' self-efficacy, positively influencing their work attitudes, engagement, and job performance. By fostering trust, support, and encouragement, compassionate leaders empower teachers to overcome challenges, contributing to a motivated, committed, and high-performing.

Compassionate Leadership and Positive Emotions

Compassionate leadership plays a critical role in fostering positive emotions among teachers, which in turn lead to enhanced work attitudes and performance. Our framework highlights positive emotions as a key element in compassionate leadership. Compassionate school principals can evoke and foster positive emotions in teachers, leading to enhanced attitudes and performance. These emotions broaden teachers' thinking (Fredrickson, 2001) and help create a trusting and supportive environment, ultimately improving resilience, engagement, and wellbeing within the school. Research confirms that when teachers receive empathy, care, and compassion, they experience greater positive emotions, benefiting both individual and organisational outcomes (Eldor & Shoshani, 2016).

The Role of Positive Emotions in Leadership

According to Fredrickson's broaden-and-build theory (2001), positive emotions expand cognitive and behavioural flexibility, helping individuals develop lasting personal resources such as resilience and self-efficacy. These resources, in turn, contribute to employee wellbeing, motivation, and job satisfaction. In the context of education, school principals who consistently demonstrate compassion create a culture where teachers feel valued and supported, allowing them to recover from setbacks, stay engaged, and remain committed to their work.

Extensive research highlights the strong link between workplace compassion and positive emotions (Dutton et al., 2007; Lilius et al., 2008). Acts of compassion, whether given, received, or witnessed, activate positive emotional spirals, reinforcing trust and strengthening relationships (Dutton & Workman, 2011). These emotions help teachers cope with daily challenges, stay motivated, and perform at their best.

Positive Emotions as a Buffer Against Stress and Crisis

Positive emotions are essential for coping with adversity and stress (Fredrickson et al., 2003). During crises, such as the COVID-19 pandemic, many educators experienced fear, uncertainty, and emotional distress. Research indicates that positive emotions not only alleviate stress but also accelerate emotional recovery, making them a powerful coping mechanism in difficult times (Tugade & Fredrickson, 2004). By fostering positive emotions, compassionate school principals help teachers remain resilient, enabling them to navigate professional and personal challenges effectively.

Beyond individual benefits, positive emotions contribute to organisational wellbeing by enhancing engagement, reducing absenteeism, and improving productivity. Employees who experience joy, pride, and fulfilment at work are more likely to develop strong interpersonal connections, take initiative, and demonstrate long-term commitment. Studies confirm that workplaces characterised by positive emotions exhibit higher levels of job satisfaction, motivation, and performance (Brief & Weiss, 2002; Gardner et al., 2004; McColl-Kennedy & Anderson, 2002).

The Link Between Positive Emotions and Teacher Engagement

Research suggests that teachers who frequently experience positive emotions are more engaged, confident, and productive (Burić & Macuka, 2018). They are better equipped to manage classroom challenges, build strong relationships with students, and stay committed to their professional responsibilities. Moreover, experiencing positive emotions in response to compassionate leadership helps teachers recover from personal and professional setbacks, reinforcing their psychological wellbeing and resilience (Fredrickson et al., 2003).

Fredrickson's (2001) research further emphasises that positive emotions have a lasting impact on employees by building essential psychological and social resources. These resources can serve as protective factors, shielding individuals from stress, burnout, and negative emotions. Studies show that individuals who frequently experience positive emotions recover more quickly from setbacks, remain optimistic, and sustain their motivation over time (Shing et al., 2016).

Compassionate leadership is a powerful tool for fostering positive emotions in schools, ultimately enhancing teacher engagement, wellbeing, and job performance. Based on the Broaden-and-Build Theory of positive emotions (Fredrickson, 2001), teachers who experience positive emotions through compassionate leadership will demonstrate higher resilience, stronger work engagement, and greater job satisfaction.

Furthermore, teachers who experience frequent positive emotions exhibit enthusiasm, confidence, and a proactive mindset, whereas those who face negative emotional experiences may become disengaged and demotivated (Burić & Macuka, 2018). Therefore, compassionate school principals can play a crucial role in shaping a positive emotional climate, which benefits both teachers and the broader school community.

Thus, organisational leaders, particularly school principals, can cultivate positive emotions among employees and teachers through compassionate leadership practices, maximising benefits for both individuals and the organisation. By fostering positive emotions through compassion, school leaders can establish a thriving educational environment that promotes both personal wellbeing and organisational success.

Compassionate Leadership and Trust in the Leader

Trust is a cornerstone of organisational effectiveness, shaping job performance, commitment, teamwork, and retention (Dirks & Ferrin, 2002; Kramer, 1999). In leadership, trust is essential, as it creates a sense of psychological safety, allowing employees to feel valued, take risks, and engage fully in their roles. Mayer et al. (1995) define trust as the willingness to be vulnerable, based on the expectation that the leader will act in the best interest of their followers. Similarly, Rousseau et al. (1998) describe trust as a psychological state comprising the intention to accept vulnerability based upon positive expectations of another's behaviour. In essence, trust reflects confidence in a leader's integrity, competence, and goodwill, fostering security and cooperation within an organisation.

Leaders cultivate trust through personalised care and attention (Jung & Avolio, 2000). When they demonstrate empathy, kindness, and genuine concern, they instil confidence in their followers, strengthening commitment and collaboration. Employees who trust their leaders are more likely to be engaged, motivated, and willing to take on challenges (Mayer et al., 1995). Research further confirms that trust in leadership enhances job satisfaction, organisational commitment, and performance, while also reducing turnover intentions (Butler et al., 1999; Dirks & Ferrin, 2002; Podsakoff et al., 1996).

Compassion plays a pivotal role in nurturing trust-based relationships between leaders and employees. Studies indicate that acts of compassion create psychological connections, strengthening workplace bonds and team cohesion (Frost et al., 2000; Powley, 2009).

Compassionate leadership fosters a supportive and trusting environment, where employees feel safe to express concerns and rely on their leaders for guidance (Dutton et al., 2007).

Trust as a Moderator in the Compassionate Leadership Process

While compassion, kindness, and care are critical elements of leadership, they do not automatically generate trust; it must be reciprocated by followers. In schools, even the most compassionate principal may struggle to achieve positive outcomes if teachers do not fully trust their leadership. To maximise the impact of compassionate leadership, school leaders must actively foster trust among their teachers. The extent to which teachers trust their principal directly influences the effectiveness of compassionate leadership in enhancing self-efficacy and positive emotions.

Trust serves as a moderator in the relationship between compassionate leadership and teacher outcomes. When trust in the principal is high, teachers experience greater benefits, including higher self-efficacy, enhanced positive emotions, and improved job performance. Conversely, when trust is low, the effectiveness of compassionate leadership is weakened, reducing its ability to cultivate desirable work attitudes and performance.

Trust in School Leadership

Trust in school leadership is vital for teacher resilience, wellbeing, and job performance. When teachers trust their principals, they are more willing to take risks, innovate, and persevere through challenges. During crises, trust provides stability and reduces stress (Kramer & Cook, 2004). Dirks and Ferrin (2002) highlight that trust amplifies leadership effectiveness, fostering sustained teacher growth and school success.

Compassionate Leadership and Teacher Work Attitudes

Compassionate leadership plays a vital role in shaping teacher work attitudes, particularly in fostering resilience, work engagement, and psychological wellbeing. These factors not only enhance teachers' personal and professional experiences but also contribute to the overall success of educational institutions.

Resilience

The term "resilience" comes from its Latin root *resiliens*, the present participle of *resilire*, which means to bounce back, rebound, or recoil. In psychology, it is defined as an individual's ability to adapt positively to challenges, stress, or trauma by utilising personal, social, and psychological resources (Masten et al., 2009). Luthans (2002) describes resilience as the capacity to rebound from failure, conflict, or increased responsibility, while the American Psychological Association (APA) defines it as the ability to adjust successfully in response to crisis or distress (Southwick et al., 2014).

Research highlights the connection between compassion, positive emotions, and resilience. Acts of compassion strengthen wellbeing and promote resilience by activating positive emotions even in the face of suffering (Peters & Calvo, 2014). According to the Broaden-and-Build Theory (Fredrickson, 2001), experiencing positive emotions regularly builds resilience, enabling individuals to recover quickly from negative experiences. Studies indicate that individuals who frequently experience positive emotions demonstrate greater resilience during adversity (Fredrickson, 2010).

In the school context, compassionate leadership fosters teacher resilience by creating a supportive and psychologically safe environment. When principals show empathy, care, and encouragement, teachers are more likely to develop resilience, manage stress effectively, and sustain wellbeing. Research also indicates that resilience is closely linked to self-efficacy, further reinforcing teachers' ability to overcome challenges (Fredrickson & Joiner, 2018; Salanova et al., 2020). Thus, by integrating compassion, self-efficacy, and positive emotions, compassionate leadership enhances teacher resilience, reduces stress, and improves overall performance.

Work Engagement

Work engagement is defined as a positive, fulfilling work-related state of mind, characterised by vigour, dedication, and absorption (Schaufeli et al., 2002).

- Vigour refers to high energy levels and perseverance, even in the face of challenges.
- Dedication involves strong involvement in work, accompanied by enthusiasm, pride, and a sense of purpose.
- Absorption describes deep focus and immersion in one's job, making disengagement difficult.

Engaged employees experience job satisfaction, motivation, and commitment (Saks, 2006), and their enthusiasm translates into higher productivity and workplace morale (Ostrem & Wheeler, 2006). Work engagement is particularly nurtured through compassionate leadership, as employees thrive in environments where they feel valued, supported, and encouraged. Gallup research further confirms that employees are more engaged when they have strong workplace relationships and leaders who genuinely care about them.

Research supports the link between work engagement and personal resources such as self-efficacy, optimism, and resilience. Studies by Xanthopoulou et al. (2007) found that employees who exhibited high self-efficacy and resilience were more likely to engage deeply in their work. Similarly, Bakker et al. (2006) reported that resilient school principals displayed higher levels of engagement, reinforcing the idea that personal resources contribute to workplace commitment.

Engaged teachers bring significant benefits to the education system, as they are enthusiastic, goal-oriented, sensitive to students' needs, and dedicated to improving learning outcomes. Research shows that engaged employees consistently perform better than disengaged counterparts, leading to increased job performance, productivity, and wellbeing (Xanthopoulou et al., 2009; Schaufeli & Van Rhenen, 2006). Thus, compassionate leadership positively influences teacher work engagement, leading to higher performance, commitment, and satisfaction.

Psychological Wellbeing

Compassion plays a crucial role in maintaining psychological wellbeing and regulating emotions, mental health, and interpersonal behaviour. Research over the past two decades has linked compassion to positive physiological and psychological benefits, including reduced stress and improved emotional regulation (Fredrickson et al., 2013; Klimecki et al., 2014). Several compassion-based interventions, such as Compassion-Focused Therapy (CFT), have been developed to enhance mental wellbeing and resilience (Gilbert, 2019; Neff & Germer, 2013).

In the workplace, leaders who prioritise the psychological wellbeing of their employees can make a significant impact, especially in times of crisis. Expressing compassion and empathy during difficult periods reduces stress, burnout, and physical symptoms, while also enhancing goal achievement and performance. Studies confirm that higher levels of compassion correlate with increased happiness and reduced depression (Shapira & Mongrain, 2010; Zessin et al., 2015).

Psychological Wellbeing of Teachers

Teaching is widely recognised as a stressful profession, with high demands leading to burnout, emotional exhaustion, and attrition (Johnson et al., 2005; Skaalvik & Skaalvik, 2015). Research indicates that one-third of teachers experience significant stress, which negatively affects their health, instructional effectiveness, and job retention (Geving, 2007; Thomas et al., 2003). Increased teacher stress has also been linked to lower student achievement (Arens & Morin, 2016; Collie & Martin, 2017).

The COVID-19 pandemic further intensified stress levels among teachers, as they were required to adapt quickly to virtual teaching, manage new technological and pedagogical challenges, and balance work-life boundaries. Studies suggest that teachers who received support from school leadership during this transition reported lower stress levels and better psychological wellbeing (Košir et al., 2022).

Given that stress is a leading cause of teacher burnout and turnover, supporting teacher wellbeing must be a priority for school leaders and policymakers. Research suggests that compassionate leadership can serve as a protective factor against stress, helping teachers cope with challenges more effectively (Brackett et al., 2010). Additionally, self-efficacy and positive emotions, which are reinforced by compassionate leadership, act as psychological buffers, reducing anxiety, depression, and emotional exhaustion.

By fostering a supportive and compassionate work environment, school leaders can help reduce teacher stress, enhance resilience, and improve job satisfaction. As a result, students, parents, schools, and the broader educational system all benefit from mentally and emotionally well-balanced teachers.

Compassionate leadership has a profound impact on teacher resilience, work engagement, and psychological wellbeing. By cultivating positive emotions, fostering self-efficacy, and providing emotional support, compassionate school principals create a work environment where teachers feel valued, motivated, and equipped to handle challenges. Research demonstrates that teachers who experience compassion from leadership exhibit higher resilience, greater engagement, and improved wellbeing, ultimately enhancing job performance and educational outcomes.

Thus, the compassionate leadership of school principals will positively influence teachers' resilience, work engagement, and psychological wellbeing, reinforcing its role as a critical factor in fostering a thriving school environment.

Compassionate Leadership and Job Performance

Compassionate leadership plays a vital role in enhancing teacher job performance by fostering positive emotions, self-efficacy, and work engagement. A compassionate leader prioritises the wellbeing of their team while ensuring tasks are effectively executed. Given that job performance is central to human resource management, compassionate school principals can significantly enhance teacher performance by creating a supportive and emotionally positive work environment (Organ & Paine, 1999).

Research confirms that acts of compassion in organisations strengthen employee performance, resilience, and commitment (Frost, 1999; Dutton et al., 2002). Organisations with compassionate cultures experience higher productivity and adaptability, especially in challenging situations. Compassionate leadership fosters an environment where teachers feel valued and supported, leading to greater motivation, perseverance, and engagement.

The Link Between Compassion, Positive Emotions, and Performance

Compassionate leadership generates positive emotions, which have been linked to improved job performance and reduced workplace negativity (Kahn, 1998; Dutton, 2003). Employees who experience care, empathy, and compassion develop greater commitment, motivation, and resilience, allowing them to perform at higher levels (Grandey et al., 2005). Studies by Fredrickson and Losada (2005) show that employees with high levels of positive emotions perform better in professional settings, demonstrating greater confidence, engagement, and communication skills.

Furthermore, a leader's ability to foster a compassionate workplace significantly impacts organisational recovery and sustained performance during crises. Employees who feel emotionally supported recover faster from challenges, leading to higher engagement, productivity, and organisational commitment. Compassion in leadership thus becomes a powerful driver of sustained high performance.

Work Engagement as a Predictor of Job Performance

Work engagement is a key factor in job performance, as engaged employees consistently outperform disengaged ones. According to Bakker and Demerouti (2007), engaged employees excel due to:

1 Experiencing frequent positive emotions such as joy, enthusiasm, and fulfilment.
2 Maintaining better physical and psychological wellbeing, enabling sustained performance.

3 Proactively creating personal and job resources, helping them manage workloads effectively.
4 Spreading their engagement to others, fostering a more productive and motivated workplace.

Studies confirm that employees with high engagement levels receive better performance ratings from peers and supervisors (Bakker et al., 2004). Similarly, Schaufeli et al. (2006) found a strong correlation between work engagement and job performance, reinforcing the idea that engagement is essential for professional success.

Teacher Work Engagement and School Performance

Engagement is particularly critical for teachers, as it directly influences job performance, wellbeing, and student outcomes. Research shows that teachers who are engaged in their work report better physical and psychological health, allowing them to perform at higher levels (Schaufeli et al., 2008).

Further emphasising this connection, Hakanen et al. (2006) found that work engagement among Finnish teachers was strongly linked to organisational commitment, demonstrating that teachers who feel valued and supported are more dedicated to their roles. Similarly, Bakker and Bal (2010) established that teachers' weekly job performance is significantly influenced by their level of engagement, highlighting the critical role of compassionate leadership in sustaining teacher motivation and effectiveness.

Compassionate school leadership not only benefits individual teachers but also strengthens the school's overall performance and reputation. When teachers feel emotionally supported, they are more likely to go beyond their standard responsibilities, contributing to a more productive and high-performing school environment.

Compassionate leadership enhances teacher job performance by fostering engagement, self-efficacy, and wellbeing. Research strongly supports the connection between compassion and improved workplace performance, showing that teachers who feel supported by their principals are more engaged, motivated, and effective in their roles.

Thus, we assert that compassionate leadership among school principals positively influences teacher job performance, ultimately benefiting both educators and the overall school environment.

Case Study: Compassion in Action

A compelling demonstration of compassionate leadership comes from Renold Pascal, Vice-Principal of St. Pauls Institute of Communication Education (SPICE), Mumbai. One day, he encountered Maria (name changed), a former filmmaker who had fallen into homelessness and was seeking financial aid. Renold Pascal, Vice-Principal of St. Pauls Institute of Communication Education (SPICE), Mumbai, faced an unexpected visitor one day. Maria (name changed), a former filmmaker, now homeless and seeking financial aid. Dishevelled and struggling, she had lost everything. Instead of merely offering short-term help, Pascal saw an opportunity to restore her dignity.

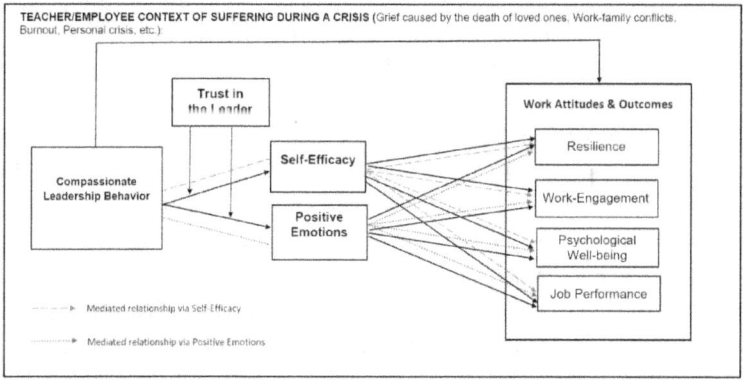

Figure 9.1 Conceptual model linking school principals' compassionate leadership behaviour to teacher outcomes.

He started with the basics, providing immediate relief and hen shifted focus to her strengths. Discovering her filmmaking background, he assigned her a promotional film project for SPICE. The result was remarkable. Maria delivered outstanding work and was compensated fairly. Within weeks, she returned with newfound confidence, well-groomed, engaged, and brimming with positivity.

Seeing her transformation, Pascal entrusted her with a bigger role: leading a filmmaking course for children and youth. She embraced the challenge with enthusiasm, delivering a highly successful program. The program's success not only restored Maria's professional standing but also brought financial benefits to SPICE.

This case illustrates how compassionate leadership fosters trust, positive emotions, self-efficacy, resilience, wellbeing, and performance. By believing in Maria's potential, Pascal not only restored her confidence but also reignited her sense of purpose. His compassion-driven leadership empowered Maria to reclaim her self-efficacy and resilience, demonstrating that leadership rooted in compassion can create lasting personal and professional transformation.

The Vice Principal's compassionate response, which boosted Maria's self-efficacy and positive emotions, was the key to SPICE's success. Bandura defines self-efficacy as "people's beliefs about their capabilities to produce designated levels of performance that exercise influence over events that affect their lives. Self-efficacy beliefs determine how people feel, think, motivate themselves, and behave" (Bandura, 1994, p. 2). Bandura's definition of self-efficacy relates to the vice principal's compassionate acts of helping a suffering member achieve personal and economic excellence.

We will now recommend a series of practical strategies, grounded in empirical research aimed at enhancing teacher resilience, psychological wellbeing, work engagement, and job performance. These strategies will focus on the critical development of self-efficacy and the cultivation of positive emotions, both of which are key mediators in the relationship between compassionate leadership and these crucial teacher outcomes.

Summary

The primary objective of this chapter was to demonstrate the impact of compassionate leadership on the work attitudes and job performance of teachers, through self-efficacy and positive emotions, particularly during crises such as the COVID-19 pandemic. Accordingly, we elucidated the dynamic interplay between compassionate leadership, particularly among school principals, and teacher work attitudes and job performance. The chapter shed light on the influence of compassionate leadership on resilience, psychological wellbeing, work engagement, and job performance. More specifically, we underscored the importance of compassionate leadership in schools, particularly during crises, demonstrating its positive impact on teacher resilience, psychological wellbeing, work engagement, and job performance, particularly when mediated by self-efficacy and positive emotions and moderated by trust in the leader. We highlighted the mechanisms through which compassionate leadership positively influences the work attitudes and job performance of teachers. The chapter demonstrated that compassionate leadership can positively impact the work attitudes and job performance of the teachers through the creation of trust, self-efficacy and positive emotions among them, particularly during challenging times. We argued that the condition of having higher trust in the leader is most likely to promote more positive emotions and self-efficacy among the teachers. Thus, we suggested that compassionate leadership of school principals would positively influence desirable teacher work attitudes and job performance through self-efficacy and positive emotions.

Further Reading

Dutton, J. E., Frost, P. J., Worline, M. C., Lilius, J. M., & Kanov, J. M. (2002). Leading in times of trauma. *Harvard Business Review, 80*(1), 54-61.
Explores how compassionate leadership helps teams navigate crises, emphasising empathy, psychological safety, and resilience.
Fredrickson, B. L. (2004). The broaden-and-build theory of positive emotions. *Philosophical Transactions of the Royal Society of London. Series B: Biological Sciences, 359*(1449), 1367-1377.
Explains how positive emotions expand thinking, enhance resilience, and foster wellbeing, which is crucial for leadership and workplace success.
Luthans, F., Avolio, B. J., Avey, J. B., & Norman, S. M. (2007). Positive psychological capital: Measurement and relationship with performance and satisfaction. *Personnel Psychology, 60*(3), 541-572.
Introduces Psychological Capital (hope, efficacy, resilience, optimism) and its impact on job satisfaction and workplace performance.
Boyatzis, R., Smith, M. L., & Van Oosten, E. (2019). *Helping people change: Coaching with compassion for lifelong learning and growth*. Harvard Business Press.
Presents a science-based approach to coaching with compassion, emotional intelligence, and sustainable personal growth.

References

Arens, A. K., & Morin, A. J. S. (2016). Relations between teachers' emotional exhaustion and students' educational outcomes. *Journal of Educational Psychology, 108*(6), 800-813. https://doi.org/10.1037/edu0000105

Bakker, A. B., & Bal, M. P. (2010). Weekly work engagement and performance: A study among starting teachers. *Journal of Occupational and Organizational Psychology, 83*(1), 189-206. https://doi.org/10.1348/096317909X402596

Bakker, A. B., & Demerouti, E. (2007). The job demands-resources model: State of the art. *Journal of Managerial Psychology, 22*(3), 309-328. https://doi.org/10.1108/02683940710733115

Bakker, A. B., Demerouti, E., & Verbeke, W. (2004). Using the job demands-resources model to predict burnout and performance. *Human Resource Management, 43*(1), 83-104. https://doi.org/10.1002/hrm.20004

Bakker, A. B., Gierveld, J. H. & Van Rijswijk, K. (2006). Success factors among female school principals in primary teaching: A study on burnout, work engagement, and performance. *Diemen the Netherlands: Right Management Consultants, 85*(4), 480-492.

Bandura, A. (1994). Self-efficacy. In V. S. Ramachaudran (Ed.), *Encyclopedia of human behavior*, vol. 4 (pp. 71-81). Academic Press.

Bandura, A. (1997). *Self-efficacy: The exercise of control*. W. H. Freeman.

Benevene, P., Buonomo, I., & West, M. (2022). Compassion and compassionate leadership in the workplace. *Frontiers in Psychology, 13*, 1074068. https://doi.org/10.3389/fpsyg.2022.1074068

Bogler, R. (2001). The influence of leadership style on teacher job satisfaction. *Educational Administration Quarterly, 37*(5), 662-683. https://doi.org/10.1177/00131610121969460

Boyatzis, R. E., Smith, M. L., & Blaize, N. (2006). Developing sustainable leaders through coaching and compassion. *Academy of Management Learning & Education, 5*(1), 8-24. https://doi.org/10.5465/amle.2006.20388381

Brackett, M. A., Palomera, R., Mojsa-Kaja, J., Reyes, M. R., & Salovey, P. (2010). Emotion-regulation ability, burnout, and job satisfaction among British secondary-school teachers. *Psychology in the Schools, 47*(4), 406-417. https://doi.org/10.1002/pits.20478

Brief, A. P., & Weiss, H. M. (2002). Organizational behavior: Affect in the workplace. *Annual Review of Psychology, 53*(1), 279-307. https://doi.org/10.1146/annurev.psych.53.100901.135156

Burić, I., & Macuka, I. (2018). Self-efficacy, emotions and work engagement among teachers: A two wave cross-lagged analysis. *Journal of Happiness Studies, 19*(7), 1917-1933. https://doi.org/10.1007/s10902-017-9903-9

Butler, J. K., Jr., Cantrell, R. S., & Flick, R. J. (1999). Transformation leadership behaviors, upward trust, and satisfaction in self-managed work teams. *Organization Development Journal, 17*(1), 13-28.

Campbell, J. P., McCloy, R. A., Oppler, S. H., & Sager, C. E. (1993). A theory of performance. In N. Schmitt & W. Borman (Eds.), *Personnel selection in organizations* (pp. 35-70). Jossey-Bass.

Collie, R. J., & Martin, A. J. (2017). Teachers' sense of adaptability: Examining links with perceived autonomy support, teachers' psychological functioning, and students' numeracy achievement. *Learning and Individual Differences, 55*, 29-39. https://doi.org/10.1016/j.lindif.2017.03.003

Dirks, K. T., & Ferrin, D. L. (2002). Trust in leadership: Meta-analytic findings and implications for research and practice. *Journal of Applied Psychology, 87*(4), 611-628. https://doi.org/10.1037/0021-9010.87.4.611

Dutton, J. E. (2003). *Energize your workplace: How to create and sustain high-quality connections at work*. John Wiley & Sons.

Dutton, J. E., Frost, P. J., Worline, M. C., Lilius, J. M., & Kanov, J. M. (2002). Leading in times of trauma. *Harvard Business Review, 80*(1), 54-61.

Dutton, J. E., Lilius, J. M., & Kanov, J. M. (2007). The transformative potential of compassion at work. In S. K. Piderit, R. E. Fry, & D. L. Cooperrider (Eds.), *Handbook of transformative cooperation: New designs and dynamics* (pp. 107-126). Stanford University Press.

Dutton, J. E., & Workman, K. M. (2011). Commentary on "Why compassion counts!": Compassion as a generative force. *Journal of Management Inquiry, 20*(4), 402-406. https://doi.org/10.1177/1056492611421077

Dutton, J. E., Worline, M. C., Frost, P. J., & Lilius, J. (2006). Explaining compassion organizing. *Administrative Science Quarterly, 51*(1), 59-96. https://doi.org/10.2189/asqu.51.1.59

Eldor, L., & Shoshani, A. (2016). Caring relationships in school staff: Exploring the link between compassion and teacher work engagement. *Teaching and Teacher Education, 59*, 126-136. https://doi.org/10.1016/j.tate.2016.06.001

Fredrickson, B. L. (2001). The role of positive emotions in positive psychology: The broaden-and-build theory of positive emotions. *American Psychologist, 56*(3), 218-226. https://doi.org/10.1037/0003-066X.56.3.218

Fredrickson, B. L. (2016). Love: Positivity resonance as a fresh, evidence-based perspective on an age-old topic. In L. F. Barrett, M. Lewis, & J. M. Haviland-Jones (Eds.), *Handbook of emotions* (4th ed., pp. 847-858). Guilford Press.

Fredrickson, B. L., & Joiner, T. (2018). Reflections on positive emotions and upward spirals. *Perspectives on Psychological Science, 13*(2), 194-199. https://doi.org/10.1177/1745691617692106

Fredrickson, B. L., & Losada, M. F. (2005). Positive affect and the complex dynamics of human flourishing. *American Psychologist, 60*(7), 678-686. https://doi.org/10.1037/0003-066X.60.7.678

Fredrickson, B. L., Grewen, K. M., Coffey, K. A., Algoe, S. B., Firestine, A. M., Arevalo, J. M., & Cole, S. W. (2013). A functional genomic perspective on human well-being. *Proceedings of the National Academy of Sciences, 110*(33), 13684-13689. https://doi.org/10.1073/pnas.1305419110

Fredrickson, B. L., Tugade, M. M., Waugh, C. E., & Larkin, G. R. (2003). What good are positive emotions in crisis? A prospective study of resilience and emotions following the terrorist attacks on the United States on September 11th, 2001. *Journal of Personality and Social Psychology, 84*(2), 365-376. https://doi.org/10.1037/0022-3514.84.2.365

Frost, P. J. (1999). Why compassion counts! *Journal of Management Inquiry, 8*(2), 127-133. https://doi.org/10.1177/105649269982005

Frost, P. J., Dutton, J. E., Worline, M. C., & Wilson, A. (2000). Narratives of compassion in organizations. In S. Fineman (Ed.), *Emotion in organizations* (pp. 25-45). Sage.

Gardner, W. L., Avolio, B. J., Luthans, F., May, D. R., & Walumbwa, F. O. (2004). "Can you see the real me?" A self-based model of authentic leader and follower development. *The Leadership Quarterly, 15*(6), 801-823. https://doi.org/10.1016/j.leaqua.2004.09.003

Geshe Thupten Jinpa. (2013). *Compassion cultivation training (CCT): Instructor's manual.* Center for Compassion and Altruism Research and Education, Stanford University.

Geving, A. M. (2007). Identifying the types of student and teacher behaviours associated with teacher stress. *Teaching and Teacher Education, 23*(5), 624-640. https://doi.org/10.1016/j.tate.2007.02.006

Gilbert, P. (2019). Explorations into the nature and function of compassion. *Current Opinion in Psychology, 28*, 108-114. https://doi.org/10.1016/j.copsyc.2018.12.002

Grandey, A. A., Fisk, G. M., & Steiner, D. D. (2005). Must "service with a smile" be stressful? The moderating role of personal control for American and French employees. *Journal of Applied Psychology, 90*(5), 893-904. https://doi.org/10.1037/0021-9010.90.5.893

Grant, A. M. (2008). Does intrinsic motivation fuel the prosocial fire? Motivational synergy in predicting persistence, performance, and productivity. *Journal of Applied Psychology, 93*(1), 48-58. https://doi.org/10.1037/0021-9010.93.1.48

Grant, A. M., Dutton, J. E., & Rosso, B. D. (2008). Giving commitment: Employee support programs and the prosocial sensemaking process. *Academy of Management Journal, 51*(5), 898-918. https://doi.org/10.5465/amj.2008.34789652

Hakanen, J. J., Bakker, A. B., & Schaufeli, W. B. (2006). Burnout and work engagement among teachers. *Journal of School Psychology, 43*(6), 495-513. https://doi.org/10.1016/j.jsp.2005.11.001

Hallowell, E. M. (1999). The human moment at work. *Harvard Business Review, 77*(1), 58-66.

Hareli, S., & Rafaeli, A. (2008). Emotion cycles: On the social influence of emotion in organizations. *Research in Organizational Behavior, 28*, 35-59. https://doi.org/10.1016/j.riob.2008.04.007

Hebles, M., Trincado-Munoz, F., & Ortega, K. (2022). Stress and turnover intentions within healthcare teams: The mediating role of psychological safety, and the moderating effect of COVID-19 worry and supervisor support. *Frontiers in Psychology, 12*, 758438. https://doi.org/10.3389/fpsyg.2021.758438

Hougaard, R., Carter, J., & Chester, L. (2018). Power can corrupt leaders. Compassion can save them. *Harvard Business Review, 96*(5), 2-5.

Jerusalem, M., & Schwarzer, R. (1992). Self-efficacy as a resource factor in stress appraisal processes. In R. Schwarzer (Ed.), *Self-efficacy: Thought control of action* (pp. 195-213). Hemisphere.

Johnson, S., Cooper, C., Cartwright, S., Donald, I., Taylor, P., & Millet, C. (2005). The experience of work-related stress across occupations. *Journal of Managerial Psychology, 20*(2), 178-187. https://doi.org/10.1108/02683940510579803

Jung, D. I., & Avolio, B. J. (2000). Opening the black box: An experimental investigation of the mediating effects of trust and value congruence on transformational and transactional leadership. *Journal of Organizational Behavior, 21*(8), 949-964. https://doi.org/10.1002/1099-1379(200011)21:8<949::AID-JOB64>3.0.CO;2-F

Kahn, W. A. (1998). Relational systems at work. *Research in Organizational Behavior, 20*, 39-76.

Klimecki, O. M., Leiberg, S., Ricard, M., & Singer, T. (2014). Differential pattern of functional brain plasticity after compassion and empathy training. *Social Cognitive and Affective Neuroscience, 9*(6), 873-879. https://doi.org/10.1093/scan/nst060

Košir, K., Dugonik, Š., Huskić, A., Gračner, J., Kokol, Z., & Krajnc, Ž. (2022). Predictors of perceived teachers' and school counsellors' work stress in the transition period of online education in schools during the COVID-19 pandemic. *Educational Studies, 48*(6), 844-848. https://doi.org/10.1080/03055698.2020.1833840

Kramer, R. M. (1999). Trust and distrust in organizations: Emerging perspectives, enduring questions. *Annual Review of Psychology, 50*(1), 569-598. https://doi.org/10.1146/annurev.psych.50.1.569

Kramer, R. M., & Cook, K. S. (2004). *Trust and distrust in organizations: Dilemmas and approaches*. Russell Sage Foundation.

Leslie, J. B. (2015). *The leadership gap: What you need, and still don't have, when it comes to leadership talent*. Center for Creative Leadership.

Lilius, J. M., Worline, M. C., Maitlis, S., Kanov, J., Dutton, J. E., & Frost, P. (2008). The contours and consequences of compassion at work. *Journal of Organizational Behavior, 29*(2), 193-218. https://doi.org/10.1002/job.508

Luthans, F. (2002). Positive organizational behavior: Developing and managing psychological strengths. *Academy of Management Perspectives, 16*(1), 57-72. https://doi.org/10.5465/ame.2002.6640181

Luthans, F., Youssef, C. M., & Avolio, B. J. (2007). *Psychological capital: Developing the human competitive edge*. Oxford University Press.

Masten, A. S. (2001). Ordinary magic: Resilience processes in development. *American Psychologist, 56*(3), 227-238. https://doi.org/10.1037/0003-066X.56.3.227

Masten, A. S., Cutuli, J. J., Herbers, J. E., & Reed, M. G. J. (2009). Resilience in development. In S. J. Lopez & C. R. Snyder (Eds.), *Oxford handbook of positive psychology* (2nd ed., pp. 117-131). Oxford University Press.

Mayer, R. C., Davis, J. H., & Schoorman, F. D. (1995). An integrative model of organizational trust. *Academy of Management Review, 20*(3), 709-734. https://doi.org/10.5465/amr.1995.9508080335

McColl-Kennedy, J. R., & Anderson, R. D. (2002). Impact of leadership style and emotions on subordinate performance. *The Leadership Quarterly, 13*(5), 545-559. https://doi.org/10.1016/S1048-9843(02)00143-1

McCormick, M. P., O'Connor, E. E., Cappella, E., & McClowry, S. G. (2013). Teacher-child relationships and academic achievement: A multilevel propensity score model approach. *Journal of School Psychology, 51*(5), 611-624. https://doi.org/10.1016/j.jsp.2013.05.001

Neff, K. D., & Germer, C. K. (2013). A pilot study and randomized controlled trial of the mindful self-compassion program. *Journal of Clinical Psychology, 69*(1), 28-44. https://doi.org/10.1002/jclp.21923

O'Donohoe, S., & Turley, D. (2006). Compassion at the counter: Service providers and bereaved consumers. *Human Relations, 59*(10), 1429-1448. https://doi.org/10.1177/0018726706071663

Organ, D. W., & Paine, J. B. (1999). A new kind of performance for industrial and organizational psychology: Recent contributions to the study of organizational citizenship behavior. In C. L. Cooper & I. T. Robertson (Eds.), *International review of industrial and organizational psychology* (Vol. 14, pp. 337-368). Wiley.

Oruh, E. S., Mordi, C., Dibia, C. H., & Ajonbadi, H. A. (2021). Exploring compassionate managerial leadership style in reducing employee stress level during COVID-19 crisis: The case of Nigeria. *Employee Relations: The International Journal, 43*(6), 1362-1381. https://doi.org/10.1108/ER-05-2020-0222

Ostrem, L., & Wheeler, D. (2006). *Engagement and trust as outcomes of servant leadership*. Gallup Leadership Summit.

Peters, D., & Calvo, R. A. (2014). Compassion vs. empathy: Designing for resilience. *Interactions, 21*(5), 48-53. https://doi.org/10.1145/2647087

Podsakoff, P. M., MacKenzie, S. B., & Bommer, W. H. (1996). Transformational leader behaviors and substitutes for leadership as determinants of employee satisfaction, commitment, trust, and organizational citizenship behaviors. *Journal of Management*, 22(2), 259-298. https://doi.org/10.1177/014920639602200204

Powley, E. H. (2009). Reclaiming resilience and safety: Resilience activation in the critical period of crisis. *Human Relations*, 62(9), 1289-1326. https://doi.org/10.1177/0018726709334881

Robinson, J. P., Shaver, P. R., & Wrightsman, L. S. (Eds.). (2013). *Measures of personality and social psychological attitudes: Measures of social psychological attitudes* (Vol. 1). Academic Press.

Rousseau, D. M., Sitkin, S. B., Burt, R. S., & Camerer, C. (1998). Not so different after all: A cross-discipline view of trust. *Academy of Management Review*, 23(3), 393-404. https://doi.org/10.5465/amr.1998.926617

Ryff, C. D., & Keyes, C. L. M. (1995). The structure of psychological well-being revisited. *Journal of Personality and Social Psychology*, 69(4), 719-727. https://doi.org/10.1037/0022-3514.69.4.719

Saks, A. M. (2006). Antecedents and consequences of employee engagement. *Journal of Managerial Psychology*, 21(7), 600-619. https://doi.org/10.1108/02683940610690169

Salanova, M., Bakker, A. B., & Llorens, S. (2006). Flow at work: Evidence for an upward spiral of personal and organizational resources. *Journal of Happiness Studies*, 7(1), 1-22. https://doi.org/10.1007/s10902-005-8854-8

Salanova, M., Rodríguez, A., & Nielsen, K. (2020). The impact of group efficacy beliefs and transformational leadership on followers' self-efficacy: A multilevel-longitudinal study. *Current Psychology*, 39(6), 2233-2246. https://doi.org/10.1007/s12144-018-9922-7

Schaufeli, W. B., Bakker, A. B., & Salanova, M. (2006). The measurement of work engagement with a short questionnaire: A cross-national study. *Educational and Psychological Measurement*, 66(4), 701-716. https://doi.org/10.1177/0013164405282471

Schaufeli, W. B., Salanova, M., González-Romá, V., & Bakker, A. B. (2002). The measurement of engagement and burnout: A two sample confirmatory factor analytic approach. *Journal of Happiness Studies*, 3(1), 71-92. https://doi.org/10.1023/A:1015630930326

Schaufeli, W. B., Taris, T. W., & Van Rhenen, W. (2008). Workaholism, burnout, and work engagement: Three of a kind or three different kinds of employee well-being? *Applied Psychology*, 57(2), 173-203. https://doi.org/10.1111/j.1464-0597.2007.00285.x

Schaufeli, W. B., & Van Rhenen, W. (2006). Over de rol van positieve en negatieve emoties bij het welbevinden van managers: Een studie met de Job-related Affective Well-being Scale (JAWS). *Gedrag & Organisatie*, 19(4), 323-344.

Schwarzer, R., & Hallum, S. (2008). Perceived teacher self-efficacy as a predictor of job stress and burnout: Mediation analyses. *Applied Psychology*, 57(s1), 152-171. https://doi.org/10.1111/j.1464-0597.2008.00359.x

Seligman, M. E. P., & Csikszentmihalyi, M. (2000). Positive psychology: An introduction. *American Psychologist*, 55(1), 5-14. https://doi.org/10.1037/0003-066X.55.1.5

Shapira, L. B., & Mongrain, M. (2010). The benefits of self-compassion and optimism exercises for individuals vulnerable to depression. *The Journal of Positive Psychology*, 5(5), 377-389. https://doi.org/10.1080/17439760.2010.516763

Shing, E. Z., Jayawickreme, E., & Waugh, C. E. (2016). Contextual positive coping as a factor contributing to resilience after disasters. *Journal of Clinical Psychology*, 72(12), 1287-1306. https://doi.org/10.1002/jclp.22327

Shuck, B., Alagaraja, M., Immekus, J., Cumberland, D., & Honeycutt-Elliott, M. (2019). Does compassion matter in leadership? A two-stage sequential equal status mixed method exploratory study of compassionate leader behavior and connections to performance in human resource development. *Human Resource Development Quarterly*, 30(4), 537-564. https://doi.org/10.1002/hrdq.21357

Skaalvik, E. M., & Skaalvik, S. (2015). Job satisfaction, stress and coping strategies in the teaching profession—What do teachers say? *International Education Studies*, 8(3), 181-192. https://doi.org/10.5539/ies.v8n3p181

Southwick, S. M., Bonanno, G. A., Masten, A. S., Panter-Brick, C., & Yehuda, R. (2014). Resilience definitions, theory, and challenges: Interdisciplinary perspectives. *European Journal of Psychotraumatology*, 5(1), 25338. https://doi.org/10.3402/ejpt.v5.25338

Thomas, N., Clarke, V., & Lavery, J. (2003). Self-reported work and family stress of female primary teachers. *Australian Journal of Education*, 47(1), 73-87. https://doi.org/10.1177/000494410304700106

Tugade, M. M., & Fredrickson, B. L. (2004). Resilient individuals use positive emotions to bounce back from negative emotional experiences. *Journal of Personality and Social Psychology, 86*(2), 320-333. https://doi.org/10.1037/0022-3514.86.2.320

Xanthopoulou, D., Bakker, A. B., Demerouti, E., & Schaufeli, W. B. (2007). The role of personal resources in the job demands-resources model. *International Journal of Stress Management, 14*(2), 121-141. https://doi.org/10.1037/1072-5245.14.2.121

Xanthopoulou, D., Bakker, A. B., Demerouti, E., & Schaufeli, W. B. (2009). Reciprocal relationships between job resources, personal resources, and work engagement. *Journal of Vocational Behavior, 74*(3), 235-244. https://doi.org/10.1016/j.jvb.2008.11.003

Zessin, U., Dickhäuser, O., & Garbade, S. (2015). The relationship between self-compassion and well-being: A meta-analysis. *Applied Psychology: Health and Well-Being, 7*(3), 340-364. https://doi.org/10.1111/aphw.12051

Zhou, H., & Chen, J. (2021). How does psychological empowerment prevent emotional exhaustion? Psychological safety and organizational embeddedness as mediators. *Frontiers in Psychology, 12*, 546687. https://doi.org/10.3389/fpsyg.2021.546687

INDEX

Note: For figure citations, page numbers appear in *italics*. For table citations, page numbers appear in **bold**.

ableism 138
absenteeism 154
accountability flow 9
affection: *cariño* 4, 9, 67-8, 72; Confucianism 79, 81
Africa 117
African American community 65-6
age 61
Aimautov, Zhussupbek 101
Alternative Provision 28, **40**, 49-50
Altynsarin, Ybyrai 99-100
American Psychological Association (APA) 156
Americanisation 59, 65
Amonashvili, Sh. 95
amygdala hijack 36
ancestral flow 9
Andreotti, V. de O. 7
Anglo-Conformity 59
Anna Freud centre 130
anthropocentrism 102
anthroposophy 100
appreciative inquiry **63**
Aquinas, Thomas 97
Arce, S. 70
Ardern, Jacinda 128
Aristotle: virtue ethics 97
Aryee, S. 82
attention: skill training **20**
Augustine of Hippo 97
authoritarianism 86-7; *see also* Confucianism
authority *see* Confucianism

Bacon, Francis 99
Bailey, E. 125
Bakker, A. B. 157, 159-60
Bal, M. P. 160
Balasaguni, Yusuf 97-8
Ball, S. 60
Bandura, A. 149, 161
behaviour: management 12; skill training **20**
Beiley, S. 95
'being-in-the-world' 102
Beisenbayeva, Aida 102
Belkhir 61
Belzung, C. 116
benevolence 87n1
'beyond-the-human' 9
Biccum, A. R. 5, 7, 128
Black Lives Matter 136
body: influence on thought 36-7
Boyatzis, R. E. 150
Boyd, Diane 118
Boyle, Robert 99
Braidotti, R. 134, 136-7, 140-1, 145
brain: 'brain-body' link 35-6; influence of the body 36-7
breathing techniques 36, 41
Breines, J. 38
British Council 77
broaden-and-build theory 149, 154-5, 157
Buddhism 4, 35, 97, 114, 124
bullying 93, 104
burnout 38, 82, 155, 158; *see also* stress

Cammarota, J. 70
Canada 5
capitalism 4, 60-1, 140
career development 84, 86
caring behaviour 31, 53 Confucianism 79, 81
cariño see affection
Carpenter, S. 61
Carroll, C. 16, **17**, 22
Castagno, A. E. 64

Centre for Creative Leadership 151
CFC see compassion-focused coaching (CFC)
CFT see compassion focused therapy (CFT)
Chatzidakis, A. 137
Chen, J. 38, 82
Cheng, B. S. 81
Chicana identity 67
children: attachment issues 120-2, *121*; care routines 119-20; child abuse 123; child development **115**; childhood 114; children's homes, designing 45-6; compassionate interactions 119-22; developmental delay 127; empowerment of 118; executive functioning skills *121*; language differences *121*; previous experiences *121*; safeguarding 123; social services **40**, 41-2, 44, 49; touch 123-5; transitions, factors affecting 120-2, *121*; vulnerable 40-50; *see also* families; youth support
China: executive leadership 80; managerial coaching 78-9; paternalistic leadership 87; traditionality 78
Christianity 97
civil rights activism 64
Clark, A. 120
class see social class
classism 61
clemency 80
Cliffe, J. 125
climate crisis 143
CMT see compassionate mind training (CMT)
coaching 16, 54; adaptive 85; compassionate leadership 39, **40**; definition of **17**, 78; developmental 84; leadership 46-50; relational 84; relational dynamics 87; styles 84; task-oriented 84, 86; tones **105**; types of 16; *see also* Confucianism; managerial coaching; mentoring
cognition types 99
cognitive behavioural therapy (CBT) 22
colleague focus 28-9
collective thriving 8
collectivism see Confucianism
colonialism 137-8
Combs, M. C. 4
Comenius, Jan Amos 99
community online open courses (COOCs) 142
Compassion-Focused Coaching (CFC) 16-18, 31; benefits of 29; emotions 21; evaluation of 29-30; leadership-related uses of 29; manual 29-30, 50; origins of 18-24; process 15-16; psychoeducation 22-3; psychological skills 24-5; reception of 29-30; use of 27-9
Compassion-Focused Therapy (CFT) 8, 16-18, 25, 31, 158; benefits of 35; compassionate school cultures 34-54; de-shaming 28, 44; objectives 35
compassion: in action 139-45, 160-1; 'beyond-the-human' **144**; challenge of 137-8; core components of 150; culture of 114; definition of 17-18, 25, 34-5, 113-14; directions of 51-2; etymology of 135, 150; fatigue 124; flows of 9, 52, **144**; other-to-self **144**; overview of 150-1; past-to-present **144**; qualities of 30, 51-3; self-to-community **144**; self-to-self **144**; skills in 41; three flows of 30, 35, 41; theory and training 19-20
compassionate correction 50
compassionate culture: four pillars of **40**
compassionate leadership: attention model *108*; concept of 106; conceptual modelling *161*; definition of 151; empathy model *108*; helping model *108*; job performance and 159-60; politics 128; positive emotions and 153-5; positive impact on organisations 151; principles 106; self-efficacy and 152-3; strategies *107*; teacher work attitudes 156-9; teachers' assessment *107*, *108*; trust in the leader 155-6; understanding model *108*
Compassionate Leadership Behavior Index 109
Compassionate Mind Foundation 16, 35
compassionate mind training (CMT) 16-18, 22, 25-8, 31; compassionate school cultures 34-54; emotions 21; flexibility 30
compassionate organisational culture: barriers to 37-9; vulnerable children 40-50
compassionate reflection 30
compassionate self 26-7, **28**, 32, 43-4; self-experiential exercises *47*; self-to-self relationships *47*, 50; self-to-student relationships 50; transition to 48-9
competition doctrine 60
competitiveness 38-9
conceptual framework 149-50
conditions for compassionate thought and action 26-7
confidence (*confianza*) 4, 9, 72
conflict resolution 43, 104
Confucianism 77-87; adaptive coaching 85; authoritarian leadership 79-83,

86; authoritarianism 81–4; authority 80; collectivism 80–2; control 80–1; developmental coaching 84; discipline 80; employee outcomes 82–3; filial piety (*xiao*) 79–81; framework *83*; harmony 80–1, 108; hierarchy 80–1; obedience 80; propriety (*li*) 79, 81; reciprocity 80; relational coaching 84; *ren* (compassion) 8–9, 79, 81; righteousness (*yi*) 79, 81; self-cultivation 79–80; task-oriented coaching 84; theoretical foundations 79–81; wisdom (*zhi*) 79; *yin-yang* balance/perspective 81–5; *yin-yang* structured compassion coaching 83–4, *83*, 86–7
Confucius 81
connatus (desire to persist) 136
connectedness 30
conocimiento **63**, 65, 70–3, *71*
constellations of practice 142
consumerism 60
contentedness 31
contextual sensitivity 8
contracts 21
Costa, M. 7
Cottis, T. 121
countering with compassion 8–9
courageousness 31
courtesy 80
COVID-19 pandemic 124, 131, 143, 148, 151, 154, 158, 162
creative tasks 104
creative tension 64
crisis management 84, 151, 154, 156, 162
critical compassion 67–8; teacher preparation 72
critical pedagogy 8, 10, 60, 62–5, 68, 70, 102
critical posthumanism: definition of 134–5
criticism 50
Csikszentmihalyi, M. 149
culture: cultural-historical frame 10, *10*; cultural identity 100; cultural perspectives 78–9; impact of 78–9

da Costa, M. 7
da Vinci, Leonardo 137
Dachyshyn, D. M. 116–18
Dafernos, M. 60
Dalai Lama 114
Davis, E. 122
de-shaming 28, 44
deadline pressure 82
dehumanisation 62
Deleuze, G. 134, 140
Demerouti, E. 159
democracy 69

Department for Education (DfE) 118
depression 124, 158
Descartes, René 99
dialogue 97
didactic principles 99
Dirks, K. T. 156
disability 61, *121*; rights movement 3; social model of 3
Disability Discrimination Act (2004) 119
distress 31; alleviation of 18; attributes for engagement with **19**; empathic 115; engagement with 18; skill training **20**; tolerance **19**, 31
Doughty, S. E. 37
drive system *see* emotion
Dulati, M. Kh. 98
Dulatov, Mirjaqyp 101
Dzhandrina, Makpal 102

early years education 4, 8, 113–30; early years team 127–30; good practice points **127**; reflective activity **129**; work discussion groups 130
early years education and care (ECEC) 113
Early Years Foundation Stage (EYFS) 118, 119, 130
earnestness 80
ecological approach: attunement 8; frame 10; posthuman frame *10*; practice *118*; principles 118
economic crisis 143
ecosystem approach 37, **144**
education: authoritarian style of 99; collective 99; etymology of 95; free 101; global model of 3; goal of 95; image (*obraz*) in 95; labour, role of 101; marketisation of 60; moral values 99; philosophies of 62; problem-posing 67; purpose of 97; research *see* educational research; scientific 99, 101; spiritual and moral 95–101; *see also* early years education; spiritual and moral education (SME) 95
educational anthropology 101
Educational Psychologists (EPs) 11–13
educational psychology 11–12, 15, 152
educational research 69–72; cultural approach **63**; data analysis **63**; data collection **63**; ethical **63**; ideal types **63**; implications for 69–72; methodologies **63**; participants **63**; practitioner pathways **63**; research context **63**; research design **63**; theoretical frame **63**
Elfer, Peter 129–30
emotion 35; CFT models 21; CMT models 21; coaching 12; drive system *23*, 39,

45; emotional contagion **117**; emotional distress 154; emotional exhaustion 158; emotional-psychological frame 10, *10*; emotional support 149; emotional turmoil 126; evolved functions of 20-1; food and 120; mammalian drives 22; positive 10, 149, 153-5, 159, 162; soothe system *23*, 39, 45; threat system *23*, 39, 45; three circles model 22, *23*, 30, 39, 43, 45; three emotion systems model 41, 45

empathy 12, **19**, 37, 81, 102, 107-9, 114-18, 130, 136, 138, 150; concept of 113; empathic distress 115, *116*; intuitive 116, **117**; model *108*; research 121, 126-7; stages of **117**

employee commitment/loyalty 150

Engels, Friedrich 99

English language 59, 120

Enlightenment era 137

environmental pedagogy **105**

equality 118

Erasmus of Rotterdam 99

ERIC 120

essentialism 62

ethics 8, 10, 77, 80, 98, 137; affirmative 9, 134, 138, 141, 143, 145-6; care 146; of interconnectedness 10; posthuman affirmative 8; theories of 99; virtue 97; *see also* Confucianism

ethnocentrism: obscurity of 65-7; as social reproduction 61-2; sociocultural concepts **62**

eugenics 137-8

Evans, Kirsty 10

evolutionary perspectives 36

exegesis 98

existentialism **105**

extended relations, concept of 140

extracurricular development 103-6

Facebook 142

factory management 59-60

fairness 11, 138

families 125-6; *see also* children; Confucianism

Farh, J. L. 81

Faulkner, M. 126

fear, pedagogy of 64

feeling: skill training **20**

feminism: Chicana methods **63**; Marxist 61, **63**

Ferrin, D. L. 156

Fichte, Johann 99

Finland 114, 160

Fit and Healthy Childhood All-Party Parliamentary Group 123

flow and frames model *10*, 14, 72, **85**

Flowers, Oliver 12

food/feeding routines 120

Foundation Stage Units 121

foundational values 8

frames of application 10

Frankl, Viktor 102

Fredrickson, B. L. 149, 154-5, 159

free market principles 60

freedom of movement 68

Freire, Paulo 67, 102, 141

Froebel, Friedrich 118

Fuller, K. 3

Galetz, E. 116

Gallup research 157

GCE *see* Global Citizenship Education (GCE)

gender 61, **63**, 68, 72, 138

generational flow 9

GERM *see* Global Education Reform Movement (GERM)

Germany 79

Gilbert, Paul 12, 16, 35, 38-9, 45

giving compassion 26

Global Citizenship Education (GCE) 6-7, 13; behavioural 7; cognitive 6; socio-emotional 6

Global Education Reform Movement (GERM) 4-6; competition 5; historical origins 5; school choice 5; standardised testing 5; symptoms of 5

Global Occupy Movement (2011) 3

globalisation 7

Goleman, Daniel 36

good faith 80

group agreement 21

group singing 104

group work 104

Guattari, F. 134, 140

Hakanen, J. J. 160

Hans's dilemmas 102

Haraway, Donna 143

harmony *see* Confucianism

hate crime 138

Healey, J. F. 62

heartful practice 116-19, *118*, 130

Heidegger, Martin 102

helping behaviour 82

Herbart, Johann 99

Heriot-Maitland, C. 18, 29-30, 35

Hewson, D. 22

hierarchy *see* Confucianism; needs, hierarchy of

high-pressure environments 37

Hobbes, Thomas 99

Hodgkins, A. 4, 126-8
Hoffman, M. 114
home learning environment 125
Homo economicus: definition of 137
homophobia 65
honesty 108
Hong Kong 78-9
hooks, bell 135
hormones: cortisol (stress) 123; dopamine (reward) 123; oxytocin (love) 123; serotonin (happiness and wellbeing) 123
hospitality, radical 141
Hosseini, S. M. 77
Hougaard, R. 151
housing charities 42
Hui, R. T. Y. 77-8
humanism **96**, 102, 137-8
humanistic psychology 101
humanity 44, 109
humour 11, 13
hurt 130; potential causes of **115**; *see also* suffering

ideal state, concept of 97
idealism: subjective 99
imagery: skill training **20**
imagination 18, 37
immigration 59, 68
imposter syndrome 140
individualism 13, 65, 142
Industrial Revolution 59
Innis, Harold 5-6
intellectualism 73
International Coaching Federation 78
International Energy Agency (IEA) 5
intersectionality theory 60-1, **63**
interstitial spaces 72
intrinsic motivation 82-3
Irons, C. 18, 35
Islam 97; philosophy 98

Jaime-Diaz, J. 4
Japan 79
job performance 150, 162; compassionate leadership and 159-60; work engagement and 159-60
job satisfaction 82, 151, 154-5, 157
Jung, Carl 100

Kant, Immanuel 99
Kapterev, P. F. 100
Kazakhstan 91-109; *Asan-Kaygy* 98; *Bukhar-zhirau* 98; *Dos bolayik* programme 93, 104; *Dospambet-zhirau* 98; *Shal-akin* 98; *Shalkiiz-zhirau* 98; spiritual heritage 98; spiritual and moral education 95-101; teachers' survey 106-8
Keyes, C. L. M. 150
Kimmerer, Robin Wall 143
kindness: culture of 107; gracious 117
King, Martin Luther, Jr.: *Letter from a Birmingham Jail* (1963) 64
kinship 134
Klimecki, O. 115
knowledge: diffusion 104; economies 6; monopolies 5; society 104; spillover 104
Kohlberg, Lawrence 102
Kudaiberdiev, Shakarim 100
Kunanbayev, Abai 99-100

labour relations 99
Latinx cultural values 4
Lazarus, R. 113-14
leadership 15-32; activities 50-3; antisocial 50; authoritarian 10, 79-83, 86; coaching 46-50; compassion, defining 34-5; compassionate *see* compassionate leadership; compassionate conceptualisation 95; Confucian 79-83; control in 85; cultural foundations of 79; focus 29; indigenous behaviours 78; internal connection 52; mapping compassionate 108-9; paternalistic 79-81, 87; positive emotions and 153-5; programme for senior teachers 49-50; prosocial 50; relational 134-45; softness of compassion 38; styles 4; training 46-50; trust and 155-6; *see also* Confucianism
Leibniz, Gottfried Wilhelm 99
Leonardo, Zeus 64
lesson structures **105-6**; advantages **105**; analysis **105**; objectives **105**; risks **106**
Li, S. 4, 80
Locke, John 99
logical reasoning 37
logotherapy 102
Lomonosov, Mikhail 99
Losada, M. F. 159
love 92-3, 104, 135-6; definition of 93, 123; professional 8, 122-5, 130
Luthans, F. 149, 156
Lynch, Kathryn 10
Lyotard, Jean-François 102

Ma, L. 80
Macedo, D. 67
Makarenko, Anton 101
Mamardashvili, Merab 102-3

managerial coaching: Confucianism and 83; cultural perspectives 78-9; definition of 77; effective 77; *see also* coaching
Marvellous Mealtimes project 120
Marx, Karl 99
Marxist feminism 61, **63**
masculinity 137
Maslow, Abraham 102, 122, 127
Mayer, R. C. 155
McGlone, F. 123
media: space-biased 6; time-biased 6
memory 18
Méndez-Negrete, J. 4, 70
menopause 12
menstruation 12
mental health 102, 109, 132, 158
mentoring: definition of **17**; peer 149
mercy 107, 109
meritocracy 60, 137-8
metacognition 36
Meyer, Paul 50
Middle Ages 94, 97-8
mindfulness 41; mindful practice, principles of 118, *118*; mindfulness-based stress reduction 22
Modern Era 94
Mohammad, A. 4
Mojab, S. 61
Montaigne, Michel de 99
Montessori, Maria 101, 118
Moore, J. R. 37
morality 80, 95; concept of **96**; connection to society **96**; core components of **96**; definition of **96**; focus of **96**; goal of **96**; methods **96**; moral behaviour **96**; moral development 102; moral education 91-109; *see also* spiritual and moral education (SME); virtues
'more-than-human' 143-4
Morgan, A. 114
Morin, Edgar 102
Mosewich, A. D. 38
motivation theory 102, 128-9, 154-5; motivational systems 35
multiculturalism 3-4
multiple selves model 22-4, **24**, 43; angry self **24**, **28**, 48; anxious self **24**, **28**, 48; compassionate self **28**, 48; sad self **24**, **28**, 48

narrative therapy 22
Nasr al-Farabi, Abu 97-8
National Society for the Protection of Cruelty to Children (NSPCC): underwear rule (PANTS) 124, *125*
Native American traditions 143

needs, hierarchy of 122, 127
negativity bias 30
neoliberalism 4-5, 7, 10, 13, 60, 137, 141
neuroscience 114
new materialism 134
New Zealand: *Kotahitanga* (unity and bonding) 116; *Manaakitanga* (ethos of care) 116; *Māori* people's values and beliefs 116; prime minister 128; *Pumanawatanga* (a beating heart) 116; *Rangatiratanga* (self-determination) 116; *Whanauntanga* (relationships) 116
nice/niceness, culture of 64-5, 67
Nichtenberg, Hermann 101
nihilism 69-70
Noddings, N. 140
non-judgement **19**
non-violence 92-3, 104; definition of 93
NSPCC *see* National Society for the Protection of Cruelty to Children (NSPCC); nursery work *see* early years education
Nysanbayev, A. 102

O'Brien, E. 62
OCB 82
Occupy movement 136
open learning systems 99
Organisation for Economic Co-operation and Development (OECD) 5
otherness, concept of 66, 143

Page, J. 122-2
pain *see* hurt; suffering
Pais, A. 7
Palmer, Parker J. 135, 141
pandemic *see* COVID-19 pandemic
Panksepp, Jaak 22
parasympathetic nervous system 36
Pascal, Renold 160-1
Pashby, K. 7
paternalism 80-1, 87; paternalistic leadership 79-81, 87
Pavlidis, P. 60
peace of mind/inner peace 92-3; definition of 93, 104
peacemaking 108
Pellegrini, E. K. 80
performance ratings 160
periodisation: definition of 94; epoch 94; period 94; stage 94
personal practice 40-2
personality theory 102, 124
Pessi, A. 114
Pestalozzi, Johann Heinrich 99
philosophy 98-9
physical environment 39-40, **40**, 44-6, 54

Piaget, Jean 138
piety *see* Confucianism
'place-acknowledgement' activities 143
'planning in the moment' 118
pláticas **63**, 66, 69, 72
Plato: ideal state, concept of 97
policy: development 43; documents 43; procedures and 42-4
Porter, Ronald 64
positive attitude 104, 108
post-anthropocentrism 138
posthumanism 102, 134, 138; critical 134-5; perspectives 135-6; posthuman frame 10; posthuman reflection walk 144
posture 53
poverty 68
power: ideology of 60; political (*potestas*) 136; relational (*potentia*) 136, 141, 145; systems of 136; types of 136
practical empowerment 149
prejudice 64
Principal's compassionate leadership in action 148-9
Proctor, S. 126
Prokopovich, Feofan 99
proletarianisation 60
psychoeducation 22, 44; CFC sessions 22-3
psychology 15; developmental 114; humanistic 101; organisational 151-2; psychological safety 82; psychological skills 24-5; psychological wellbeing 158-9; positive 13; positive organisational behaviour 149-50; social 114; transpersonal 101; *see also* educational psychology
psychotherapy 16, 35
punitive approaches 12-13
Purvanova, R. 128

qualities 51-2
questions 25-6

race 59-61, **63**, 72; racial segregation 64, 66; white fragility 65
racism 61, 64-6, 69-70
Radugin, A. 102
Ramachandran, S. 108
re-encountering compassion 3-4
reason, role of 99
reasoning: skill training **20**
receiving compassion 26
reciprocity 70; *see also* Confucianism
Rector Aranda, A. 70
reductionism 4
reflection prompts 30-1

reflective practice 10; coaching and 16; definition of 15-16; language of 17 ; supervision and 16; prompts **144**
relational accountability 8, 10
relational focus 8
relational leadership *see* leadership
relaxation techniques **105**
relentless welcome, concept of 141
religion 61, 97, 117
Renaissance Era 94
research: design 94; methods 94; objectives 93; questions 93-4; *see also* educational research
resilience 8, 32, 72, 82, 149-50, 154, 156-7, 162; definition of 156; etymology of 156
respect (*respeto*) 4, 9, 68-9, 72, 107-8
responsibility for others 108
restorative practice 139
rhizome concept 140-2; rhizomatic structure *142*
right action 92
righteous behaviour 93, 104; definition of 93
Rogers, Carl 102, 118
Romero, A. F. 70
Rousseau, D. M. 155
Ryff, C. D. 150

'sad passions' 136
safe spaces 139; concept of 64
Sahlberg, P. 5
Saint-Exupéry, Antoine de 100
Scandura, T. A. 80
Schaufeli, W. B. 160
school 152; climate 109; ethos 12-13; performance 160; schooling, culture of 68; special schools 10-13; uniforms 138; *see also* education
Scotland 120
Seitheshev, A. 95
selective perception **62**
self-cognition 91-109, 110; combined lesson criteria **105-6**; spiritual and moral education 103-6; subject 92; subject project 93-4; values 92
self-cultivation 79-80
self-determination 68
self-efficacy: building 153; compassionate leadership and 152-3; definition of 161; teacher 153; theory 10, 149, 162
self-empowerment 68
self-esteem 11
self-focus 27-8
self-knowledge 102
Seligman, M. E. P. 149
Seneca 97

sensitivity **19**, 151
sensory skill training **20**
sexism 61, 65
sexuality 72; *see also* gender
Simos, G. 45
sincerity 108
Singapore 80, 86
Singer, T. 115
skill development 22
slavery 137-8
slow pedagogy 120
'slowing things down' 27
Smith, J. 77
Smith, J. B. 145
social class 59-61, 65, 69-72, **63**
social constructivism **105**
social distance **62**, 66
social environment 44-6
social inequity 66
social justice 8, 10, 118
social media 141-2
social processes 39
social reproduction: ethnocentrism as 61-2; guide for deconstruction of *71*; institutions of **62**; theory 72
social services **40**, 41-2, 44, 49
socialisation 66, 70
sociocentric approach 101
sociohistorical theory 8, 60
sociological theory 61
Socrates: dialogue 97
Solovyov, G. 102
Solvason, C. 125-6
soothe system *see* emotion
soothing techniques 27
soul, generosity of 80
space theory 101
special educational needs (SEN) 10-11, 106, 120, 124, 126
special schools 10-13
Spinoza, Baruch 99; *Ethics* 134-7, 143
spiritual and moral education (SME) 8, 91, 95-101; classical period 98-100; concept of 95-101; contextual approaches 102; goal of 103; historical timeline *103*; key thinkers 99-102; non-classical period 100-1; post-non-classical period 101; pre-classical period 97-8; self-cognition 103-6; whole person, development of 100
spirituality: concept of **96**; connection to society **96**; core components of **96**; definition of **96**; focus of **96**; goal of **96**; methods **96**
St. Pauls Institute of Communication Education (SPICE) 160-1

staff: interactions 42-3; meetings 42-3; morale 149; wellbeing 40-2
standardisation 13
Steiner, Rudolf 7, 100, 118
Steiner education 121
Stepin, V. S. 95
Stevenson, H. 3
storytelling 104, 109; strategies **105**
stress 82, 150-1, 153-8
structural-political frame 10, *10*
student focus 28
suffering 21, 31, 113-14; attributes for engagement with **19**; skill training **20**; *see also* hurt
supervision 16; definition of **17**; metaphor of 22; *see also* reflective practice
supervisor guidance 50
support 81; emotional 149; youth 42
Svinth, L. 123
sympathy **19**, 136
systemic focus 29
systemic inequity 13

tactile defensiveness 124
Taiwan 80; Ismaili people/religion 117; *Nazrana* (offering) 117; *Zakah* (charity) 117
Taylor, J. 29-30
Tazhibayev, Tolegen 102
teachers: engagement and positivity 154-5; preparation 59-72; psychological wellbeing 158-9; work attitudes 156-9; work engagement 160; *see also* teaching practice
teaching practice 138-9; adult education 139-42; further education 139-42
team meetings 42-4, 39-40, **40**, 54
test scores 60
theological approach 97
theoretical foundations 149-50
thinking environment 138-9, 141, 146
Thomas, Rebecca 148
threat system *see* emotion
threat-base mindset/mode 42; *see also* emotion
three circles model *see* emotion
Thupten Jinpa, Geshe 150
TikTok 140
toilet training 119-20
Tolstoy, Leo 100
Tolyq Adam, concept of 99
Toraygyrov, Sultan-Makhmut 101
touch: affectionate 124, *124*; affectionate-controlling 124, *124*; appropriacy of 124; assisting 124, *124*; controlling 124, *124*;

educative 124, *124*; functions of 123; tactile defensiveness 124; types of *124*
training 54; compassionate leadership 39, **40**; distress and suffering **20**; leadership 46-50; train-the-trainer sessions 42
transdisciplinarity 102
transitional objects 121
transpersonal psychology 101
trust (*confianza*) 4, 10, 68-9; building 149; compassionate leadership process 156; leadership and 155-6; school leadership 156; trusting group, foundations for 21
truth 92-3, 104; definition of 93
Tsui, A. S. 80
Tumak, O. 94
Twitter 141-2

undercommons, spaces of 141
UNESCO 5; International Commission on the Futures of Education: Looking Ahead Towards 2050 91; Pedagogy of Cooperation and Solidarity (2021) 92
Ungar, Michael 37
United Nations (UN) 5; Global Education First Initiative 6
United States (US) 70; managerial coaching 79; minority groups 68; school system 62, 73
Ushinsky, Konstantin 101
Uusitalo, L. 114

Valikhanov, Shokan 100
values 12, 92; cardinal 99; moral 99
Vigilancia 65-6
virtue ethics 97
virtues 80
visualisation techniques 27
Vitruvian human 137-8; definition of 137
voicing behaviour 82
vulnerability 143; vulnerable persons *see* children
Vuorinen, K. 114
Vygotsky, L. S. 125

Waldorf educational approach 100
Wei, H. 4, 80
wellbeing 8, 151; care for **19**; emotional 128, 149, 152; employee 82; long-term 37; multidimensional model of 150; organisational 154; psychological 154, 158-9, 162; resilience and 150; school policies 12; school services 13; staff 39, **40**, 54
West, C. 69
West, M. A. 95
WhatsApp 140
wheel of compassion 50-1, *51*
widening participation agenda 140
Winnicott, D. 121
wisdom 31, 51, 53, 116-17; *see also* Confucianism
work engagement 150, 157, 162; absorption 157; dedication 157; definition of 157; job performance and 159-60; teachers 160; vigour 157
Working on What Works services 13
workshops 46-7

Xanthopoulou, D. 157

yin-yang perspective *see* Confucianism
Yoon, E.-S. 5
youth support 42; *see also* children
Yunkaporta, T. 139

Zharykbayev, Kubigul 102
Zhu, Y. 80
Zhumabayev, Magzhan 101

For Product Safety Concerns and Information please contact our EU representative GPSR@taylorandfrancis.com
Taylor & Francis Verlag GmbH, Kaufingerstraße 24, 80331 München, Germany

www.ingramcontent.com/pod-product-compliance
Lightning Source LLC
Chambersburg PA
CBHW080806300426
44114CB00020B/2846